RIDING BY THE SEAT OF MY PANTS:

A Solo Motorcycle Journey
From Alaska To Argentina

2010 – 2011

Brian Gibbons

ISBN: 978-1-910662-59-5

Focus Motivation Publishing

www.focusmotivation.co.uk

Acknowledgements

This was meant to be a solo ride, which apart from brief interludes when I shared the road with a companion or two, it was. However, as with all major endeavours, it would not have been possible without the help, support and encouragement of countless individuals. I would like to extend special thanks to my son Dan for his constant motivational support throughout the journey. To my best friends Tony and Tim for always being there when I needed them. Tony was instrumental in the planning stage and Tim along with Kris, were prepared to bail me out if I got into trouble. To Sean, my benefactor and friend without whose help it would have been much more difficult. To Mick and Anne who always encourage me in everything I do and were always the first to post comments on my blog. To Danny, Sue and Paul, my biker friends who were with me in spirit. To Tony and his wife Ren whose help was invaluable in preparing me, and my bike for the trip. To Bill in Phoenix, for his amazing generosity and friendship. To Paul in San Ramon, for taking in a total stranger and helping with my bike's mechanical problems. To Garry and his family in Mexico City who opened their home to me and treated me as one of the family. To Nathan in Canada who gave me much need respite. To my Couchsurfing family, Myrna and Layton in Kelowna, Canada, Payette and J.C. in Petaluma, California, Sally and Larry, in San Diego, Francine and Carl in Bakersfield, Arizona, Luis in Leon, Mexico, Luis in Guatemala City. You all treated me as a friend and touched me deeply with your open hearts and generosity. To Brian and Wendy in Canada for taking pity on me and buying me dinner. To Barbara and Ron for their kindness in buying me lunch on the river trip in California. To my temporary riding companions, Mark, Lenny and Andy, thanks for your great company and support on the road. To the stranger riding a BMW in Canada who donated his spare oil can to me. To the amazing mechanic in Peru, who diagnosed and then fixed my chain problem. To the Tuk Tuk driver who ferried me around and found me people to help fix my bike. To the wonderful Santiago and his lovely wife Paula who looked after me and fed me in Argentina. To the total stranger who picked up my bike and followed me for two hours to ensure my safety after my altercation on the Dalton, whoever you were, you were a Guardian Angel that day. To "Mad Dog" in Belize, for diagnosing and fixing my electrical problem. To Steve aka the "professor" and all the members of The Chain Gang for all their help and advice at the rally in Oregon. To Tim and Angela, from Seattle, for your help and hospitality. To Micky and her team of physios at "Healing Hands" in Antigua for getting me back on the road. To Graham Styles of Brainrotting.com who provided much needed inspiration and advice. To my brother Steve for his painstaking proof reading and suggestions for improvement. To all the many people I met on the road who extended me friendship and kindness and to everyone who sponsored me and donated their hard earned money for a good cause. I thank you all.

The Northampton Hope Centre

Charity Registration No. 1015743

Northampton Hope Centre began back in 1974 when local man Michael Mulligan started a free food handout for rough sleepers from the back door of Bishop's House in Marriott Street. This grew over the years into the Northampton Soup Kitchen and finally developed in the Hope Centre, a Day Centre offering a wide range of services and practical support to Northampton's homeless.

CONTENTS

Prologue

23rd March 2011

"It's bad," Tony said. "She has a big tumour. I'm following the ambulance now. We're on our way to The John Radcliffe Hospital, in Oxford"

I looked at the clock. It was 11.00 p.m. My mind was confused. I tried to take it all in as I jumped out of bed and threw some clothes on, giving Jane a kiss as I left.

I'd been back from my epic trip only a few weeks. Tony had said that Claire, his wife hadn't been feeling well and kept complaining of headaches and dizziness. The doctors had diagnosed migraine or menopausal problems. The truth is, she had a brain tumour the size of a fist and needed brain surgery.

Had I not arrived home four months sooner than anticipated, I might have been in Patagonia as this trauma unfolded.

I'd arrived back in the U.K. on the 19th February on a bitterly cold, wet, rainy day. On that very day, although I didn't know it at the time, my friend and fellow speaker, Clive Gott had suddenly died at the age of 52 from a suspected heart attack. Three days later on the 22nd February a huge earthquake had hit Christchurch, New Zealand where my friends Tim and Kris live. They had been lucky to survive the devastation. A few short weeks later, I was racing to the hospital in Oxford. What on earth was happening?

Since I'd arrived back home, everything seemed to be turned upside down. If ever I needed a reminder of why I had embarked upon this journey this was it.

Life is short. Life is precious. Don't waste it.

Introduction

"Twenty years from now you will be more disappointed by the things that you didn't do than by the ones you did do. Explore. Dream. Discover."

- *Mark Twain*

My biggest fear had always been to end up on my deathbed, whenever that time might come, with a feeling of regret. Of chances not taken, potential not realised, dreams not followed. It was these fundamental drivers that underpinned the whole reason for taking on this adventure. Many people have dreams, goals and ambitions but fail to achieve them through fear; in whatever guise it appears to them. Fear of failure, fear of success, fear of criticism. They often excuse their inactivity and point to a lack of time or resources or they inhabit the fantasy island of "one day I'll......"

One day I'll work for myself...

One day I'll apply for that job...

One day I'll write that book...

One day I'll move abroad....

I didn't start riding motorcycles until I was fifty years old and it was during a trip to the Bike Show at the NEC in 2006 that I found myself at the GlobeBusters stand. It was here I had met Julia Saunders. She had ridden around the world with her husband Kevin, and together they were the Guinness world record holders for the fastest time around the globe and also the fastest time riding the Pan American Highway from Alaska to Argentina. In that conversation, a seed was planted.

I came away feeling inspired and thinking how incredible that would be to do something similar. One day I'd love to do something like that, I thought. Of course I'd watched Ewan McGregor and Charley Boorman going the *Long Way Around* on their epic motorcycle trip and thought at the time, wow, one day I'll do something like that.

These thoughts sat at the back of my mind for years until I read a quote from Goethe and came to the realisation that I was fast running out of potential "one days".

Rest not! Life is sweeping by;

Go and dare before you die.

Something mighty and sublime;

Leave behind to conquer time.

- *Goethe*

At about the same time I had come across an interview with a man who was dying of terminal cancer and was recording his last thoughts on video. It was profoundly moving. In the video he came out with a statement, which touched a nerve in me and to this day has a major impact on my decisions. He said,

At the end of it all we will all have two questions we need to answer:-

- Who will I need to have been?

- What will I need to have done?

In order to feel that my time on earth was well spent.

In that moment, I decided I just had to do this. I wanted to do something *mighty and sublime*. I wanted to do something I could reflect back on with immense pride and satisfaction. The decision made, I Googled flights to Alaska, checked out all the information I could on Horizons Unlimited, a website for overland motorcycle travel, and slowly a plan began to take shape. There was massive risk attached to this potential one year long adventure, not least of which was what would happen to my business if I left it for a year? The recession was already starting to bite, work was thin on the ground and here I was planning to take a year out. Was this a sensible thing to do? I had many nights of fitful sleep as the enormity of the undertaking seeped into my unconscious mind. And yet, I kept being drawn back to the deep desire to do something special. Something significant. Helen Keller's famous words kept coming back to me,

"Life is either a daring adventure or it is nothing at all"

In my work as a motivational speaker, management trainer and coach, I often encourage people to step out of their comfort zones and tap into their full potential. I had given myself many challenges in the past, including an epic battle with Kilimanjaro three years previously, but I felt this plan was even more audacious and came with even bigger risks attached to it. The only question that remained was whether I was prepared to accept the risks involved. If the answer was yes, then I just had to figure out how. As someone once said, "If you have a big enough WHY, you'll soon find a HOW."

I knew **what** I wanted to achieve and I was very sure **why** I wanted to do it. The how was just going to be a matter of logistics and planning.

Getting funding was going to be the first priority. How was I going to afford it? Unlike Ewan and Charley, I wasn't going to be given everything for free and be backed by massive sponsors. In fact I would have to fund everything myself, and so I spent many hours in conversations with my close friend Tony, who also happens to be a coach.

"I could re-mortgage my house or take some money from my pension" I said to him as we sat in the sauna one day after a gym session.

"Or you could ask someone for the money" he added, "let's focus on possibility thinking"

We both hold strong beliefs when it comes to the universal laws and the power of the mind. In my training sessions I teach a process of goal setting where I talk about the immense power of the subconscious mind to solve problems and seek out powerful goals, so I just knew I would find a way to make all this happen. The series of circumstances that subsequently unfolded are perfectly described in this quote by William Murray, leader of the Scottish Himalayan Expedition in 1952. He said this,

"Until one is committed, there is hesitancy, the chance to draw back, always ineffectiveness. Concerning all acts of initiative (and creation), there is one elementary truth the ignorance of which kills countless ideas and splendid plans: that the moment one definitely commits oneself, then providence moves too. A whole stream of events issues from the decision, raising in one's favour all manner of unforeseen incidents, meetings and material assistance, which no man could have dreamt would have come his way."

Once you are committed and begin to take action, things start to happen. A series of serendipitous events occurred shortly after our conversation in the sauna. I was having lunch with a friend of mine who had been on my management training courses many years before. Sean had subsequently gone on to run a very successful business. Over lunch I was excitedly telling him of my plans and what I was proposing to do,

"Whatever happens I'm going to do it!" I said as I excused myself and went to the washroom.

I came back to my seat and was just finishing my drink when Sean said,

"I've been thinking about what you're planning. It sounds amazing and I want to lend you the money!" he said with a smile.

I just looked at him and before I could respond he added,

"You don't have to worry, you can pay me back whenever. There's no hurry. I just feel I've got a lot from your courses and this is a way of helping you out"

I couldn't thank him enough. In one sentence, Sean had just eliminated the principle hurdle. It's incredible what happens and who turns up to help you once you commit to something.

I still had many other things to resolve in the six months I had given myself to prepare before my June departure date. I'd decided that June would be an optimum time to arrive in Alaska because even in the summer months, the weather in the Arctic Circle can be extremely inclement. So arriving home after my lunch with Sean, I set about the task with renewed energy and focus. I had decided to add even more importance and meaning to the trip by raising money for The Northampton Hope Centre, a local charity who do great work with the homeless and disadvantaged. I had spent the last couple of Christmas Days there helping out, and so with their blessing, "The Journey for Hope" was born and became the title of the blog I would write to keep people back home up to date with what was happening.

To raise more awareness for them I appeared on local radio and was featured in the local newspaper to publicise the trip. Exposing your dreams and goals to a wider public also increases the pressure to complete what you set out to do, and I was well aware that the more people I told, and the more publicity I garnered, the more important it was to fulfill all the expectations. I remember sitting in the lounge of a pub being interviewed by a local magazine,

"It seems a massive undertaking. Especially travelling solo. Are you not worried if something goes wrong?" the young reporter asked.

"I'm sure things will go wrong," I replied with a smile, "there will be problems with the bike. It's inevitable, but one of the things I wanted to do was step out of my comfort zone and challenge myself!"

I didn't realise it at the time, but there would be many, many occasions in the coming year, when I would rue the bravado of that comment while sitting in the warmth of an English pub.

My desire to do the trip solo was a concern for many people, particularly given my total lack of mechanical ability,

"Why don't you go with a friend or join an organised trip like GlobeBusters?" They would often ask. The truth was, I didn't want to ride to someone else's itinerary and I really did want to challenge myself to see what I was capable of.

Apart from the technical and mechanical deficiencies there was also the small matter of not speaking Spanish, the predominant language of every country from Mexico onwards. This situation was exacerbated by a long standing, limiting self belief, that I was no good at languages. I had successfully nurtured this belief for years. It seemed that this journey would be the opportunity to create new empowering beliefs about my abilities, both linguistic and mechanical. The simple truth was, I would have no choice.

I immediately sent off for a "teach yourself Spanish" course, which I downloaded onto my ipod. At the same time, I set about learning as much as I could about the workings of the single cylinder BMW 650 Dakar motorcycle. This was the bike many experts had encouraged me to use because it was reputedly very robust and easy to work on if something went wrong. This of course presupposed I would know how to fix it if it did go wrong! Having signed up for a motorcycle maintenance class at the local college and found it to be disappointing, I had to re-think my strategy, so I put a post on one of the many motorcycle websites asking for help. I received a response from Tony, who happened to be a BMW motorcycle mechanic and lived only twenty minutes away! Serendipity? He offered to help me and refused to take any money, despite spending hours and hours at nights and weekends trying to impart as much knowledge as possible in a brief amount of time. I kept him supplied with his favourite brand of cigarettes in return for his expertise, and ever so slowly, I did begin to build my confidence.

In the meantime, I booked myself on a very demanding two day off road riding course in Wales, as many of the roads I would be encountering on the journey would be unlike anything I had previously experienced. This turned out to be probably the best investment I would ever make.

CHAPTER 1

The 6 Ps:

"Proper Planning Prevents P**s Poor Performance!"

I'd been formulating lists for months and by this stage I should have been spending most of the time ticking them off, but I seemed to be adding as much as I was ticking off, which was slightly disconcerting. The run of poor weather had affected my plans to get work done on the bike and I must admit that I expected to be much more up to speed with all things mechanical than I was at the time. Technical successes so far included:- Upgraded standard horn to a mighty 132 decibel (they'll certainly hear me coming!) - upgraded seat for more comfort - installed sealed unit battery (for less maintenance) and completed 12,000 mile service.

Still to complete:- change steering head bearings (no idea what they were but I knew it was a big job!) - check valve clearances (big job!) - fit off road tyres and heavy duty inner tubes - upgrade to heavy duty DID X ring chain(more robust than standard) - fit LED rear bulb - upgrade footpegs (I'd be standing on them quite a lot) - learn how to use the BMW diagnostic tool, and generally learn how the bike operates and how to fix it when it goes wrong. All the above had been worked on with the help of Tony Evers, who was not only a superb mechanic but also a man of immense generosity of spirit. He had worked tirelessly for many, many hours attempting to get me from a raw novice to someone capable of surviving on his own. His patient wife Ren just kept supplying us with endless cups of tea and sympathy. It all seemed to work in Tony's garage, but what about the Dalton Highway in Alaska, one of the most remote and desolate stretches of road in North America?

As the time pressed on, I was acutely aware that I was on on a very steep learning curve. The build up to departure day also involved renting out my house. I'd considered placing all my worldly goods into storage but after consulting the letting agents was informed that a fully furnished rental property would be more attractive, and within days they had found me the perfect tenants! An older couple (I didn't want wild raves upsetting my lovely neighbours) who wanted to move in quickly. With all the paperwork duly completed I could relax a little and tick a major task off my ever increasing "to do" list.

A few days later I had a call from the agents to say one of the prospective tenants was very ill and they could no longer take the property. So it was back to the drawing board and with time running out I had to consider the possibility of leaving my home empty and hoping they would find a suitable tenant while I was away. With only a couple of weeks to go I received the good news that I needed. We had new tenants lined up!

I was due to spend the last week before departure at my girlfriend Jane's house, and as I gazed around my home for the last time, I wondered what the next twelve months would bring. It was with a sense of slight trepidation that I pulled the front door shut for the last time, climbed into my heavily loaded car and drove away. The final week was spent doing last minute shopping for essentials, including three pairs of special, all singing, all dancing, fully wicking, quick drying underpants! Jane, being a top Image Consultant was tasked with consulting on all my wardrobe requirements (in other words, they were her idea). Her living room was strewn with a year's worth of clothing and accessories including countless leads, batteries and chargers for my camera, camcorder, mobile phone, ipod, helmet cam, laptop, etc. All of this stuff and miscellaneous odds and ends had to fit into two panniers, one tank bag and a holdall which would be strapped to the back of the bike. It had to be minimalist packing. Sadly, this meant keeping books to a bare minimum, apart from a couple of travel guides for Canada and Alaska. It was going to be a tight squeeze.

The last few days were spent in a kind of surreal, suspended animation. Busying ourselves with last minute logistics and making sure all the paperwork was in order. Checking and re-checking passports, visas, bike documents, insurance, and all the while counting down the clock to D Day. Throughout this whole period I was constantly amazed by how Jane was coping with the fact that we wouldn't be seeing each other for up to a year. She just focused on getting me organised and making sure I was as prepared as I could be. In the spare time we had we would go for a walks and talk about the coming trip,

"It will all pass faster than you think," I said, trying to reassure her.

Judging by how quickly the whole plan had come together from inception to execution, I knew I was right, while at the same time thinking, a year sounds a long time and I have a very, very long way to go. That night after dinner we were sitting and chatting about the length of time I would be away,

"I've been thinking," I said, as I sipped a glass of red wine, "I don't think it's fair to expect you to wait for me for a year. This wasn't your choice, it was mine."

We'd been seeing each other for only eight months before I started planning the journey and now here I was about to leave her for up to a year.

"If you want to go out with someone else I would understand" I added, not at all wanting that to happen.

"I don't want anyone else," she said, leaning forward and giving me a huge hug, and then reached into her bag saying, "I've got something for you. I wasn't sure about this. I wasn't sure you would wear it."

She handed me a small box, inside which was a silver St. Christopher medal.

"It's to keep you safe!" she added, "turn it over."

On the back was engraved the words to an Alicia Keys song from an album I had given her on Valentine's Day. It read,

"Through distance and time, I'll be waiting"

"Of course I'll wear it," I said, choking back the tears, "I'll never take it off!"

D Day

Just after lunch we loaded Jane's car and headed off to Heathrow. I was due to fly very early the next day so we decided to spend our last night together at a hotel near the airport. The anticipation, nerves and the accompanying slow drip adrenaline started to build up as the afternoon progressed. We seemed to be just marking time, which in fact we were. We couldn't really enjoy the time. There was too much tension. We had a couple of drinks, an early dinner and eventually got to bed at about 11.00 pm. We had to be up at 2.00 am the next morning so I didn't expect to get much sleep. I was right.

An unnecessary alarm went off and we both got up and dressed without saying much. I'm not naturally talkative first thing in the morning and today was even worse. When I'm going somewhere I generally like to get on with it and get going. The tension and stress was almost unbearable. I had the combined nervous anticipation of the journey itself coupled with the knowledge that I would be leaving this amazing woman that I loved, for a year. I felt sick. I was sweating, dehydrated and had a headache. Thankfully the wait for the check in desk to open wasn't too long, and as soon as I checked my bags in we said our goodbyes. I'm not one for prolonged, emotional goodbyes. Besides there was nothing we hadn't already said. There would be plenty of time for tears later. I went through security, found the nearest seat and slumped down. I was physically and emotionally exhausted.

Whenever I fly, I can't fully relax until I get on the flight. When that happens I know I'm on my way, so I was relieved to see the "boarding now" sign signalling it was time to board my flight to Frankfurt. I hate delays. I settled into my seat and breathed a huge sigh of relief. I would soon be on my way. Sadly, fate decreed otherwise as our scheduled take off time came and went and we hadn't even pushed away from the terminal.

"Unfortunately, ladies and gentlemen we have a technical problem with one of the engines. We are working on it and hopefully we will be away as soon as possible."

Brilliant. Just when I thought it was safe to relax. I was concerned about the possibility of missing my connection to Anchorage and began to get even more anxious as people started to speak to the cabin crew and begin unloading their luggage. This was not the start I was hoping for. After what seemed an eternity, we pushed away from the terminal and finally got a newly assigned take off slot. By this time I was working really hard to compose myself and tried not to become too stressed. Not my strength. When we finally reached cruising altitude, I spoke to the steward,

"I've a connection to make in Frankfurt. Will I make it in an hour?"

"It's possible, but you need to really hurry when you leave the plane."

It's **possible**? Fuck. All this didn't augur well for the start of my big trip. The plane had barely touched down in Frankfurt when I was straining at my seatbelt cursing the pilot for not taxiing faster. When we got the clearance to disembark I grabbed my hand luggage including my precious helmet and started to run to my embarkation gate. Sod's Law dictated it would be miles away and I strained my hamstring on the concourse as I dodged past crowds of irritating passengers ambling along,

"Get out of the fuckin' way!" I muttered under my breath as I finally limped the last hundred yards and arrived at the departure desk with two minutes to spare sweat rolling down my brow,

"Mr. Gibbons! We've been waiting for you!"

"Sorry," I gasped, "technical hitch at Heathrow."

It was with a huge sense of relief that I slumped into my seat. I hope the rest of the trip is a damn sight less stressful than this I thought. As we climbed up into the clouds, it occurred to me that if I sprinted the length of the terminal and only just made the flight, what were the chances of my luggage being as swift as me? Still, there was nothing I could now except relax and enjoy the flight. I was finally on my way. Looking in the in flight magazine I came across a map of north and south America showing the destinations that Lufthansa fly to, and as my finger traced the length of the Pan American Highway, I reflected upon the enormity of the undertaking I was embarking upon.

CHAPTER 2

Holed up in Anchorage!

I arrived in one piece in Anchorage on Sunday. Unfortunately I couldn't say the same for my luggage. Apparently it had been reluctant to leave the safety of Frankfurt Airport. Lufthansa assured me it was winging its way to me, and all being well it was due to be with me in five hours later. This would have been good news for two reasons. 1. I couldn`t start my trip without my riding gear. 2. I had now worn my underpants back to front and inside out and was running out of options. Sadly, I had been misled and it took almost two days for my luggage to appear.

The weather, which had been beautiful and sunny when I had arrived two days previously, had become wet and windy and was forecast to stay around for the week, which would make the infamous Dalton Highway (414 miles of dirt road) an interesting experience.

While acclimatising and getting over jetlag, I thought it mandatory to explore and experience all things Alaskan. So far my dining requirements had been totally taken care of by one "authentic" Alaskan eatery. All I can say is, this was not a place to diet. Good wholesome food (and obviously plenty of it) and the smallest beer they served was a pint! I made the mistake of ordering BBQ pork ribs and got a plate big enough to feed a small army. Unfortunately, I became that small army and wasn't so small anymore. If my gear didn`t arrive soon, I may be too big to get into it.

While waiting for my luggage to arrive I busied myself with the bureaucratic headache of releasing my bike from U.S. Customs and FedEx. This involved reams of paperwork and form filling, which has to be my least favourite pastime. After a fairly lengthy process I was given the necessary stamps and made my way to the FedEx building. Passing through security I handed my paperwork to a young woman who took a cursory look and asked,

"Do you have any tools to open your crate?"

"Tools?" I responded incredulously, "uh, not exactly."

Why would I bring tools with me, I muttered under my breath as I followed her into the warehouse. I naively assumed someone would be there to do that kind of stuff. She escorted me through more security where we liberated a huge claw hammer and wire cutters from the high security FedEx toolbox and I set off following her as she drove my precious cargo on a forklift truck to a safe place 600 yards from the depot (security apparently, didn`t want me running amok on my dangerous goods in their depot).

She finally deposited my crate in a "safe" car park and left me to it. It was with a sense of nervous anticipation that I attacked the crate with the huge claw hammer, hoping that my bike would be intact. In no time at all I had hacked my way through the crate and freed my precious cargo.

Stage one complete, I said to myself.

Lufthansa permitting, I would set off early the following day for the next stage, a ride of 362 miles north to Fairbanks. It would take two days of hard riding just to get to my starting point of Prudhoe Bay on the Arctic Ocean. This was the most northerly point in Alaska that can be reached by road. From then on it would be due south all the way to Argentina.

Fairbanks and beyond.....

At last! The journey had really begun. I set off really early (couldn`t sleep) for my first stop in Fairbanks 362 miles away. It was a relief to eventually get on the road. The next challenge would be coping with the huge mileages that would define Alaska and Canada. There would be no option but to just keep going. Alaska consisted of vast tracts of rugged wilderness dotted with small enclaves of civilisation. Day one would be the first of many long days in the saddle.

After a couple of hours riding, I stopped for breakfast at Trapper Creek Trading Post. An interesting place, it was full of old blokes with beards and baseball caps. The only woman there was the waitress, no beard but a nice neck tattoo. It was like a scene from the film, Deliverance. Fortified by (my now staple) breakfast of eggs (over easy), bacon, hash browns, toast and coffee, I pressed on to Fairbanks arriving late afternoon at my destination of the Go North Camp. It was a kind of cross between a camp ground and a hostel and good value at $25, even if it did entail sharing a cabin with three other blokes.

It was here that for the first time I experienced the peculiar Alaskan phenomenon of twenty four hours of daylight. The strange and slightly unsettling total lack of darkness. You know the kind we get used to at home? It gets to night time and the sun goes down. Not in Alaska. There was no darkness! It was like trying to sleep with the light on. It couldn`t be done. Another early start was obviously on the cards.

17th June

As expected it was indeed an early start. I was up at 5.45 am and on the road before 7.00 am. Before leaving Fairbanks I pulled into the local supermarket to buy another one gallon petrol can for the long haul up the Dalton Highway, which was notoriously short of "gas" stations. I rode for about half an hour before turning on to the Elliot Highway. Glancing down at my GPS it said next turn in 321 miles! I knew then, this was a serious road trip.

CHAPTER 3

The Dalton Highway - "The Road to Hell!"

After riding on tarmac for about an hour I took a right turn and headed onto the dirt of the infamous Dalton Highway,

Well, this is it, I said to myself, this is where the real challenge starts.

I stood up on the foot pegs to stabilise the bike and my heart rate increased noticeably as a steady drip of adrenaline seeped into my system. The Dalton Highway is famous for its unpredictability. Commonly referred to as "The Haul Road," it is essentially 414 miles of dirt and gravel; notorious for huge trucks kicking up clouds of dust in the summer and in the rain it can turn into a quagmire. Either way it would not be a pleasant experience when you're on two wheels. Because conditions can change rapidly and its severe reputation, when I set off that morning I was a little apprehensive to say the least.

My first destination was the little outpost of Wiseman, about seven hours away. Although this first leg wasn`t as bad as I expected, it was still unlike any previous motorcycling experience I had encountered. Unless you've been there it is difficult to grasp the scale of the Alaskan wilderness. For seven hours I rode alone save for the occasional big truck coming south as I tracked the Alaskan pipeline northwards. Although this part of the Dalton was relatively straightforward there were several occasions when I was glad I'd invested two invaluable days with the BMW Off Road Skills course in Wales. Learning how to control the bike on unstable ground was to prove essential, and if I was to make it safely to Prudhoe Bay and the Arctic Ocean I was going to need every one of the skills I had spent two days trying to master. I didn't know it at the time, but my inexperience on dirt was to prove very costly indeed.

There are only two places to refuel on the Dalton, the first available stop is The Yukon River crossing at about sixty miles, and on such a long ride it's important to stop and fill up at every opportunity. I refuelled and after having a coffee break I was about to leave when I saw a couple of riders coming from the north,

"Hi! How's the road ahead?"

"Not too bad, but be careful on the last eighty-five miles. It's very cold and the weather wasn't too good"

Thanking them and wishing them good luck I noted that one was riding a Harley. If he can do it on a Harley, then surely I'll be fine on my better suited BMW? I thought to myself, trying to bolster my fragile confidence. I fired up the engine and headed north, looking for all the world like an intrepid solo adventurer, but inside feeling like a complete novice with my confidence ebbing and flowing at an alarming rate. It was disconcerting to experience these wildly fluctuating mood swings, from high confidence to extreme anxiety. I just hoped that when I needed it, my confidence would be there.

The Arctic Circle

After another uneventful sixty miles or so I reached an important milestone. At latitude 66 degrees and 33 minutes I had just reached the Arctic Circle!

An obvious photo opportunity was called for and I rode my bike off to the right where I found the famous signpost. Jumping off my bike I set up the camera and took a couple of quick shots before the mosquitoes found me and attacked with several squadrons. I decided not to dwell and made a speedy exit feeling rather satisfied with myself that I'd actually ridden into the Arctic Circle. As I pushed further north it became noticeably colder as I expected, so I decided to plug in the heated jacket and gloves I had thankfully bought at the NEC Bike Show a few months earlier. I didn't realise it at the time but they would turn out to be one of my better purchases.

Made it to the Arctic Circle!

I arrived in Wiseman in the early afternoon after my last petrol stop at place called Coldfoot. This would be the last place to fill up before Prudhoe Bay and was located a few miles south of Wiseman. I quickly found my pre-booked accommodation at the Arctic Getaway, a small cluster of wooden huts tucked away in the wilderness a few miles off the beaten track. My host was a rather dour Alaskan named Bernie who had been running this place for twenty years and was clearly at home in this beautiful but rugged and isolated part of the world. After showing me my hut for the night he went off to cut more logs for the fire while I busied myself unpacking, showering and lubricating my chain. This was to become my ritual from then on. Regardless of how tired I would be feeling at the end of a long day's ride, my motorcycling mentor Tony, had instilled in me the importance of looking after the chain. However, this was to be the only time I did it under a full head mosquito net.

I had been warned about the Alaskan mosquitoes and they certainly lived up to there evil reputations. These were no ordinary mosquitos. These were specially trained "Stealth Mosquitoes." There would be no early warning signs of the steady buzzing sound to set you on your guard. These were silent and deadly little bastards that seemed to love freshly imported English flesh. My son Dan had bought me a full head net and despite looking a little odd, I was very thankful for its protection.

Setting off early (as usual) after a hearty plate of bacon, eggs, toast and coffee (as usual) the weather was fine, bright and sunny. It`s always nice to have a good start when you`ve got 243 miles of demanding riding ahead of you, particularly when you know that the last 85 miles are the worst. After an hour`s riding I could see the Atigun Pass looming in the distance. This is Alaska`s highest mountain pass (4,800 ft). It was shrouded in ominous dark clouds and it was with a sense of foreboding that I pressed on. An ever increasing sense of isolation weighed on me with every mile I rode. I felt I was heading further and further away from civilisation (and help) if anything were to go wrong. Truth be told, the feeling of anxiety was to become my constant travelling companion.

I quickly left behind the bright, sunny skies and for the next six hours experienced every kind of weather. Climbing the pass it started to rain and got heavier as I descended the other side. From then on the conditions on the road began to deteriorate. In a day`s riding I experienced sun, rain, wind, dust, heavy mud, fog and a bitterly cold wind as I headed deeper into the Arctic Circle. Thank God for my heated jacket.

Climbing through low cloud and mist on a very muddy section, I was peering through the gloom with the kind of intense concentration that saps your mental and physical strength, my whole being in tune with every twitch and slide of the bike's back wheel, when I saw some way in the distance what looked like a light. A single light? It must be another biker. The thought of a kindred spirit in this bleak and desolate terrain helped enormously. I wasn't riding quickly because of the conditions but I noticed I was gaining on the lone rider in front.

My God, he's going significantly slower than me, I thought, as I pulled briefly alongside and threw a wave. There was no wave back. This was a man intent on one thing only, staying upright. His eyes were focused with steely determination on the patch of dirt road in front of him. As I passed him I realised why. He was riding a road bike with road tyres. No wonder he was finding it difficult. He must be crazy!

The encounter with the lone biker was the first human contact for hours! About an hour from Prudhoe I stopped to put more petrol in the tank and it was bitterly cold. I'd seen nothing for hours apart from a couple of herds of Caribou crossing the road ahead of me and one lone Arctic Fox staring at me from the side of the road. What a God forsaken, desolate place this was. I was getting chilled to the bone even with my heated clothing. I wanted to record as much of the trip as possible so I did a piece to camera showing the desolate terrain and quickly pushed on to Prudhoe, desperate for some warmth.

I occupied my mind by counting down the mile markers. These were short wooden poles placed at the edge of the road at each mile point to help the ice road truckers keep on the road during white outs and blizzard conditions. That was their function during the winter, but now, here in the summer they provided a welcome sign that I was nearing my destination. Eventually, out of the gloom, signs of civilisation gradually appeared.

Thank God for that.

The thought of a nice warm shower and hot food was massively comforting. Prudhoe Bay is deceptively huge and sprawling. It stretches for miles around so, frustratingly it took a while to orientate. Despite my near hypothermic state, my first priority was to refuel and so I rode around for a while getting colder and colder trying to locate the one petrol pump and get the job done now. I instinctively knew I wouldn't want to be doing this first thing the next morning. I was so cold it took me a while fumbling with my keys and the petrol cap but eventually, fuelled up I made my way to my hotel. I use the word hotel loosely, because it looked more like a bunch of portacabins stuck together. I don't think the designers of Prudhoe Bay were into style.

It was a good job I'd booked ahead of time because there was precious little room anywhere. After showering, I was having a coffee in the canteen when the receptionist asked me,

"Excuse me. Are you the motorcyclist?"

"Yes I am. Is there a problem?"

"No I just wondered if you wouldn't mind sharing your room tonight? Another motorcyclist has just arrived, he hasn't booked a room and is too tired to go on."

"No problem. Where is he?"

"He's just unpacking his bike now. I'll send him to your room"

Two minutes later there was a knock on the door and in walked Austin from Chicago. He was the one I passed hours before in the fog and mud! After swapping Dalton stories and showering we made our way to the restaurant,

"What on earth possessed you to try and ride a road bike up the Dalton?" I asked over dinner.

"Somebody told me it was possible and I thought I'd try it," he replied with a rueful look. I just looked at him,

“I know, I know,” he said, shaking his head.

“What time are you heading off tomorrow?” I asked, hoping for a bit of company on the dreaded return trip.

“Straight after breakfast?” I offered.

“As soon as I wake up! I want to get out of here as soon as I can!”

Both of us weren`t relishing the return journey at all, now we knew just how bad it could be, we were hoping for better weather in the morning. Sadly, we were to be disappointed!

Toe in the Arctic Ocean!

But first I had a task to perform. I promised if I made it to Prudhoe Bay I would at least dip my toe in the Arctic. Well, you have to haven`t you? The weather was colder than normal (according to the locals) with a biting north wind that cut right through you, despite several layers and my big jacket. Because of the high security around Prudhoe, (the U.S. protecting one of its valuable assets) it wasn’t possible to go anywhere unsupervised, so to reach the Arctic Ocean you had to join an official tour. Prudhoe Bay itself is a vast complex and although the bus tour took over an hour it was a fascinating insight into another world. It might be a Godforsaken, windswept and bitterly cold place but it is so big it produces 20% of North America`s oil. Personally, I couldn`t wait to put it behind me as soon as possible, and the more miles between me and the Arctic, the better.

The next morning I was up early. Filled with trepidation and a good deal of anxiety about the road back. My anxiety increased when I looked over to where Austin was sleeping and saw an empty bed. He must have slipped out really early. I know he was very worried about the road conditions and wanted to leave before the road works began. We'd noticed on the way up that much of the road was being resurfaced or reconstructed, which basically meant huge tractors and diggers churning up vast amounts of mud so that one side of the road was 2 feet higher than the other making the terrain extremely difficult to cross over on a motorbike. Several times I had almost lost control and crossing over to the other side. Adrenaline had become my constant companion on the Dalton.

I left at 6.00 am and was thankful I'd fuelled up the day before. I just wanted to put as many miles between Prudhoe and me as I could. If anything the weather was slightly worse and again bitterly cold. I spent most of the first 85 miles stood up on the pegs as I counted off the mile markers. Unfortunately, the connector from my heated gloves to the battery wasn't long enough to do this with ease and somewhere over the first twenty miles it fell off. By the time I'd noticed my gloves cooling down it was too late. I stopped and walked back down the track in a fruitless attempt to find it, after a cursory look I knew it would be pointless and more important, time consuming to continue so I pressed on and hoped the weather would get milder the further south I rode.

After about 170 miles I saw the Atigun Pass in the distance, again it seemed to be shrouded in low cloud, even denser than the way up, and as I climbed it became even thicker with visibility down to forty or fifty feet in parts, the last place you wanted to meet an oncoming truck. This is the type of riding that takes immense mental concentration and is extremely fatiguing so I was thankful and relieved when I descended the other side and finally came out of the low lying cloud.

I made it back to Wiseman with only a few more heart stopping moments meeting diggers coming my way and having to cross the heavily rutted and thick mud to avoid them. The last few miles were completed in torrential rain so when I finally pulled up at The Arctic Getaway I was drenched, tired and not a little grumpy. After showering and cooking up a pasta dish I sat down to work on my blog and did a piece to camcorder reflecting on the journey so far. The ride up the Dalton had certainly been the most demanding riding of my life and without the experience off the BMW course and my heated clothing, it may well have proved too difficult.

As I put my head on the pillow that night, despite the 24 hr daylight, I slept the sleep of an exhausted but satisfied man. I had achieved the first part of the plan and had ridden to the Arctic Ocean. The hardest part of the infamous Dalton was now over. I fell into a fitful sleep not realising just how wrong I was going to be.

CHAPTER 4

The Dalton bites back......

The next day, fortified by another hearty breakfast I headed south down the Dalton re-tracing my steps. I filled up with fuel at Coldfoot Camp and rode off in welcome sunshine for the next fuel stop at the Yukon River crossing. I was beginning to enjoy the solitary nature of the Dalton and was maybe lifted by the belief I'd done the hard bit and the weather was improving. After a few miles I glimpsed in my wing mirror and noticed something flapping in the breeze. It was my rain suit that I hadn't strapped down properly. I made a mental note to do that at my next stop and thought no more of it. The rest of the ride to the River crossing was proving peaceful and almost meditative. It felt like I was the only person alive on the Dalton and I was quite enjoying the solitude when I suddenly felt a bump and a jerk as if I'd ridden over something which was strange because there was nothing on the dirt track at all. I slowly pulled up and quickly glanced in my mirror.

There was nothing flapping. My rain suit wasn't there. But how could that have fallen off? I was a little confused as I dismounted and sure enough the suit had gone, but to my horror I saw where it had gone. It had got caught in my chain and had been pulled through the chain and sprocket and completely destroyed my rear master cylinder.

"Oh, fuck, fuck, fuck!" I shouted to no one, my heart racing with adrenaline fuelled panic, "why the fuck did you let that happen?"

I berated myself for the stupidity. Now I had no rear brake at all and my earlier confidence vanished in a heartbeat. The solitude I was enjoying now became my worst nightmare. I had always been plagued by the thought of my bike breaking down in the middle of nowhere. As I attempted to pull myself together and calm my emotions, I pulled as much of the torn and melted rain suit residue from the chain and assessed the true damage.

O.K. I have no rear brake but at least nothing else is damaged which means I can still ride. I'll just have to be extra careful and nurse it until I get back to Fairbanks, I concluded.

Remounting and gingerly heading down the slight incline, I was still annoyed with myself for not stopping immediately and securing the rain suit when I first spotted it flapping. This internal dialogue continued for some time. The main drawback of solo riding is being alone in your helmet for hours everyday. It can be a very scary place. As Milton observed,

"The mind is its own place, and in itself can make a heaven of hell, a hell of heaven."

I was to become adept at the latter. One of the main personal objectives of the whole trip was to become better able to "go with the flow." I recognised a weakness of mine was the need to control things, so I deliberately set out on a journey where I knew things would go wrong and I wanted to be able to accept them when they did and not get stressed by them. I was falling short of my objective.

I continued down the Dalton and with every passing mile my confidence grew little by little. Indeed, I was feeling almost euphoric. The infamous Haul Road I had watched on television's "Ice Road Truckers" was almost complete. The road I had read and worried so much about was virtually over. I had conquered the infamous Dalton! I was only seven miles from the end after completing 821 of the most challenging miles I had ever experienced, and it was in this state of self congratulatory naivety that it all went horribly wrong.

I'm still not exactly sure what happened. I remember riding into some heavy mud as I came over a rise probably carrying a little too much speed and without a rear brake. Maybe I forgot and grabbed a heavy handful of front brake, which destabilised the bike? I'm not sure, but the net result was the front started to wobble and twist violently and I just knew I couldn't control it. I was going to crash.

The next thing I knew, I was lying sprawled out on my back in the mud. There was total silence. The bike was few feet away on its side and both panniers had broken off and spilt their contents all over the dirt road.

With adrenaline still coursing through me I conducted a very quick personal check of my arms and legs to check that nothing was broken. Apart from a very sore wrist I seemed O.K. The next thing was the bike. At first glance it didn't seem too bad but as I got closer I noticed the handlebars were badly bent on the left side.

"Oh fuck!" It must have been a seriously heavy impact to bend them that much I thought. Then the negative thought process kicked in.

What am I going to do now? Only a week into the trip and it's over. I planned this for a year and now what's going to happen? I've broken the bike and I'm miles from civilisation. Then it began to rain.

I tried to pick the bike up but it was lying downhill and was too heavy, my feet just couldn't get traction in the mud and I didn't know whether it would start even if I did get it upright. As the rain continued to fall I just stood there trying to figure out what to do. At that moment, in the middle of this wilderness I heard the sound of an engine. I turned round to see a 4x4 truck coming up the dirt road. The driver pulled up in front of my bike and jumped out,

"Are you O.K.?"

"Yea, just a bit shook up, but I'm not sure about the bike."

Together we righted it and put it on the side stand. He was used to riding dirt bikes and after a few attempts managed to get the engine fired up.

"Thank God for that. At least it starts, but is it rideable?" I asked, deferring to his obvious expertise.

"Let's see if we can straighten the bars. I used to do this all the time when I rode dirt bikes."

I was reassured by his confidence. Sadly, this wasn't to be as easy as his dirt bike. He was a big man, maybe 6 '2'', but he couldn't budge it. I would have to try to ride it as it was.

"Where are you heading?"

"Back down to Fairbanks," I replied.

"Dalton 1 BMW 0"

"Let's get all your gear on the back of my truck and I'll follow you back to make sure you're O.K."

He had just driven the seventy five miles from Fairbanks taking his young son on a fishing trip.

"That's really kind, but what about your son and his fishing?"

"Aw, there's always time for fishing!"

I couldn't believe his generosity and kindness. I honestly don't know what would have happened had he not shown up.

With the rain providing a steady drizzle I climbed back on the bike and checked if everything else was working. Apart from a slight bend in the clutch lever it seemed O.K. I set off gingerly down the muddy track still in a state of shock, trying to keep the bike pointing forwards with a significant bend on the left handlebar. Unsurprisingly, I now felt very anxious on the increasingly muddy surface and was extremely thankful I had only seven miles of the Dalton left. At the same time I was desperately upset to have got this far and with only a few miles left to have made such a stupid error. These and a myriad other negative thoughts and feelings occupied my mind for the hour or so journey back to Fairbanks and by the time we arrived back at the camp ground I was simultaneously relieved and exhausted.

As we unloaded my gear from his truck I thanked him profusely and offered him some money for all his kindness, which he refused, and I don't know why, maybe I was still in shock, but I didn't get his name. To this day he remains a total stranger who turned up at the right time to help me. Serendipity.

I checked back into the camp I had left several days earlier and decided I needed a few days to recover. My priority was to get the bike fixed so I could continue the journey and fortunately, Fairbanks had the only BMW dealership in Alaska. The next day

I took the bike in and asked them for an estimate on time and money to do the necessary repairs,

“New rear master cylinder and new handlebars, that'll be about $600,” said the service manager.

“Any idea how long it will take?” I asked, trying to be philosophical about the financial pain.

“Three to four days if we can get the parts ordered.”

“O.K. can you call me on this number when it's done?”

There was nothing I could do except use the time to recover and reflect on the past few days. I decided against mentioning this particular trauma in my regular blog. I didn't want to worry everyone at home unnecessarily, but I had to tell Jane. Having been out of contact for the duration of the Dalton I knew she would be worried until I'd checked in. The camp kitchen area was the only place there was a wifi connection for Skype, so I headed straight there to let her know what was happening,

“I was getting worried,” she said. “Are you O.K.?'

“Yes, fine. Just had a little problem,” I replied, trying to play down the situation.

“I thought so. What's happened?”

“Well, I had a bit of a small crash on the Dalton, but I'm O.K., just a sore wrist. The bike needs a bit of attention though.”

We had a long chat and I hoped I had put her mind at rest. Thank God for Skype! I wasn't aware at the time but it was to become a lifeline for me over the next few months.

As I signed off I didn't mention my growing concern with my right wrist. It was slightly swollen and had developed a nagging ache. I was hoping there was nothing broken, if so, that would prove to be a big problem at this early stage. It was yet another thing to worry about and feed my underlying and constant anxiety. I would have to get it checked out for my own peace of mind.

The next day I caught a taxi to the hospital expecting to be there at least a whole morning as is customary in the U.K. As I walked through the sliding doors I was met with silence! The room was empty apart from the reception desk,

"Good morning! How are you today?" said a cheery receptionist.

Wondering whether they had opened specifically for me that day my eyes flitted quickly around the room for the usual suspects – drunks, kids with bandaged arms, the tattooed masses, etc.

"Fine thanks. Just got a problem with my wrist." I said rather distractedly.

"What exactly is the problem?

I explained what had occurred and was given a form to fill out.

"Please take a seat over there and someone will be out to see you soon."

Two x rays, and a consultation later it was confirmed that I hadn't broken the wrist but rather it was badly sprained and I was recommended a brace to wear for a week or so. Mightily relieved and still somewhat bemused by this empty hospital I enquired where I should pay for the treatment? I took the paperwork to the desk and got it processed. The total came to a $1,000 dollars!

"Bloody hell! No wonder this place is empty."

I'd already checked through my insurance documents to clarify my position and I knew that if the sum exceeded £500 I had to phone the U.K. to get permission to go ahead. The exchange rate meant that I was just under that amount so I naturally thought everything would be O.K. Little did I know that a can of worms had just been opened and wouldn't be closed for nearly a year.

I spent the next few days recovering, writing my blog and waiting for the call from the garage. When the due date had come and gone I called them,

"Any news on my 650 Dakar?" I asked hopefully.

"Let me take your details and check for you."

"Yes, unfortunately, they sent the wrong bars so we had to re-order."

My heart sank. I was eager to get back on the road and get over this disappointing interlude.

"We're really sorry about this and we'd like to loan you an 800 GS so at least you can ride around for the next couple of days."

Not that I could really go anywhere of significance, at least it was an olive branch of a kind so I took them up on their offer. In truth, it was just good to be back in the saddle to get my confidence restored.

Eventually the call came, "your bike is ready for you to collect sir."

"Fantastic! I'll be right down!" I said. While waiting for the dirt of the Dalton to be washed off the bike I sat outside sipping a coffee and chatting to the service manager.

"Yea, we'll be real busy tomorrow. The Hoka Hey is coming

through here."

"Hoka Hey? What's that?" I asked.

"There will be a couple of thousand Harley riders. They're riding from Florida to Alaska and whoever gets here first wins $500,000."

"Wow, that's some prize money!"

The Service Manager was clearly cynical about the whole event and I was about to ask him why when I spotted a familiar face and bike pulling into the car park,

"Austin, you made it! How are you?"

My room mate from Prudhoe was looking good and so was his bike. No wonder he wasn't there when I woke up that morning to leave Prudhoe Bay. He told me he'd left at 3.00 am as he couldn't wait to get out of the place! But at least he'd got back in one piece,

"Sorry to hear about your spill. Is there anything I can do to help out?"

"No I'm O.K. now but thanks for the offer. Good luck on the journey back home!"

"You too! Ride safe!"

After relieving me of another substantial chunk of money I thanked the service manager and rode back to the camp and quickly loaded my gear. I had already planned the next leg and was keen to put in some miles.

CHAPTER 5

Oil leaks and long days in the Yukon

After my extended stay in Fairbanks the journey recommenced with a two hundred mile run to a little place called Tok. Another place in the middle of nowhere. Not for the first time it reminded me of the wild west when a stranger rides into town. I rode through the town slowly scanning left and right looking for possible accommodation and refreshment and within a couple of minutes I was through the town and out the other side. I'd noticed a store with some kind of café attached so I did a quick u turn and headed back into town. I pulled up in front of the store, killed the engine and dismounted. As I did so I glanced down at the chain and noticed a small drop of oil appearing, and then another.

"Oh fuck!" my heart rate increased and yet more adrenaline started to seep into my system again.

The discovery of an oil leak created an anxiety which stayed with me for quite a while and the negative voices began flooding into my consciousness,

"Shit, the nearest BMW garage is nearly a thousand miles away."

Not sure how bad it was I bought extra oil and determined to nurse it along to the nearest garage of any description. It was about this time that my lack of mechanical ability and knowledge really exposed me and was to prove very damaging to my levels of confidence throughout the whole trip. The truth is, most engines leak a little oil and it is of no significance and the amount wasn't huge anyway, but when you're in a fragile mind set it becomes easy to "catastrophise" and I became very adept at "mountain climbing over molehills."

The downside of solo travel again became apparent. What I really needed was someone to remind me that it wasn't anything to worry about, but "someone" wasn't there. Not for the last time did echoes of a long lost conversation ring in my ears,

"Yes, I want to do it solo. I want to challenge myself and step out of my comfort zone."

Yea, right. Bollocks to that. Right now would be a good time to have a travelling companion. Pushing these thoughts to the back of my mind I needed to focus on finding accommodation for the night and the weather which had been fine in Fairbanks had become changeable. Cold, blustery, wet and fairly miserable, much like my mood. Enquiring at the store I was directed to a motel down the main street.

"Yes, we have one room left sir. That'll be $97."

"I'll take it," I said quickly at the same time thinking Alaska was really making a hole in my savings, but I needed the comfort of a decent bed and a good meal.

I'll save money when I start camping, I rationalised. I had brought a tent to use when the climate was more favourable. As I was unpacking the bike two more riders pulled up and checked into the rooms on either side of me. It looked like I might have some company tonight. The thought of conversation with like - minded people raised my spirits and so at the first opportunity I engaged them in conversation,

"Hi, where are you both heading?

The younger of the two was in his 30s and rode a BMW 1200 Adventure,

"Back to Anchorage," he replied, "just had a couple of weeks riding through Canada. How about you?"

I briefly related my story, "Hey, that's an amazing trip! I would love to do that!"

The second rider, Jim, was probably in his early 60s and rode a Harley. He was also heading back north.

"Do you drink beer?" Paul asked.

I felt like saying, "Is the Pope a Catholic?" But thinking the reference might have been lost on him, I nodded, "Yea I sure do. Can we get some around here?"

"There's a general store down the road. I'll just ride down and pick some up"

Five minutes later he arrived back with his panniers loaded with cans. He broke off one from the pack and offered it to me,

"Thanks very much. It's great to have some company!"

For the next few hours we sat outside our respective rooms chatting about life, the universe and everything – as you do. The two were not related; they weren't even riding together. They'd happened upon the same place at the same time and yet they shared one common trait. They had an interest in all things military.

"My biggest regret," Paul said, "was not having the opportunity to serve my country."

Jim nodded "Yea, my time in Korea was the best."

"Really?" I added somewhat bemused. Maybe I'd stumbled upon two archetypal rednecks. But no, these seemed both normal and intelligent people. I decided not to pursue the line of thinking that was running through my mind but rather, enjoy some company and sip a couple of beers. Meeting other riders coming the opposite way also gives you the opportunity to discover critical information about road conditions ahead but even before I had time to ask Paul volunteered,

"Be really careful on the road to Haines. There are some real bad frost heaves for about twenty miles this side of Destruction Bay."

"You bet," chipped in Jim, "I almost fell right in one. You really need to slow down and concentrate."

The damage caused by intense frost had buckled the road in places leaving huge cracks and holes. I thanked them for the advice and a short time later thought it time to turn in and get a good rest before my usual early start. Early starts became my routine. I much prefer to be on the road early and if possible stop early wherever I am so I can at least enjoy the place I'm staying in for a little while before moving on, but in Alaska it was a necessity because of the vast distances between any form of civilisation. It would mean riding hard all day. At least the route was straightforward – just follow the Alaskan Highway 1!

After breakfast with my two companions we wished each other a safe ride and I headed south. After a couple of hours on the road with nothing but wilderness surrounding me, I noticed in the distance a signpost welcoming me to Yukon Territory and like nearly all road signposts in this part of the world was peppered with bullet holes! A short while later I happened upon a border checkpoint. Slowing down I noticed a few vehicles coming the other way and lining up to cross into Alaska. It was a little confusing as I hadn't been asked to stop and there seemed no obvious checkpoint to do so. I rode on down a slight incline of gravel and stone, standing on the pegs to gain traction. I hated this kind of terrain. Ever since my altercation with the Dalton, my confidence on any unstable road surfaces had completely vanished, so I rode with intense concentration and yet more adrenaline for the next two hundred yards.

Counterintuitively, this kind of riding requires the rider to be totally in tune with every twitch of the back wheel. The rider is an extension of the bike and necessitates an instinctive and relaxed feel as opposed to the natural tendency to tense up. Very difficult to do when you are almost frozen with anxiety and fearful of falling. Having negotiated the worst bit I pulled up next to a sign welcoming me to Canada! How could I be in Canada when I haven't officially left Alaska? Am I in Canada illegally? Glancing back at the checkpoint I was faced with a dilemma. Do I push on anyway and if stopped plead ignorance or go back and check it out?

"Shit, I'd better go and check," I said out loud, not relishing riding back up the incline through the gravel again. So carefully turning around I rode back up to the checkpoint but instead of lining up behind the other vehicles I cut across to the road I'd entered on as if to bypass the checkpoint. This manoeuvre clearly caused a flurry of official activity and in no time several, armed border guards rushed out,

"Hey buddy what are you doin'?" one guard said while flagging me down.

"Sorry, but I couldn't find passport control," I replied as innocently as I could.

It turns out that confusingly, the actual border crossing to enter Canada was a few miles further on. Thanking him and apologising for almost causing an international incident I headed back down the road slightly relieved but frustrated and annoyed they hadn't made it clearer.

Sure enough, a few more miles brought me to the official entry point which, for the first of many border crossings proved fairly easy. I was now officially in Canada! I had ridden all the way across Alaska. I was congratulating myself on this milestone, when the back of the bike kicked away dramatically as I hit yet another patch of gravel and in a heartbeat my whole system was flooded with adrenaline,

"Fuckin' 'ell Brian. Concentrate!" I shouted out loud in annoyance. It was yet another reminder to be constantly vigilant. As stunning as the scenery was, I was constantly reminded to be alert for subtle changes in road conditions (not wanting to repeat my Dalton experience) which, when you're riding six to eight hours a day would take its toll on mind and body.

From Tok to the little outpost of Haines Junction was an uneventful but fairly arduous seven hour ride followed a day later with another seven to eight hours to Whitehorse, the capital of the Yukon. The Yukon is about twice the size of Great Britain with a total population of 30,000 and 26,000 live in Whitehorse!

"You're about the bravest fucker I know!"

I rode into town pretty tired and my lower back was aching so I planned on spending a couple of days off the bike for some much needed rest. I also knew that Whitehorse had the only motorcycle dealership for hundreds of miles and I was very keen to get the oil leak fixed and maybe change my tyres from the off road ones to a more dual purpose set. I quickly found a suitable hotel (meaning as cheap as possible) and locating the exact position of the garage, planned to be there first thing the next day. The priority now was to explore the town.

I bought myself a little diary to record various thoughts and observations. Apart from writing the blog I'm not one for keeping a journal. I don't really have the necessary self discipline to do it on a regular basis, but I thought it might be worth recording my thoughts so I could look back and see what was really going on without the softer, rose tinted memories we often hang on to. I found a nice, funky coffee bar, a great cappuccino and muffin and for the first time on the trip put pen to paper with my real feelings. Without the luxury of a riding partner as a sounding board, the diary was to prove a dumping ground for all my nagging fears, anxieties and concerns. This first entry was on June 28th,

"Just reflecting on the last two weeks on the road. Crashing on the Dalton really shook my confidence and sent me into a downward spiral of worrying about everything – the bike, my health, whether I can complete the trip. It really put into perspective just how big a challenge I've taken on. A long arduous run of 7/9 hour days constantly worrying about the oil leak and what if the bike breaks down in the middle of nowhere! Going with the flow is proving really tough to live by. I feel disappointed in my lack of ability to deal with all this stuff more resourcefully….."

It felt strangely cathartic pouring out all the pent up feelings and emotions, almost as if I'd lightened my load a little.

"Thanks! That was a great cappuccino. I'll be back tomorrow!" The young girl smiled and thanked me, "you're welcome!"

First thing in the morning I rode to Yukon Yamaha where I got them to check for the oil leak,

"You might as well do an oil change while you're replacing the tyres," I added.

Unlike in the U.K. oil and tyre changes would have to be planned with more forethought. This would be a taster for what was to come. In Mexico and beyond, finding the right tyres (or any tyres) would prove more problematical.

$600 later I rode back to the hotel with my brand new tyres and an accompanying sense of relief that my biggest concern had been resolved. No more worrying about oil leaks. It was all sorted.

That night I headed out to a local bar for a beer and a bite to eat.

With the locals being extremely friendly, conversation was easy at the bar.

“Hi, where are you from?” Slurred a slightly drunk chap sitting next to me at the bar.

“England.”

“England!” he said very loudly. Do you think inebriation makes you slightly deaf?

“Jeez, you’re a long way from home. Whadya doing here?”

I explained the purpose of the trip and he insisted on buying me a beer and said I was either ex military or slightly crazy doing the trip on my own.

“Those people down there are dangerous!”

He was shocked I wasn`t carrying a gun or any weapon at all. I told him it wasn`t an English thing to do! He just shook his head.

“You`re about the bravest fucker I know.”

I must admit I didn`t know whether to take it as a compliment or what.

CHAPTER 6

Bear Paranoia in the Rockies

The next day, confident the bike was now O.K. I headed for Watson Lake, a ride of some 207 miles through some appalling weather and worse roads. The spectre of the Dalton sat on my shoulder every time I saw dirt or gravel covered roads. The inconsistent nature of the roads served to keep me focused at all times. One minute I'd be riding comfortably along great tarmac and then for no good reason I would hit an extended patch of gravel. It seems scattering 50 – 100 metre patches of gravel across the road is the way they construct the highways.

Pulling into a petrol station for a break I met up with an American Harley rider who was one of over eight hundred riding from Key West, Florida to Homer, Alaska (9,000 miles). This was the "Hoka Hey" race the service manager in Fairbanks was telling me about. I had a chat with him and wished him a safe ride before pushing on to Watson Lake.

I rode into town and then did my usual recce of the town to find the cheapest accommodation. Alaska and Canada were proving to be very expensive and I was mindful of my budget and the distance I still had to travel. I eventually found "cheapish" accommodation in an old 1940s airbase (ironically run by a German couple who had lovingly restored it). Unpacking the bike, I discovered the leak was back. Now the only place to get it looked at was going to be Calgary (a long, long way). The anxiety returned like a trusted and loyal friend.

"I wouldn't worry too much," the owner said, "I've had a BMW for years. These Rotax engines are bombproof. They go on forever."

I sincerely hoped he was right and temporarily, at least, I felt more confortable. As with most of the small towns in this part of Canada, there was precious little to see, but at least in Watson Lake there was the famous "Signpost Forest." This was the town's main attraction. Don`t ask why, but signposts from all over the world are placed there.

With rain hammering down all night, I prepared myself for another day of riding in the rain as I set off early for Fort Nelson.

So far, although I knew I was heading into bear country, I had ridden hundreds of miles without a bear in sight. My main focus had been on the bike and the oil leak and indeed that was on my mind as I rounded a bend in the road when I noticed something moving up ahead by the side of the road. I slowed slightly and squinted into the distance,

"Shit! That looks like a bear to me," I muttered, "a brown one too. It's a Grizzly."

My heart temporarily taking up residence in my mouth and beating with increasing tempo I watched as the Grizzly slowly lolloped across the road a hundred yards ahead of my by now slowing bike. This first bear sighting focused my wandering mind completely and from then on I spent the ride scouring the open road ahead glancing to left and right checking out the thick forest on either side. It occurred to me that this would not be a good place to breakdown, which then automatically fed on my insecurities and bear paranoia became my new best friend.

Yet again serving to remind me of my vulnerable position. I made a mental note to stop at the next town and arm myself with some Bear Spray. Over the next hours, my mind occupied itself with different bear scenarios and what I would try to do if I did breakdown and how I could avoid becoming bear meat. I'd of course heard all about the fact that bears are more scared of us than we are of them. Oh really? I beg to differ.

"Don't worry, they are shy creatures and if you make a lot of noise they will run away," I was confidently informed by an expert in Alaska, "unless, of course, you get caught between a bear and its cub."

"What happens then," I asked.

"It'll attack you," he said in a matter of fact way, "and a grizzly can do over 30 mph uphill," he added unnecessarily.

Note to self – don't get caught in that predicament.

To add to the bear paranoia, the black bears behave completely differently. The key difference between the two is that if you play dead with one kind they will basically leave you alone after a while, but with the other kind if you play dead they will eat you! I'd been told all this but now I had a big problem. I couldn't remember which one did which. If it's a black bear do I run away or play dead? I couldn't remember. My sense of unease and jitteriness increased as I rode past several black and brown bears by the side of the road over the next few hours. By the time I rode into Fort Nelson, I was wet, cold and emotionally drained.

Fort Nelson sounded quite quaint but it wasn't and to make matters worse it poured down for two days. With nothing much to do I found a nice pub (Dan`s Pub) and hunkered down to watch baseball and Canadian Football (like American, but they think it`s better!)

The next day brought a minor break in the weather so I got up early but had to wait until the shops opened to buy some Bear Spray.

I handed over my $40 for a large gold aerosol can.

"Exactly how does this work?" I enquired of the owner. For some reason I felt compelled to get up to speed with such potential life saving information. Knowledge is power.

“Well first of all,” he said, “you have to make sure you’re upwind of the bear.”

Oh that’s great. So in the middle of a potential bear attack I have to have the wherewithal to ensure my correct positioning!

“Otherwise the pepper spray will blow back in your direction,” he added. I nodded sagely.

“Then you point the spray like this, pull the restraining safety pin and press this button.”

“Simple,” I said.

“Yup. That’s pretty much it.”

“Does it work?” I enquired, desperately wanting an “every time” kind of response.

“So I’m told,” he answered with a shrug of his shoulders.

I left the store feeling marginally better now I was “tooled up” and decided to pack it into my tank bag for easy access. As I rode out of town and back into the wilderness, it crossed my mind that, in the event of a bear attack, you would have to be amazingly calm in the face of a seven foot Grizzly, bearing down upon you at 30 mph, to check the wind, stand firm, and keep a steady aim without losing control of your bowels.

“I wouldn’t worry about bears. It’s the moose that’s the biggest killer on the roads.” The barman had helpfully informed me at Dan’s Bar.

All this good advice helped to really concentrate the mind during the day’s ride. On top of keeping a lookout for bears, stray moose, buffalo, deer, gravel, and pot holes, I was totally knackered by the time I reached Dawson Creek.

During a petrol stop en route I noticed a BMW 1200 GS parked next to what looked like a big trike but it had two wheels at the front instead of the back. Peering over it with curiosity the riders came out of the café.

"An interesting machine!" I said smiling.

"Yea, that's Wendy's. It goes like a rocket!"

"I'm Brian!" He said.

"So am I!" I replied.

It turns out that Brian and Wendy were ex pats from England now living in Canada.

"Where are you heading?" Brian asked.

"Dawson Creek," I replied.

"So are we! Fancy meeting up for a beer tonight?"

"That would be great!" I said, eagerly grabbing the chance of a bit of company.

They were such a lovely couple, even though Brian had been having technical problems with his BMW, they took pity on me and bought me dinner - the best ribs I'd ever tasted!

That was the last of the good life. Having decided I was way over budget and needed to severely economise, the day after I set off for Prince George determined to find a campsite. Another long and very tiring leg eventually found me arriving in town at about 5.00 pm. Maybe I was just very tired, but I pulled up to a junction to check the GPS for a campsite and lost concentration. The bike went down with a crash! Another blow to the ego and a snapped front brake lever (still, you don`t need the end two inches anyway). By which time I`d had enough and went to the cheapest, seediest downtown motel there was, which luckily was just round the corner. Shower, lube the chain and find a bar. Deja Vu?

The following day I was going to be heading to Jasper in the Rockies. A famous ski resort and a place I`d heard a lot about. While packing the bike (for the mandatory early start) I noticed a problem with the pannier racks from the drop the day before, so it was out with the tools. A couple on a big Honda Goldwing motorcycle were also staying at the Motel. Tim and Angela were on their way back to Seattle and they kindly helped me put the racks back on straight,

"I have a 650 back home. They're great bikes. Where are you headed?" Tim asked.

"Jasper for a couple of days and then I'm not sure."

"If you're passing through Seattle you're welcome to stay," he said offering me his card.

"Thanks very much. I'll be sure to call if I'm passing that way."

I was just finishing tying my bag on the rear rack when Tim asked,

"Are you going to the rally?"

"What rally is that?"

"The BMW rally in Redmond, Oregon?" he answered. "It's the biggest in the country. There'll be 6,000 riders there. You really should go. It might be useful to you."

"It sounds like a good idea," I replied.

"If you like, you could stay over at our place and we could ride down there together?"

"That would be great!" A bit of company on the road for a couple of days would be more than welcome after the endless solitary days.

"Why don't I give you a call when I reach Seattle?"

We settled on a loose plan and both went our separate ways. Once again I was struck by how helpful people just kept turning up!

Tim and Angela

Just like Brian and Wendy, the world`s full of kind, generous bikers! Thanking them for their help I set off for Jasper and was soon soaking wet (again).

The beautiful Rocky Mountains hid themselves behind dense clouds and swirling rain. Still, it did clear up in time to pitch my tent and armed with my Bear Spray I went to bed knowing tomorrow it would be better.

Sadly, the inclement weather didn't relent. In fact it rained all night and pretty much most of the next day. It was cold, grey and pretty miserable, so with nothing else I could do (Jasper itself was two miles away), I went back to the temporary comfort of my sleeping bag. The grey and heavy rainclouds matched my mood. This didn't fit at all with my picture of the Rocky Mountains, however, I'd discovered there was a hotel in Jasper that offered massage, so in desperate need physically and mentally I'd booked one for the afternoon. The incessant rain forced me to put back my appointment for an hour in the hope that it would relent.

As I lay in my sleeping bag with only the sound of the rain occupying my thoughts I reflected on the belief that I was supposed to be "living the dream" as some people had indicated. Indeed I was privileged to be able to attempt such a journey and at the same time I was also consumed with a kind of guilt for feeling so self pitying. Thankfully, the sound of silence shook me out of my negative thought process as the rain finally abated. I jumped on the bike and headed into town and eventually located the hotel only to be told that I was thirty minutes late. It turns out that I had passed through another time zone entering Alberta and hadn't adjusted my watch.

"Oh for fucks sake!" I muttered under my breath.

"Do you still want to go ahead?" the therapist asked.

"Yea, sure. Might as well," I replied, now totally pissed off.

Lying on the bed trying to shake off this massive feeling of irritation, my mind was attempting to make sense of what was happening. It seemed the universe was offering me countless opportunities to learn to "go with the flow" and I just kept on fighting it and constantly losing. The scary thing was, I was only three weeks into this journey and so far every fear, vulnerability and weakness (that we all have buried deep within us) had been discovered, unlocked and given free reign. Almost totally consuming me at times, and this was only North America. I reflected that in terms of going with the flow I was yet again failing miserably. It seemed so simple at home listening to Byron Katie and "Loving What Is." As I climbed off the massage bed, I made a mental note that this had to change.

Thankfully, the day after broke with blue skies and at last I could see the real beauty of the Rockies. My damp spirits of the day before had lifted with the clouds and I was feeling much more buoyant as I walked the two miles into Jasper. As pleasant as the walk was I was also aware of how desperately quiet the road was and remembering I was still deep into bear country, my senses were alert to any slight sound or movement from the trees on either side of the road,

"Shit! I've forgotten my bear spray," I said out loud. Speaking to myself was now an accepted phenomenon. Somewhere in my mind, I recalled that singing and making a noise was also a deterrent. Unfortunately, the only song that sprung to mind was a Monty Python song, so I deterred any local bears with rousing choruses of, "Sit on my face and tell me that you love me..."

"Welcome to bear country!"

Don't ask me why. It just popped in my head and refused to leave.

It seemed to do the trick as I arrived in one piece in Jasper and immediately went on my usual quest of finding the nearest wifi.

I found a great cafe/bakery and ordered a cappuccino and pastry only to set up my netbook and find their wifi was down! Finishing my breakfast I resumed my internet search. I quickly found another spot, but had to order a full cooked breakfast in order to use their wifi! C'est la vie! These are the challenges of being on the road. Staying on top of my e mail, Skype, blog, etc, sometimes proved difficult. I took a brief tour around the town and then headed back to camp with the forests resonating to the sounds of Monty Python. Why change a winning formula?

On the way to my pitch I came across three other BMW riders. I spent some time chatting with them and when they also suggested I attend the big BMW rally that would be taking place in Oregon, it seemed I was destined to be there. Meeting kindred spirits seemed like a good idea. It would also give me a few days off the bike and maybe I could pick up some advice about Mexico and further south. With that in mind, I created the first real plan in three weeks. Redmond, Oregon it was!

From Jasper, I rode about three hours to Lake Louise. The route took me along the beautiful Icefields Parkway, which is the road connecting Banff National Park with Jasper National Park. Mile after mile of stunning scenery finally brought me to Lake Louise campsite which was so popular I had to queue to get in and managed to bag one of the last sites. As with Jasper, the site was situated outside the town and necessitated a two mile walk to get provisions and wifi connections. My routine was now well drilled - pitch the tent, stow any food in the bear proof lockers and walk into town to find wifi!

On the way to Lake Louise

In the evening I attended an outdoor lecture on "A Year in the life of a Grizzly" on the basis that knowledge is power. I wanted to know what I would have to deal with in the event of a bear encounter. This campsite had bear warnings all over the place despite being surrounded by an electrified fence. It felt like camping in a mini Jurassic Park!

Returning to my tent a much wiser traveller, I noticed another bike next to my pitch so I wandered over to investigate,

"Hi, where are you from?" I asked the couple who were busying themselves preparing some hot food on their camping stove.

"England!" Grinned Dave as Jill popped her head out of their tent and added, "Manchester."

"Manchester? I'm from Blackburn," quickly adding, "originally!"

We exchanged stories from the road and blog addresses. They were leaving the next day for Calgary and the world famous stampede.

"Why don't you come with us?" Dave asked, "We've got a spare room?"

I must admit to being sorely tempted. It would be nice to have some company on the road but I had committed to "Couch Surfing" in a place called Kelowna two hundred miles to the south and my hosts were expecting me. (Also, I needed to get my oil leak checked out at the BMW garage). Thanking them for the kind offer, I wished them well, headed back to my tent and contemplated my forthcoming Couch Surfing experience.

CHAPTER 7

Couch Surfing in Kelowna – Tea and hot tubs in Surrey!

Before I left England, I had been following the exploits of a fellow motorcycling adventurer named Graham Styles. He had posted some brilliant videos of his Pan American trip and had kindly agreed to meet up so I could pick his brains about my journey.

"What you really need to do is sign up for Couch Surfing."

"Couch Surfing?"

"Yea, it's a global, online community of people who offer to accommodate you for a night or show you around," he responded, "you should check out the website."

And so that's exactly what I did. I uncovered a huge, online community of people all over the world who were more than happy to take in total strangers

A couple of weeks beforehand I'd logged on the site and punched in Kelowna and found several people offering to host. For some reason I was drawn to a lady called Myrna Park and when I checked her bio discovered she was into motivational speaking and training so I dropped her a line explaining about The Journey for Hope and asked if she would be kind enough to let me stay as I was passing through her town. She replied saying she would be happy to host me and gave me her phone number asking me to call when I was on the way.

"Hi Myrna! This is Brian!"

"Hi Brian, how are you?"

"Great thanks. Just thought I'd give you a call. I'm at a garage about an hour away from you, but when I arrive in Kelowna I have to drop off my bike at the BMW garage to check out my oil leak"

"That's no problem. I'll get Layton to pick you up from there. You can`t miss him. He`s a tall man with a beard and will be driving a pink car!"

I'd just dropped off my bike when sure enough, a big bear of a man rolled up in a pink hot rod! Enter Layton Park, speaker, author and humourist!

"You must be Layton!" I said thrusting out my hand,

"You must be Brian!" He said, smiling and shaking my hand vigorously, "let me take your bag."

"Wow, that's some car!" I exclaimed as he popped the boot of what looked like a souped up, open topped, hot rod in bright pink.

"Yea, it's my favourite toy! Jump in."

Myrna and Layton

And so began a fascinating two days were they treated me as one of the family, introduced me to their friends and even took me as a guest to a local meeting of the Canadian Association of Professional Speakers (CAPS). Myrna created some fantastic, healthy salads (best food I`d had in weeks!) and Layton regaled me with stories of his books and bikes. Myrna and Layton were two extraordinarily talented and generous people. We talked about quantum physics, personal development and the journey (literal and metaphorical) I was on. They created a haven for me to recover after many days of hard riding. It was just what I needed. Coincidence? I don`t think so. I was so comfortable there, I didn`t want to leave! But too soon, I had to get back on the road. Myrna insisted I soak my neck scarf and T shirt with water to combat the stifling heat (30-35 degrees!) and warned me about dehydration. With a commitment to stay in touch, I waved and headed off over the mountains towards Vancouver.

"Body Modifications?"

After a long, hot and sticky ride I finally arrived in Surrey (about thirteen miles from Vancouver). Nathan and Sandra who were both family friends, had kindly offered to accommodate me for a couple of days. I was met at the door by Nathan`s Dad, John who greeted me with a cup of tea and sandwiches (and also, a few beers!) It felt like being back in England (apart from the weather of course). By the time Nathan and Sandra had got back from work I was feeling remarkably relaxed.

"Who wants to go in the hot tub?" Nathan asked.

"Hot tub?" I said. This is the life I thought.

"Yea," he answered, "I had one put in in the back garden!"

So that was that! We all jumped in the hot tub and I started to feel the stresses of the road slip away. The next day, Nathan`s business partner, Sarah also came over and we had a fantastic barbecue and I think I decimated their beer supply. Nathan and Sarah run a company called "Body Mods". Yes, that`s right, they`re in the business of body modification, and I don`t mean going to the gym! They sell "things" that you either stick on or in your body. You get the idea. I was considering having a tattoo of a BMW 650 Dakar across my back and maybe a couple of piercings, but in the end I decided to book a massage instead. There`s only so much pain I can take.

I had a brilliant time and was once again overwhelmed by the generosity and hospitality I received, but after a couple of days of R+R, it was time to hit the road again. I was due to attend the big BMW rally in Redmond, Oregon two days later. On the way down I had arranged to stay overnight in Seattle, with Tim and Angela, the couple I had briefly met in Prince George.

The U.S. border was only a few miles from Surrey and as I approached I was mentally preparing myself for the 3rd degree. I`d heard about many U.S. and Canadian citizens getting a grilling and was warned not to get caught with anything controversial in my luggage, so I kept reminding myself,

"Whatever you do, you must declare the bear spray. You must declare the bear spray."

I rolled up, the guard checked my passport, asked me about the trip I was on, wished me luck and waved me on! Easy! Of course, I completely forgot about the spray.

I needed to change some currency and was advised to go to the nearest casino where I would get the best exchange rates.

"You can't miss it," Tim told me, "It's a huge building on the right side of the road."

Sure enough, after a few miles, signs started appearing advertising the opportunity to gamble! It seems that the local

Native American tribes were given the chance to generate income through opening and running casinos as a kind of retrospective compensation for stealing their land and consigning them to the reservations.

I pulled up in the car park and feeling rather scruffily dressed for the plush, opulent surroundings wandered through huge rooms with wall to wall slot machines and found myself in the main room. Here were the crap tables, roulette wheels, blackjack and poker tables and at the far end of the room I spotted the tellers dispensing chips and cash. I handed over my Canadian Dollars, pocketed my U.S. equivalents and headed for a small coffee bar I had spotted on the way in.

Replenished with a cappuccino and muffin I headed back onto the highway. I hit Seattle just in time for rush hour on the freeway, which slowed me down a little but also gave me more time to check the sat nav. It was in these circumstances that having the aid of technology certainly eased the stress of navigating around big cities. Tim had given me his address and I knew he lived on the outskirts of Seattle but it took much longer than I anticipated crossing the city at that time of day, nevertheless, I still got to Tim`s before he did. I didn't know it at the time but he was stuck in traffic a couple of miles behind me. After unpacking and showering, Tim drove us to a little Mexican restaurant and insisted on buying me dinner. Over dinner we talked about our love of bikes and it transpired that like me, Tim was a late adopter and had got into motorcycling late in life. Nevertheless, he turned out to be a very accomplished rider and mechanic. The following day we both set off for Redmond, Oregon and it was comforting to be riding with someone who not only rode the same bike, but also knew how to fix it if something went wrong!

It was really nice to have a bit of company on the road for the first time in a month. Tim, knowing the roads so well took us on a scenic route via several volcanoes including the famous Mount

St. Helens which erupted in 1980. The roads and scenery were spectacular. The route to Oregon was longer than I anticipated and because of deviating slightly to take in the sights we ran out of time and ended up camping overnight when it was clear we wouldn`t be getting to Redmond that day.

CHAPTER 8

Oregon: "Feeding the 6,000!"

We were both up very early the next day eager to get to the rally, which was only a couple of hours away. Despite the early start, the temperature was already climbing significantly. By the time we arrived in Redmond it was a sweltering 95° and it pretty much stayed that way for the next three days. After pitching our tents we went for a walk to orientate ourselves when I suddenly started to feel very weak, slightly nauseous and unstable on my feet. I recognised immediately the signs of dehydration and heat exhaustion. Taking on plenty of water in these conditions was essential, and I had compounded the problem by riding for hours, and obviously losing a lot of fluids. Clearly I had been neglecting myself. This was an important lesson to learn given where I would be riding in the next few months. Sitting in the shade and sipping lots of water eventually had the desired effect and I could begin to enjoy being immersed in this spectacular event.

The only bike rally I had ever been to was back home in England when I attended the Horizons Unlimited meeting in Ripley. I went with my friend Dan to learn from the masters of overland motorcycle travel and pick their brains in preparation for this trip. There must have been at least two hundred people at that event, but here at Redmond, was a completely different proposition. This rally was huge. In the end, over 6,000 bikers arrived.

I spent my time picking people`s brains and attending as many technical seminars as I could. There were BMWs of all shapes and sizes and all the bikers seemed to congregate with riders on similar bikes. Because Tim and I rode 650s we camped with the rest of "The Chain Gang", a group so called because we all rode chain driven bikes rather than shaft driven. The group has its own web site and inspirational leader in the aptly named "Professor" aka Steve Johnson, an engaging, charismatic former teacher, who generously helped me with some mechanical issues and was always there to answer any questions I had, and there were many!

Being surrounded by so many experts, I felt confident enough to strip the panels off the bike and do some very basic maintenance including cleaning my air filter and chain. It was quite funny, as people passing, seeing the bike stripped of its panelling, kept asking what I was working on! (As if I knew what I was doing!) I didn`t have the heart to tell them I was just poking around.

I met some very interesting people who gave me good advice about entering Mexico. The consensus was – don`t hang around near the border towns (drugs, shootings, etc), avoid the big cities and whatever you do, get off the road before sunset. All this gave me plenty of food for thought.

I felt much better for having the three days off the bike, socialising, resting and having a few beers (well I was told to drink plenty of fluids). It was quite sad to see everyone packing up to leave on the final morning. I exchanged e mail and blog addresses and it seemed all too soon it was time, yet again to get back on the road. I`d spent the past couple of days wondering where to go. I could head east and take in a couple of National Parks or west and head for the coast and Pacific Highway 101. In the end, the weather decided for me. It had been so intensely hot I decided to head for the cooler air of the coast.

CHAPTER 9

"Random Acts of Kindness"

The coast was indeed cooler! Having stripped off all my lining and waterproof inners in Redmond, I hadn`t gone more than forty minutes before I was stopping to put them all back on again. I decided to head for a place called Gold Beach, mainly because it sounded nice. It turned out to be a little bit further than I wanted to travel (having made the decision to slow down the pace and make more stops along the way) so I resolved to stop at the first town that looked pleasant and find a place to stay for the night. These criteria formed the basis of all my decision making for the rest of the trip. And so it was that I happened upon the little seaside town of Bandon.

I followed my usual routine of riding around first to check out any nice coffee shops and cafes, and it looked perfect. I negotiated a favourable rate at a nearby motel and went for a "cappuccino stroll." By this stage of the week my body was beginning to complain. Cumulative hours were taking their toll on my back, so finishing an excellent cappuccino and a lovely slice of home baked banana cake, I went in search of a massage.

I'd discovered that on a trip of this scale, if I didn`t put looking after my body as a high priority it rapidly deteriorates. A nice helpful lady in a shop made a call for me and put me in touch with a local massage therapist called Suzanne. I called her, but being a Sunday she wasn`t at work. When I explained I was only in town overnight she agreed to come back into town and see me! What a nice, kind thing to do, I thought. My belief systems support the notion that people turn up in your lives when you need them. And so began a series of serendipitous meetings with total strangers who all played a part in supporting me on my journey.

The massage was exactly what my body needed at the time and more importantly, the conversation I had with her was just what my spirit needed too. We talked about the journey, physical and spiritual, positive affirmations and even quantum physics (although we didn`t refer to it as such!) She reminded me to create each day using affirmations instead of living in fear. Basically, she reminded me of all the things I knew about and had let slip. As I was leaving she gave me a piece of writing which she thought I might find useful and inspiring to help me along the way. It was brilliant and so relevant. Not for the first time did I regret not being able to carry with me even a few of the many books I have at home to help regulate my attitude when faced with challenging times.

As a student and teacher of self development, this whole experience was becoming an object lesson in the need for the right resources to help navigate this thing we call life. It was becoming ever clearer that no matter how mentally strong you are, when faced with challenges and being inundated with Automatic Negative Thoughts (ANTS) it is essential to somehow keep putting in the good stuff. At home I surround myself with positive uplifting people and literature. Out here, with nothing to occupy me but my own thoughts, I was becoming horribly exposed. I had also to contend with a minor health scare as for the last three days I had been passing blood when I went to the toilet giving me something else to worry and fret about. It was beginning to wear me down. How many other things were going to challenge me? If I'd have been at home I would just go to the doctors and get it checked out. I wondered why all this was happening.

I left feeling calmer and more relaxed than I`d done for weeks and headed back into town for dinner. I'd noticed earlier a restaurant on the harbour front and so I decided to treat myself to a fish dinner and nice glass of wine. As I sat overlooking Bandon harbour I reflected on the last couple of weeks and concluded that this was all supposed to be fun and right now it just wasn't. While sipping my chilled Chardonnay and eating Snapper two thoughts crossed my mind,

"What's the matter with you Brian? What more do you need?"

The next morning I was having breakfast before heading off down the road, when a mother and daughter came into the cafe and sat on the next table. Sharon and Marlyn were perusing the menu and debating what to eat for breakfast.

"I can highly recommend the breakfast croissant!" I advised.

"Really?' Sharon replied, "is it that good?"

"You bet! In fact, I could probably eat another one!" I said with a smile.

"Where are you from?" Asked Marlyn.

"England!" I replied explaining about the journey, "what about you?"

They were originally from New York but now lived in Miami and came to Bandon for their vacations. They asked me about the reason for my journey and were so thrilled at what I was doing, they promised to sponsor me. We talked about many things for about an hour, and because it seemed appropriate, I showed them the copy of the writing I`d been given the night before. They loved it so much Sharon sent Marlyn around town to find a place to get a photocopy. They were such lovely, warm people and they said that they were so glad to have met me and it had made their day. Promising to e mail them with my blog details I headed off with my faith in human nature positively reinforced again.

Since my session with Suzanne I had made a decision to slow

down and hoped that taking the pressure off would enable me to "smell the roses" and start enjoying the journey more than I had up to now. Instead of driving myself and putting in the huge mileages and long hours in the saddle I would make more stops and spend more time off the bike. With this new philosophy in mind I headed only fifty five miles down Highway 101 to the town of Gold Beach.

I enjoyed the coastal ride down the 101 with the strains of "Ventura Highway" on my ipod, ringing in my ears I arrived at Gold Beach and was surprised to see that it didn`t really live up to its name. Nevertheless, it was pleasant enough. I was riding slowly down the main street when I saw a sign "Rooms from $35" – Perfect, just what I was looking for! I was getting off my bike to take a closer look when a couple on another BMW pulled up behind me for a chat. It turned out, they too had been to the rally too. We had a brief chat and they gave me their number and offered me a place to stay if I wanted at their home which was about 150 miles further south. Isn`t it incredible how you can meet perfect strangers and be invited as a guest into their homes? I thanked them for their kindness and wished them a safe ride back.

Unfortunately when I enquired about the cheap rooms, Luis the owner, had none left!

"I`ve only got that one over there and it`s $85."

I explained that it was way over my budget and told him of "The Journey for Hope." He thought for a second and said,

"You know what, it's a good thing you`re doing – I`ll give it to you for $48."

This was certainly the best rate I would get in town. I asked if he had wifi, but sadly he didn`t. I told him about my blog and how an internet connection was so important so he rang around town to see if he could find someone who would give me a good rate! Eventually he found one for $54 + WiFi. I had to take it. I thanked him very much for all his help and was about to get on my bike when he said,

"Good luck with the trip!" and he shook my hand with a $20 bill in his palm and said, "Have dinner on me tonight."

I was half way through saying "I can`t possibly….." but instead, I just gave him a big smile and thanked him warmly for his kindness. Once again, a total stranger went out of his way to help.

Luis

I`d decided that if anyone showed me kindness or offered any help on this trip I would just accept it and thank them. I'm a great believer in Karma; what goes around, comes around.

Sharon had advised me to book on a river trip if I stayed in

Gold Beach, so having done nothing "touristy" since I'd arrived from England, I decided I would. The following day I booked on an eighty mile, jet boat trip up Rogue River with lots of white water thrown in for fun. It was an excellent day and gave me an opportunity to focus on something other than riding a motorcycle for a few hours. I was seated at the back of the boat next to a couple from Fresno, California. We exchanged a few words before setting off and then it was "hang on to your seats stuff." Great fun. We stopped half way for dinner and I settled down with a book waiting for my food to arrive. I was the only single person on the boat and Barbara (one of the couple next to me) came over and asked whether I would like to join her and her husband Ron for dinner. I said I would love to and so we spent an hour or so chatting about travel and work. Ron was an accountant and Barbara worked with the victims of juvenile crime. After hearing what I was doing they seemed so impressed and excited for me they offered me a room with them if I was passing through Fresno and also paid for my dinner! I just seemed to be constantly coming across lovely, kind and generous people.

Setting off the following day, I headed down the coast for a town called Eureka. By now I'd got into a routine of getting up early and getting some miles in before stopping for breakfast. For some reason I decided to pull off highway 101, and headed down into a little harbour side cafe for breakfast. It was a quiet place with only one person eating. While waiting for my eggs and bacon, the waiter asked me where I was from and where I was going. I told him about the trip and we talked about the homeless in his area and how he had done some work for them. The only other person who was eating turned out to be the owner of the place, a tough, resilient lady called Elaine Righetti. In the course of the conversation we got involved in, she related how she had lost her husband only recently after 44 years of marriage. That led us into discussing the challenges that life throws up and how we deal with them. We had both concluded that above all, life was for living and you have to grab it while you can and live it to the full. She took down my details and promised to sponsor me and also gave me breakfast on the house!

This was yet another example of the kindness and generosity of total strangers. It was interesting that after my "dark nights of the soul" and my battles with the ANTS, I was now beginning to meet so many total strangers who, by their very generosity of spirit seemed to be the perfect antidote to my self indulgent, pity party. There was clearly a key lesson to be learned and maybe, this was what part of the journey was all about.

CHAPTER 10

“California Dreamin`”

My route south down the 101 brought me into California and to the town of Eureka. At last I`d found it! Unfortunately I couldn’t find a suitably cheap place to stay. Eventually, after riding around for a while I ended up in the less salubrious part of Eureka and got a motel room for $44. The area was a bit rough and had a distinctly unpleasant feel to it, with sticky carpets in the room and clientele who looked “interesting.” I chained my bike right outside the door that night and after a fitful night`s sleep I headed out of town at a brisk pace searching for the “real” California.

I rode for another one hundred and seventy miles south down the 101 through a national park with giant Redwoods finally arriving in the little town of Fort Bragg where I stayed for two nights, mainly because I found a good value motel that was really clean! It also allowed me to catch up with my e mails, source a replacement laptop battery and buy some automatic transmission fuel for the chain. I had become almost obsessive about keeping the chain in good order and while I was at the rally, several people had recommended ditching the standard chain lubricants and instead just using ATF, which was much cheaper. My new laptop had also developed a problem. It was just refusing to carry a charge. It was clear I needed to stay in one place for a couple of days and do some maintenance. I’d located a small computer shop a short walk from my motel although I wasn’t massively optimistic they would have an exact battery match for my laptop.

“Hi, how can I help you today?” Said the cheery man behind the counter.

“I’ve got a problem with my laptop,” I replied, pulling my computer from its bag, “the battery’s completely dead and it just won't charge. I don't suppose you carry Samsung batteries for a laptop like this?" I enquired hopefully.

"Mmm, let me see," he said checking the make and model. "Unfortunately, we don't have any in stock at the moment but I can order one for you. It will be here next week."

Looking rather despondent and disappointed I explained my situation.

"Well, the other option is you can have mine! I've got the exact same laptop and have just put a brand new battery in last week. I could sell you that one if you like?"

"That's perfect!" I said, hardly concealing my elation and thinking how serendipitous. In this small shop in this small town, this man had exactly the same laptop as me. I love it when a plan comes together!

It felt good to deal with all the little things that had been on my mind, and I was in much better spirits when I got back to my motel. My last task was to liaise with my next Couch Surfing hosts who lived in the town of Petaluma, which was a two and half hour hour ride down the highway.

Couch Surfing in Petaluma!

My hosts in Petaluma were Payette and J.C. Payette being named after a river in Idaho (discovered by a French explorer) and J.C. being named after, well..... J.C. We'd communicated via e mail and arranged to meet up by the river where the town's annual festival was being held. I had Payette's mobile number so my plan was to use the GPS to locate her house, drop off my heavy biking gear and ride down to the town in something lighter and more comfortable. With temperatures reaching the high 90s, I arrived at their house, which was situated at the top of a very steep hill. A cursory look round confirmed there was nobody home and I guessed they would be down at the festival, so I quickly changed outside in the street and piled up my gear and bags on the decking outside their house, confident it would be safe and headed down to the river.

“The Rivertown Revival Festival” was in full swing as I pulled up. I killed the engine, dismounted and locked the bike. My next challenge was to locate my hosts in the throngs of people wandering around. This proved more difficult than I imagined. For some reason I just assumed I would bump into them! I rang Payettes’ number without any luck and just decided to enjoy the festival, have a bite to eat and then later make my way back. Eventually, they would show up I thought.

I enjoyed the music, had a beer, and watched a fascinating demonstration of robot wars. Huge, home made robotic machines being operated by hand held remote control units. It was like something from Terminator 2. Tearing myself away from the surreal display and needing to get out of the intense heat, I decided to head back to the house and try my luck. Arriving back at their house I noticed a 4x4 in the driveway, at least someone was home. I rang the bell and was greeted by James Taylor’s doppelganger. It was an uncanny resemblance of the great tunesmith,

“Hi, I’m J.C.” he said gesturing me to come in.

“Thanks very much, I’m Brian.”

“Do you wanna beer?”

What a perfect welcome! I took a couple of sips of my beer and then said,

“You know what I really could do with first is a shower! Is it possible I could just freshen up?”

“Sure, no problem. Let me get you a towel,” he said leading me downstairs to a basement shower room.

“This is your bathroom,” he said, “make yourself at home. Take your time.”

After a very quick shower (didn’t want the beer to get too warm), the conversation flowed as easily as the beer. Payette arrived a while later and we settled down to a sumptuous home cooked meal. We covered lots of topics - travelling, computers, politics, ecology and commune living, well into the night and well into another six pack of very fine Alaskan Amber (which I promised to replenish the following day). Before I got into discussing religion, I thought it time to turn in as they both had an early start the next day. Sunday was their designated kayaking day. They would get up early, drive to the sea and paddle with some kindred spirits to a secluded bay, where they would eat food and drink wine and then paddle back. A very pleasant way to spend a Sunday! Meanwhile I caught up with internet stuff, did all my washing (aren`t clean clothes great!) and picked up some more beers. I would be leaving early the following day,

“I’ll be leaving early tomorrow so I’ll be as quiet as I can so you won’t be disturbed. I just want to thank you so much for all your amazing hospitality!” I said to both of them before heading off to bed.

It was another fascinating Couch Surfing experience.

I got up early the next day and leaving as quietly as I could, loaded the bike and headed towards San Francisco. I`d posted a request for help in servicing my bike on the “Chain Gang” website. One of its members, very kindly, not only offered to help me work on the bike, but also give me a room for the night, and so I was heading for San Ramon, in the Bay area of San Francisco to meet Paul.

Thank goodness for the GPS! Negotiating the bridges and freeways of San Francisco was an interesting challenge! I'd arranged to meet Paul at 10.00 am and as I pulled around the corner, there he was waiting, garage door open and ready to go! I rode straight in, pulled my helmet off and introduced myself properly.

"Thanks Paul, I can't tell you how grateful I am for this!"

"You're welcome. Just pleased I can be of help."

Paul turned out to be not only a top bike mechanic, but also a top aircraft mechanic. A local multi millionaire employed him to look after his two private jets, so when he wasn't keeping the jets flying, he was riding his Triumph Tiger motorcycle on dirt roads for fun and helping out people like me. We got going pretty much immediately. With Paul's help we stripped the bike down to get to the valves. Doing a valve check was not only a very important job; it was also way beyond my limited ability.

The valves were obviously still very hot after the ride and needed to be cold to check the clearances, so while they cooled down, we jumped in his truck and he took me round to several shops so I could get the parts for the service. The day went so quickly we didn't even have time for food. We stopped off to buy something for dinner and headed back with two huge steaks (which he cooked to perfection) and an extraordinary bottle of wine. I couldn't resist it - $1.99! I thought it was a mistake, so I checked again,

"Excuse me. Does this say $1.99?"

"Yes, sir, $1.99. It's our own brand."

By a country mile, the best value wine I've ever tasted!

The following day we finished off by changing the oil, replacing the throttle cable and cleaning the bike. As Paul hosed the front of the bike, the water turned brown as the residue of the Dalton Highway was washed away.

"My God! Look at all that mud!" I exclaimed, "I've been carrying all that since Alaska."

Paul washing the dirt of the Dalton from my bike

"Yep, it sure looks like it."

"Thanks for all your help Paul you've been brilliant!" I asked him what I could do to repay him but he wouldn`t take any money for all his troubles.

"Think of it as my contribution to your journey." He said.

So thanking him once again, I wished him the best of luck with the "hot date" he was going on that night - an attractive, belly dancing member of Mensa! Who wouldn`t be fascinated?

And so, the road was calling again and the delights of Santa Cruz were beckoning. I extricated myself from the environs of the Bay Area with the aid of the GPS and once again hit the coast road to the delightfully named Santa Cruz. Sadly it turned out to be less than delightful and so I just used it as a brief overnight stop before following Highway 1 to Carmel.

CHAPTER 11

"Has anyone seen Clint?"

Looking for Dirty Harry.....

Before I had left the U.K. my friend Tony had recommended Carmel as a nice place to visit.

"And on your way there you must do the 17 Mile Drive." He added, an apparently beautiful route around Pebble Beach Golf club. Unfortunately, 17 Mile Drive ended up as 17 Yard drive as security turned me away,

"We don't allow motorcycles," grunted a rather officious uniformed guard.

His demeanour didn't allow for the obvious question, "Why not?" So, slightly disappointed, I went in search of Clint Eastwood.

"Dirty Harry Burgers and a fistful of fries......"

The town of Carmel is famous for its former mayor (Mr. Eastwood) who not only still resides there but owns a fair chunk of properties including a restaurant and bar, quaintly called The Hog's Breath Inn. The town also attracts the affluent, who flock there to buy antiques, oil paintings, designer clothes and expensive wines. So obviously, I knew I'd fit right in! Initially, I was just going to have a look around and then head further south for cheaper accommodation. This was easier said than done. Car parking spaces were at a premium. It would have been easier trying to park in Central London. With the temperature rising by the minute as I slowly crawled round, and with sweat testing my ice breaker T shirt to the limit, I finally found a parking spot very close to a motel. Out of curiosity I went in to ask their rates. As expected, it was out of my range, but I thought, nothing ventured nothing gained, so I went in and spoke to a nice lady on reception.

"You know something, I'd love to stay here but I'm on a very tight budget."

I explained about the Journey for Hope, "is there any way you could do me a better rate?" I said, giving her my best smile.

"Let me check with my manager," she replied disappearing into the office.

"I can give you $40 dollars off the room rate?"

I hesitated for two seconds, "I'll take it thank you!"

It was still relatively expensive, but this was Carmel and I was in Clint country.

After unpacking and showering the first port of call was to find The Hog`s Breath Inn. Secondly, I needed to check out the beach. Having duly orientated myself with the important landmarks, it was back to my very nicely appointed room to catch up with the blog/e mails. Several hours later, after writing my blog, downloading my video footage and dealing with technical laptop problems, I went in search of Clint.

"So is Clint going to be in tonight?" I enquired of the barman at The Hog's Breath Inn, "Oh yes, I'm sure," he replied with a smile.

"If he does, what will he drink?" I said out of curiosity.

"He always drinks this," replied the barman, pulling down a bottle of expensive Cabernet Sauvignon.

I'll bet he does, I thought, "In that case give me a pint of your finest pale ale and tell him when he comes in I'll buy him a drink."

"Sure," he replied busying himself pouring my beer.

Suffice it to say, he didn`t show. I waited and waited. I sampled his best beer and wine and even the famous Dirty Harry Burger. I think the latter explains why he doesn`t eat there anymore. Slightly disappointed, but pleasantly mellow, in a four pints of IPA kind of way, I wended my way through the beautiful people spilling out of the many over priced, Mediterranean - themed restaurants and made my way back to my motel.

The following day`s ride was a pleasant meander further south to the town of San Luis Obispo, or SLO as it was referred to in all the town`s literature. Initially I thought it was a reference to a SLOwer pace of life! Which would have been a useful practice to adopt on the road, as I discovered when I had an unpleasant altercation with a wasp at 55 mph (not sure what speed the wasp was doing, but it was a head on collision). Luckily I was wearing my sunglasses! The impact took the left lens out and left the wasp trapped between my head and helmet. Not content with destroying my rather pricey shades, it then proceeded to sting me in the temple until I could slow down, find a safe place to pull over, take off my gloves and then my glasses and then my helmet. It`s times like this you wish you were a Harley rider with an easier to remove open faced helmet. Still, never mind, I thought to myself, it`s only pain (oh, and $90 + tax for new glasses).

SLO turned out to be a really nice town. As I wandered downtown, I noticed a hive of activity in the main street. I`d arrived just in time for the weekly Farmer`s Market! It started at 6.00 pm and went on till 9.00 pm. As it was already 5.30 pm and obviously "beer o`clock," I thought it mandatory to sample what SLO had to offer in the way of ale and company.

With a very fine IPA to quench my thirst I sat and watched a moto cross programme on the TV above the bar. Very gutsy women riders throwing themselves over huge leaps (making the Dalton Highway look like a wimp`s day out). I exchanged some observations with a man sitting next to me. It turned out that he used to ride moto cross when he was younger. The conversation developed (as it does over a beer), and so I asked him how he came to be in SLO.

"My parents were both drug dealers and so we had to move around a lot to escape the law." He said, in a matter of fact kind of way.

"Are you being serious?"

"Yea, they were both in and out of prison in several states. As a kid I went to lots of different schools. Thought it was normal I guess."

Happily, they had now cleaned up their acts and achieved a measure of normality and he`d survived that childhood and was applying for a job in a nuclear power plant (I didn`t want to throw in any Homer Simpson references), so I bought him a beer and left to sample the delights of the now buzzing Market.

They certainly knew how to run a street market! Fantastic food, great music and a real community feel. $4 for a ¼ BBQ chicken and coleslaw! That sorted my dinner out and it was also quite healthy I thought. Sadly, it was followed by a chocolate and banana crepe, which although not exactly health food, was nevertheless absolutely delicious. It's incredible how IPA beer can sharpen an appetite. I decided it was time for bed before the real munchies took over.

The next day I was leaving the beautiful coast and heading inland to Bakersfield for what would be my third experience of Couch Surfing. I'd put a search in for the California area and Bakersfield had come up. This was fortuitous, as it was more or less en route to my next destination, which was going to be Las Vegas. Francine had kindly responded to my request and so began a two hour ride across the sweltering desert.

CHAPTER 12

Baking Hot in Bakersfield

As I headed east, away from the cooler coast, the temperature steadily climbed to 90°+! I had to stop at every available place that could offer me shade. Petrol stations, diners, anywhere I could escape the blistering heat to take on more fluids and soak my T shirt in water. I must admit to getting some strange looks as I used the toilets to strip off and soak my T shirt in cold water. This allowed only a brief respite from the intense heat and usually lasted a few miles before completely drying out.

Normally, to cool myself on the road, I ride with my visor up (trying to avoid wasps, of course), but in this intense heat it was like putting your head into a fan oven, the rush of hot air began to cook my face so I had to ride visor down for the duration. I arrived in Bakersfield just after 4.00 pm and eventually located Francine`s house after a few dead ends. Sometimes the GPS lost the plot a little and for no good reason took me completely the wrong way, leaving me to resort to the old fashioned way of communicating with the natives! I was so glad to get off the bike and into a cool house. Francine welcomed me like a friend showed me around the house and said,

“Please help yourself to whatever you need. This is your house now.” And so began yet another extraordinary Couch Surfing experience.

Francine and Carl were an amazing couple who epitomised the entire spirit of the Couch Surfing concept. Francine was Greek by birth and still retained that Mediterranean love of all things to do with family and community. Their house was almost an open house for whoever happened to be passing. Everyone who came to the door was welcomed, invited in and offered food and drink. She was passionate about life, food and above all sharing everything she had. She had also been looking after foreign students who came to the U.S. to study. At the time of my visit they already had a long term surfer, Maria from Austria, who was there to improve her English.

After settling in and showering, I chatted for over an hour with Francine while we awaited Carl's arrival from his trip to L.A. We soon discovered how much we had in common in our values and philosophies of life. Which of course was no real surprise. The Law of Attraction was alive and well!

It was continually fascinating to me how you could meet a total stranger, and within minutes feel completely at home with them. When Carl arrived, one of the first things he said was,

"Would you like a cold beer?" Perfect!

Carl, Francine and Maria

That night they took me out to a very upmarket and plush, downtown hotel where they`d arranged to meet up with some of their friends in the rooftop bar. We had a fabulous night with great company, great beer, great location and a fascinating insight into the Bakersfield Friday night scene. The Padre Hotel rooftop bar was clearly where the "beautiful people" congregated. It was the perfect place to people watch.

The following day was spent primarily indoors because of the baking heat, although we did venture out to the local supermarket, which thankfully was just around the corner, to replenish food and beer stocks! Each evening (and morning come to think of it) both Francine and Carl busied themselves in the kitchen creating superb culinary dishes. I ate like a king for three days!

At least the heat enabled me to catch up on blogging and e mails. On my last day, after what seemed like hours pouring over my laptop, Francine said she had a surprise for me and could I take a break for a while. Obviously, being open to anything and everything that happens on this journey I said yes. So she drove me downtown and ended up at a massage therapists. Knowing how beneficial this stuff is to me she had arranged for a good friend of hers, who also happened to be a massage therapist, to set aside some time to see me and sort my back out (again). After a beautifully relaxing and re-energising session with another fascinating person I asked how much I owed and was told,

"It has all been taken care of by your wonderful friends!"

What exceptional people. I was sad to be leaving this new family I had got to know so quickly, but the next day I would be making for Las Vegas.

I got up early the next day in order to beat the heat before it got to pressure cooker intensity. Francine, Carl and Maria all got up especially early to see me off. I was very moved by their amazing generosity of spirit and kindness. It had been a real positive and uplifting experience being with them, but the flesh pots of Sin City were calling me, so just out of curiosity, I had to see what all the fuss was about. From the sublime to the ridiculous. Viva Las Vegas!

CHAPTER 13

"Welcome to Sin City!"

It didn't take long for the temperature to start building as I approached the Mohave Desert and pretty soon it was pushing into the 90s. After a couple of hours riding and sweating profusely, the outskirts of the city began to appear, or more accurately, the casinos began to appear! The landscape seemed full of huge hotel complexes, with their own roller coasters (obviously, a mandatory appendage) just springing up out of the desert. It was almost surreal.

As I entered the city, the temperature was now over 100°. I'd sourced a hotel online who were offering a good deal on room rates, the aptly named Sahara Hotel. It was one of the original hotels/casinos on the strip (many years ago!). In its heyday, it was **the** place to stay. The Rat Pack, The Beatles and everybody who was anybody had stayed there. Now it was my turn. At the front desk I was informed by a rather surly receptionist that the rate was in fact higher than I'd expected (tax for this and taxes for that, extra for wifi) so I decided to try elsewhere, after all Vegas is full of hotels/motels. An hour later, after a fruitless, hot and sticky tour of the south strip with temperatures now at 104°, I returned to The Sahara, swallowed my pride and checked in!

After a very welcome shower, I was eager to get out and explore this very strange, but oddly compelling place.

The hotels are designed to create a self sufficient environment. If you want to gamble, you need never leave your hotel. You can get everything you want under one roof - food, drink, clothes, haircut and a tattoo (yes, for some reason the tattoo business in Las Vegas is huge). They even had huge banks of screens showing live baseball, football, basketball, horse racing and any sport that you can bet on and people would spend several hours watching the games having placed bets on the outcome. That's all some people actually did in Las Vegas. I don't think some of them ever left that part of the hotel!!

Eventually, after sampling the mandatory $1 beer, I forced myself away from the seduction of the Sahara and ventured further afield. Stepping out of the beautifully air conditioned hotel into the 100° + furnace was always a shock to the system, but I needed to explore the famous strip, so I bought a 24 hr bus pass and headed for where the rich and famous spend their money. The Bellagio and Caesar's Palace were clearly object lessons in decadence and made The Sahara look distinctly shabby.

I stared in disbelief at The Eiffel Tower hotel, yes, they've built their own version! Welcome to Las Vegas, the city where anything is possible! Someone must have gathered a bunch of designers and architects and said,

"O.K. guys, money no object, see what you can come up with."

Welcome to Sin City!

And believe me, they did. Each new hotel, bigger, better, more opulent and outrageous than the one before.

Having done my duty representing the English (since there was a distinct shortage of Mad Dogs), I retreated to the cool of O`Neill's Casino (or was it O`Reilly`s? Not sure, but it did have a digital counter on the wall counting down the days to the next St. Patrick`s Day) for another $1 beer. I watched with fascination as a steady stream of punters wandered from casino to casino dodging the line of little Mexicans wearing T shirts emblazoned with,

"Hot Babes! Girls to your door in 20 minutes."

In one twenty yard stretch, I was handed about forty cards with pictures of beautifully airbrushed ladies and their telephone numbers. I was looking for someone to do swops with so I could collect the full set. Sadly, I had no takers so I finished my beer, left the cards on the bar and went back to my hotel to recover and plan my next outing – the strip by night!

Las Vegas by night assaults your senses. It`s one of those things you have to do just once in your life. In a relatively cool 88°, I went down to The Bellagio and watched the fountain display, got discounted tickets for a show called The Mentalist, a comedy revue and a highly recommended topless revue that had been running for years. Obviously it would have been a shame to pass it up. So that was each evening's entertainment sorted! The topless revue was first up and after couple of beers and a pleasant meal I headed for the theatre. I must have been early as there were so few people queuing I was right on the front row. The lights dimmed, the music struck up, the curtains parted and a bevy of beautiful, semi naked girls spent the best part of ninety minutes gyrating in front of me. They must have been doing it for years because it was slick, professional and the least sexy thing I have ever witnessed. As I left, I hoped that The Mentalist would be more entertaining the following night. I spent the rest of the night wandering around soaking up the surreal atmosphere of the rest of the strip.

The next night I wasn't to be disappointed as The Mentalist was indeed Mental! It was an absolutely brilliant display; right up there with the U.K.'s own Derren Brown.

I wanted to get to bed before midnight because the next day would be an early start, so I headed back to the hotel and found the Big Screen group still waiting on the outcome of their bets on the live baseball. Happy that everyone was in their place doing what they should be doing, I set my alarm for a 5.45 am start. Leaving in 80° heat was as good as it was likely to get!

The next day I was heading for the little town of Seligman on the historic Route 66.

CHAPTER 14

Route 66, The Grand Canyon and "Close Encounters of the Mystical Kind"

Over three hours in blistering heat brought me into the time warp that is Seligman. A curious little town that probably only exists now because of the nostalgia attached to the old Route 66. In the days before the major interstate highways, Route 66 was **the** prime road from the east to the west and Seligman was a thriving town on that route. Nine thousand cars a day used to pass through taking east coast migrants to sunnier climes in California and what they hoped would be a better future.

In the 60s and 70s it was a well travelled route for families on their way to the new and exciting Disneyland. And so it prospered until Interstate 40 was constructed a few miles away and the nine thousand cars dwindled to fifty and Seligman all but died. A local hero called Angel Delgardillo, successfully campaigned to put the town back on the map and so it became "Seligman and the historic Route 66." Its raison d`etre is now to remind tourists of the nostalgic 50s and sell them Route 66 memorabilia. That said, I quite liked the ghost town feel of the place!

Nostalgia isn't what is used to be....

My deluxe motel was anything but, and I did notice a couple of squashed cockroaches outside my room, but maybe they were a throwback to the 50s too? After checking in, I was keen to grab a quick shower and explore this strange nostalgic museum of a town. I stripped off, stepped into the shower and turned the water on. Nothing happened. Not a drip. I quickly dressed and hurried to the reception,

"There doesn't appear to be any water in the shower" I said, hardly concealing my irritation.

"I'm sorry but we've just heard there's a damaged water main. There is no water anywhere in town until it's fixed," he said apologetically.

"Well how long will that be?" I responded, feeling slightly more pissed off than before.

"We're not sure. Possibly five or six hours," he answered, "and that means the restaurants won't be able to serve food either."

Seligman

No shower or cooked food for five hours! There was nothing I could do but accept the situation and make the best of it, so I took my camera and wandered the streets of Seligman to learn as much as I could about the area and what was so great about this historical town. It reminded me of an abandoned film set. Every building and shop was stuffed with memorabilia, but there was hardly anyone around. Having completed my tour of the shops I discovered there was a petrol station about a mile out of town where I could buy some beer and sandwiches, so I jumped back on the bike and went to collect my dinner for the night.

With nothing much to do that evening, I decided an early night would be in order only to be woken by a very loud bang at 2.00 am. The loudest thunder, and closest lightning strikes I`d ever experienced. I was hoping it would blow over by morning for my next leg to the Grand Canyon. Sadly, it was not to be. The forecast predicted heavy rain and thunderstorms over the Grand Canyon area for the next two days. Which was a little unfortunate, because I was going to be camping for the next two days at the Grand Canyon!

A hearty breakfast was called for before the foray into the cold and wet. And it was over breakfast that I met Rowie and Rhys from England. A really lovely young couple, with a great story to tell! Both were musicians. Rhys was a violinist with the London Symphony Orchestra and Rowie was a cellist and played in a quartet. They both lived in Kingston on a barge (or two barges to be precise). When I met them they were coming towards the end of their road trip and had just visited the Canyon,

"We just got engaged!" Rowie said, hardly containing her excitement.

"That`s fantastic! Congratulations!"

"Yes, he proposed at the edge of The Grand Canyon! We`d just watched a thunderstorm across the Canyon and there was a break in the clouds. And you won`t believe it, but a ray of light broke through the clouds in the shape of a heart! He got down on one knee and proposed!"

I don`t think they`ll forget that experience any time soon! What a great memory to have. I felt quite uplifted after chatting to them. They were off to Vegas and I was off into the rain!

So from the searing heat of Las Vegas, I rode to The Grand Canyon in the pouring rain and got thoroughly soaked and cold. It turns out my waterproof Goretex lining wasn`t waterproof after all!

If there`s one thing I really don`t like about camping, it`s pitching a tent in the pouring rain. So I was mightily relieved when I got to the campsite and it stopped raining. My main concern was spending two days at one of the wonders of the world and not being able to see anything! I put the tent up as quickly as possible (just in case) and went in search of the canyon. I was hoping to catch a glimpse of it if the cloud broke and at the same time was hoping not to be disappointed by what I saw (this had been on my "bucket list" for a long time).

I walked up to the rim in low lying cloud and as I reached the edge, the clouds parted, revealing a scene so breathtaking I was lost for words (a couple of expletives may have slipped out by accident though). The sheer scale of it was incredible.

I`m not going to even attempt to describe what I felt in that moment because I couldn`t put it into words. And even as I busied myself with fruitless attempts to capture it on film like everyone else, I knew that just being there was sufficient.

It was interesting to note that, apart from a few fenced off viewing points, there was little or nothing between the 100s of visitors and sheer drops of 1,000s of feet! I`m surprised there aren`t more fatalities there, given the fact that most of us seemed to want to get a close as possible to the edge for the "ultimate" shot.

Thankfully, the forecasted rain and thunderstorms didn`t appear, and so I visited the canyon several more times over the two days at different times of the day including sunset. Each time was equally spectacular, but nothing will surpass the memory of that very first view.

After two days of nourishing my spirit and soul I headed south for further spiritual enlightenment in the mystical vortex of Sedona.

Red rock, auras and stars......

With the storm clouds gone and the weather back to normal, I set off from the Canyon under a warm 80° sun and blue skies. By the time I reached the outskirts of Sedona it was already 90°, but somehow felt hotter because of the extraordinary red rock that makes up Sedona`s environment. The ride down the valley was stunning and as I entered the town itself, I could see why it has such a reputation. It was a beautiful little town surrounded by spectacular rock formations.

Unfortunately, it is also an expensive place to stay! However, I had shopped around on the internet and found a good deal on a little motel called The Baby Quail Inn, which happened to be owned by Dick Curtis, a former actor, all round entertainer and director. Dick was a very sprightly and engaging eighty two year old who had worked with many stars of stage and screen, including John Wayne, Nat King Cole, Ella Fitzgerald and countless other stars. I could have listened to him for hours as he regaled me with stories of his time in Hollywood and on the stage.

My time in Sedona was all too short, but I did take some advice and rode up to The Chapel. What a perfect location for a church, perched high on a hill surrounded by stunning views! The heat limited my options to see things on the bike and I vowed to return and see the rest of this beautiful place in the future. It would appear that my Bucket List was getting longer by the day.

I knew that Sedona was famous for attracting those interested in all things mystical and spiritual, but I wanted to find out more. What was so special about this place? I know you could get psychic readings, auras read, crystals, psychic massage (and no, I didn`t try it – too expensive!) and all kinds of healing, but why this place? I was curious, so I found a lady called Jules who was more than happy to explain while I did a video interview with her for my blog.

Whether you`re a believer or not, this was certainly a very special place and the ribs I had for dinner were excellent. And so was the beer. Oh, and the glass of wine too. In fact, I `m sure I had a spiritual experience that night. Yes, I`m definitely going back!

While in Sedona, I had posted another request for help on The Chain Gang website. I was having a recurring problem with my horn. Before I left England I had an extra loud horn fitted, because when you get down to Mexico and Central America it`s really important to be heard, and for some reason it had just stopped working. My knowledge of all things electrical is about as deep as my knowledge of Vortexes, so I turned to The Chain Gang for more help. I got an immediate response from Bill in Phoenix, who not only offered to help me fix the horn, but offered me a place to stay as well. I looked at my map and saw the distance from Sedona to Phoenix wasn`t that far, so I gratefully accepted.

CHAPTER 15

"Hydrate or die" – Welcome to Phoenix!

Unfortunately, Bill worked shifts and wouldn`t be home until 3.00 pm. the following day. I`d heard about how fierce the heat was in Phoenix so I set off, slightly anxious about how I`d cope riding in the heat of the day. Up to now I'd developed a coping strategy for the fierce heat. I would get up very early and get on the road before sunrise to get as many miles I as I could and my rule was when the temperature hit 100°, it was time to stop for the day. Which meant that I could be looking for a place to stay by breakfast!

"By the time I get to Phoenix...."

As it turned out, I was right to be anxious. It was mad hot! I`d never ridden for so long in that kind of heat and I wouldn`t recommend it. I didn`t realise that Phoenix is America`s fifth biggest city and it took much longer than I expected to reach Bill`s place. It was such a relief to step into air conditioned heaven!

One of the first things he did was offer me a cold bottle of water (and I`m sure I drank gallons while I was there!).

"In Phoenix we say, hydrate or die!" Bill informed me. And that was just commuting to work!

After showing me to his guest room and a quick change we got started on the bike and fault finding the horn problem. As with Paul, Bill made it look so simple, and after checking various components with his multimeter (I really must figure them out) he concluded that the relay was corroded. Within an hour of arriving, Bill had fixed the problem! Genius! Which I was thankful for as we could then get out of the 100° heat of the garage!

“My God! How do you manage to live in this heat?”

“You just get used to it,” he responded casually.

“Not when you come from England,” I responded.

Bill had re-arranged his work schedule just so he could help me out. He had a really fascinating job working as chief technician on a flight simulator used for training airline pilots. His job was to ensure the simulator kept “flying”.

After showering, we were discussing plans for dinner that night when Bill`s girlfriend Lori would be home,

“What kind of food do you like?”

“Any kind. I really don`t mind.”

“Do you like beer?”

Dangerous question!

It just so happened, Bill was a big beer fan. Proper beer, not the Bud, Miller, Coors stuff, and he knew a bar that had an amazing selection of micro brewed beers. He was eager to take me there and I was all too eager to go.

So that night Bill and Lori treated me to dinner - superb beer and chicken wings! My loose plan had been to set off the next day but Bill and Lori insisted that I didn`t need to rush off and frankly, it was too tempting to stay and keep cool for a while, so I gratefully accepted their kind offer to stay a while longer. Lori did some washing for me (clean clothes again!) and Bill dug out some instructional DVDs on how to change tyres and how to repair the water pump. The fact that Bill’s bike was also the exact same model as mine was a huge bonus.

Bill working on my bike

While we were out shopping for a few bits and pieces for the bike we just happened to pass by a huge beer warehouse with another amazing collection of weird and wonderful micro brewed beers. Naturally we had to get a couple. It would have been foolish not to.

That night Bill had arranged for Lori and me to meet him after work and go for a flight. The simulator is a very impressive and expensive piece of equipment. Think of it as a very advanced Disneyworld ride, except that the pilots that are trained on it spend $15,000+ for the privilege. It`s so realistic that you could go straight from the training and fly a real plane.

Bill was obviously an expert on the simulator and regularly flew a couple of hours a day.

“O.K.” he said as we strapped ourselves in the cockpit, “where do you want to go?”

“You’re the expert Bill. You choose.”

“JFK airport.” He replied decisively, “we’ll take a flight around the airport and buzz the control tower!” He added, warming to the notion.

“Great!” I said with a big smile, “just like Top Gun!”

He taxied the 747 down the runway gradually increasing speed and as we reached top speed, with the whole plane shaking we lifted off. Not surprisingly, it felt just like the real thing. He then took us for a quick flight around JFK airport before handing the controls to each of us in turn. It was then his turn to play “God”! He would sit at his own controls and change the environment we were flying in at the push of a button. From blue skies to thick fog, to thunderstorms and turbulence! It was a brilliant experience and what`s more we both landed it without crashing!

I had such a great time with Bill and Lori I didn`t really want to leave. They made me feel so welcome and at home. Bill was so knowledgeable and helped me enormously with route planning ideas. He had spent many hours planning his own journey down the Baja peninsula in Mexico, which he was hoping to do sometime in the near future, so his thoughts were invaluable. He did all that to help me, despite having the shadow of possible redundancy hanging over him. He`d been informed on the day I arrived, that his company were downsizing. Which meant that some people would be out of a job and of course they didn`t specify who, they just left the entire workforce to worry for a few days. Thankfully, Bill`s expertise and knowledge were clearly still needed. Nevertheless, it was a worry for a couple of days, but he just ignored it and focused on helping me.

From Phoenix, my route was going to take me back west to California. I had arranged to meet up with my friends Tony and Claire who were taking a holiday In Carlsbad, California and I had also organised another Couch Surfing stay in San Diego.

The next day I was up early, again, in an attempt to "beat the heat". I was heading for San Diego and that meant getting across the Arizona desert and there wasn`t going to be an easy route. The frustrating thing is that the actual distance could easily be done in a day`s riding, but the heat is such that I had to do it in two stages which meant three day`s riding.

To combat the intense heat and keep my fluid intake up while I rode, I`d bought a hydration pack the day before. This proved to be another vital purchase. You wear it as a backpack and drink through a plastic tube as you ride. It could be a life saver on long desert rides. Bill filled it with ice and water to keep me going and promising to stay in touch, I headed out to the blistering heat of the desert.

CHAPTER 16

"Surfs Up!" – San Diego and Carlsbad

I try to maintain my "100° policy," that is, I ride until it gets to 100° and then get off the road and find somewhere to stay until the next morning. This usually meant riding until 9.00 am at the latest. Bill found my whole strategy hilarious,

"You're going to stop over in Gila Bend?" he said incredulously, "but that's only seventy five miles from here?"

"That's true," I replied, desperately trying to justify the pathetically short hop, "but I can't stand the heat!"

He just laughed and shook his head. And so it was, that I rolled into Gila Bend, a tiny little, one street town at precisely 9.00 am. As I pulled off the main highway and rode into the town to look for a cheap motel, I did consider pushing on through the desert to Yuma City my next staging post, but to be honest the thought of another 116 miles in that baking heat didn't appeal. Besides which, I rationalised, it would give me plenty of time to catch up with my blog and the far more time consuming task of editing video footage and uploading it. Luckily, Gila Bend offered absolutely nothing to distract me from these critical activities.

The following day I set off early again for the race across the desert to Yuma City. Thank God for my newly purchased hydration pack which was a worth its weight in gold and was to remain so for the duration of the trip. Arriving in time for breakfast, I checked into a Motel 6 and was relieved to notice that Yuma was considerably larger than Gila and would have more to occupy me for the rest of the day.

So after three days racing across the Arizona desert in short bursts with two overnight stops, I finally reached the outskirts of San Diego and my next Couch Surfing experience with Sally and Larry.

Larry was involved with Motorola doing technical wizardry and Sally was a languages specialist and was involved in innovative ways of training teachers how to teach languages to children.

My arrival coincided with their son Alan announcing his engagement, and an impromptu trip to the races at Del Mar with several of their friends. I seemed to have been swept away on this surreal whirlwind of activity. I arrived, unpacked and showered and was then whisked off to breakfast at a very popular Jewish deli/diner and then to downtown San Diego to pick up their friend Alexis and then onto another friend`s place to pick up the race tickets and then on to the races!

This is the strange thing about the Couch Surfing experience. It means you are stepping into a total stranger's life for a brief time, which can be a little disconcerting if you are the shy, retiring type. Here in San Diego, it felt like I was gate crashing the busy and hectic life of total strangers. Which of course I was! But they were all so welcoming and friendly it just seemed natural. I had a fascinating conversation with Alexis who worked as a coach and facilitator with major companies. He was a very bright and engaging man and because we had similar professional interests we spent quite some time in between the races, chatting about our work as we wandered around the racecourse looking for beer and hot dogs.

Though not being a huge horse racing fan, it was nevertheless an interesting experience and I didn`t lose any money on the horses, and just as with Las Vegas, it was a fascinating place to watch people.

I only planned to stay one night as I had to go to Carlsbad to meet up with my friends Tony and Claire Whittle and their boys Mark and James. However, that night, Sally told me that she was piloting an innovative method of teaching Spanish and invited me along if I was interested. It would be the following weekend so I readily agreed. Any help before going into Mexico would be a real bonus. I had been attempting to learn Spanish with a programme I'd put on my ipod months ago, but I'd let it lapse, and now felt an impending sense of urgency with Mexico around the corner. So with my Spanish lesson booked I headed for the coast and the short ride to the surfing hotspot of Carlsbad.

As I negotiated the five lane freeway out of San Diego at my standard 55 mph, (easily the slowest vehicle on the road with even big trucks passing me) I was looking forward to seeing my good friends, catching up with news from home and just relaxing for a few days.

I arrived slightly earlier than expected in the plush environs of the Grand Pacific Pallisades Hotel and so I parked my bike on the entrance driveway, took off my heavy jacket and sat on a bench to wait their arrival. I felt a little incongruous in my dirty riding gear and unkempt appearance and probably stuck out a little as the steady stream of guests arrived in their 4x4s. The brief respite did give me time to reflect on the strange feeling to be meeting my good friends who had flown from the U.K. while I had ridden all the way from Alaska and the Arctic Ocean. I was enjoying the warm and satisfied feeling of my achievement when a car pulled up next to my bike. The Whittle family had arrived and obviously spotted this dodgy looking character with a rather dishevelled appearance.

Tony and Claire treated me to an excellent Chinese meal that night and I spent a lazy few days drinking beer, chatting, walking on the beach and lounging by their pool. Almost like a proper holiday! Initially I had been sleeping on a pull out bed in their lounge but after a couple of nights I decided to check into a nearby, cheap and cheerful (well cheap anyway) Motel 6. It would have been too much of a prolonged imposition to share their living space for a whole week and besides, I had become accustomed to being on my own and having my own space. I was also worried about the luxurious surroundings making me too soft for the culture shock of Mexico.

Tony and Claire

It was great to have a proper break from the constant riding, and having my friends around provided a welcome distraction from the building apprehension I was feeling about the next leg of the journey into Mexico and beyond. I was highly aware that from here on in I would be entering alien territory. Everything would change the instant I crossed the border and I knew that the journey so far had been the easy bit and things would ramp up considerably as I journeyed further south.

I must admit to feelings of rising anxiety when I allowed my mind to wander onto this new mental territory. The brief sojourn with Tony and Claire was the perfect antidote and while I was in my little motel room I busied myself with the practicalities of the blog and pouring over maps of Mexico trying to decide what route to take, recognising that whichever route I was going to take it was going to be “muy caliente!” – very hot! The days in Carlsbad were spent by the pool or the beach, while Mark and James checked out the surf. In the evenings we would try out some of the local restaurants, or sometimes stay in while Tony treated us to one of his culinary specialities all washed down with copious amounts of fine wine.

My time chilling with Tony and Claire passed all too quickly and it was a strange feeling leaving to carry on with my journey, while they were going to be heading home from holiday. For a brief period of time I had felt normal, being around familiar faces, now it was back to the routine of the road with only my own thoughts to accompany me.

But first, I had a very special Spanish lesson to focus on back in San Diego. I arrived back at Sally and Larry`s in the afternoon and we chatted by their pool before the other students arrived. A friend of Sally`s and fellow languages teacher, Monique arrived for a brief chat and then was persuaded to stay for the evening lesson. She was a woman of immense character who despite dealing with the bereavement of her husband was amazingly upbeat and positive about life and we had a fascinating conversation about life’s challenges and the moments of serendipity.

The Spanish lesson was like no other language lesson I`d ever had. It was fun and Sally made it so interesting and easy to learn. The fact Larry plied us with fine red wine throughout, merely added to the enjoyment.

Now that`s how Spanish should be taught!

Again, time passed so quickly and I had to be up at 5.00 am the next day (for another dawn race against the rising sun) so I thanked Sally and Larry for their magnificent hospitality and turned in for an early night, feeling a little more comfortable with my basic Spanish. The real test would come in a few days time.

CHAPTER 17

"Bearings, gun fights and border crossings"

I had decided to enter Mexico from Arizona in order to find a smaller border crossing because I wanted to make it as painless as possible. Besides, I`d heard a lot of horror stories of the drug war that was taking place in and around the major border towns where shootings were commonplace. Bill and Lori in Phoenix, had offered me a room if I wanted to stay with them before heading for Mexico and Bill said he would give the bike a quick check over before I set off.

Knowing the score this time, I set off in the dark from San Diego and reversed the route back to Phoenix via Yuma and Gila Bend. I arrived in Phoenix early in the morning. It was great to see Bill again and we caught up over a quick breakfast in Dunkin` Donuts. He was in the middle of putting his bike together and as he greased the swing arm bearings on his bike he casually said,

"We should take a look at yours while you`re here."

I looked at his bike scattered all over the garage in bits and said,

"Isn`t that a big job?"

"Not really. Just a few bolts to unscrew," he replied, making it sound so simple.

"Yea, I suppose you`re right."

And so began a simple check of the swing arm bearings on my bike. He was right. In no time at all we had the swing arm off, but as he inspected the bearings, his face adopted a serious frown. All the bearings were rusted and stuck, with no movement whatsoever. This wasn`t looking good.

"What do you reckon Bill?"

"We need to order a whole set off new bearings for the swing arm and links."

After ringing a couple of dealerships, we had to place an order because no one stocked those type of parts. With any luck they would arrive the next day, if we were out of luck they would have to be flown in from Germany and could take several days. I was desperately trying to "go with the flow" and accept the fact that things don`t always go to plan. Once again, the universe was trying to offer me the lesson of going with the flow and once again I was content to fight against it. I wondered just how long would it take for me to learn this important lesson?

I had an unsettled sleep that night, wondering how it would go the next day and whether the parts would arrive.

A quick call in the morning brought the good news that the key parts had arrived! The next major hurdle was going to be removing the rusted bearings and fitting the new ones. For this job we had to go and buy a six ton press! With temperatures rising and sweat pouring we managed to figure out how to put the press together. I bought it as a flat pack and relied heavily on Bill's ability to decipher what looked like Chinese characters in the instruction booklet. After the assembly came the very delicate task of removing the old bearings, fitting the new bearings and locating them within a millimetre. It was like keyhole surgery. Feeling pretty redundant throughout the whole process, all I could do was hand Bill the necessary tools and keep my fingers crossed, but finally, after about six hours of sweating and hoping, the job was done. Believe me, the beers tasted good that night. I can't imagine what would have happened some way down the road if Bill hadn't sorted the problem,

"That was the hardest thing I've ever done on these bikes," he said to me later.

On the bright side, as a token of my thanks I donated the press to him so at least he had a six ton press at his disposal for future similar problems!

Bill was keen to accompany me to the border and even though I was now a day behind schedule, we decided to use the next day for a test ride for both our bikes.

It had been a while since Bill had been on his bike and he was eager to put it through its paces, so he took me for a ride to Superstition Mountain which was on the old Apache trail and included a steep dirt trail section. In this environment Bill was in his element, so I let him race off and kick up some Dakar dust while I just concentrated on staying upright. By the time I`d got down to the bottom, I think he`d had a nap and done some maintenance work on the bike!

"Where have you been? Holding up traffic?" He chided me when I eventually arrived at the bottom.

"Better safe than sorry!" I replied, more than happy with my snail's pace.

It was a great ride out and the first time I`d been on dirt since the infamous Dalton Highway. Satisfied that his bike was running smoothly Bill declared himself ready for the ride to the border. It`s always best to cross any border early in the day to allow for any bureaucratic delays, so we decided to stop overnight at a little town called Bisbee which was about twenty five miles from the border.

"This route takes us right through Tombstone," I said excitedly, pouring over Bill's map.

"It sure does!"

"That's brilliant. I've always wanted to see the actual place where the gunfight at the O.K. Corral took place!"

While we were fuelling the bikes on the way back from the ride we met a couple of Harley riders who came over for a chat,

"Where are you heading?"

Bill told them our plan to cross the border at Douglas.

"There`s a one and half hour delay at Douglas."

"How come?"

"There`s been some shootings just over the border a couple of days ago."

Just great. I`d chosen Douglas because I thought it was quieter and safer.

"Have you got a gun?"

"I`m English. We don`t carry guns!"

"If I were you, I`d buy one."

"I wouldn`t know what to do with one," I replied, trying to inject a little levity into what was sounding deadly serious (pun intended).

"Just point and shoot!" added Bill with a smile.

"Thanks Bill!" As an image flashed through my mind of me armed with my trusty bear spray facing down a bunch of drug running banditos.

"Well, what do you think?" Bill said afterwards.

"I think we should stick to the original plan."

"I agree," he said.

And with those images playing in my mind we rode back to Phoenix.

The next day we were up early. We packed the bikes, took the mandatory photos and met Lori for a quick breakfast of coffee and donuts, before heading for the town "that wouldn't die."

Bill and me on the way to Tombstone

Tombstone was a fascinating place. They have retained the original street which is now Arizona's second most popular tourist attraction (after The Grand Canyon). There we met Wyatt Earp, Doc Holliday and had a great lunch in Big Nose Kate's saloon. After lunch and with a huge storm brewing and heading our way, we just had time to watch a re-enactment of a typical shoot out with some of the worst actors we'd ever seen! Still, it was all good fun. Jumping on our iron horses, we rode out of town and tried to out run the storm to Bisbee, which we managed with only minutes to spare.

Bisbee is an interesting little place that`s now famous for attracting artists, hippies and bikers. We spoke to one local in a bar, who told us,

"To get a woman in this town you have to be an artist or ride a bike!"

Apparently the local ladies were very attracted to extreme stereotypes – bohemian artists or roughneck riders! Since we were neither, we settled for a quiet night and a few beers.

We`d stumbled across a quirky little hotel with themed rooms and had the pleasure of sharing the "Geronimo" room. He probably stayed there when he came to Bisbee for a few beers. That night we sampled several of the local ales and ended up in a strange bar with live music. The music also attracted a lot of strange people. I could have sworn Charles Manson`s doppelganger was there, with long, wild hair and an upside down cross tattooed on his forehead. Yes, Bill and I fitted in perfectly!

I would have liked to stay longer but thought it wiser to head back given that tomorrow was the big day. Needless to say, it wasn't the best night's sleep I'd ever had. A combination of beer and apprehension about the border crossing made for a disturbed sleep.

Over breakfast the next morning we made small talk and I must admit to feeling a little under the weather. Slightly hung over and being faced with Bill tucking into a hearty plate of bacon, eggs and grits didn't help at all. Whenever I'm feeling anxious about anything, I hate delays. I just wanted to get going and get on with it. As soon as breakfast was over, we headed south for the border town of Douglas.

I followed Bill for the twenty five mile ride and really wished he was coming with me. I`d thoroughly enjoyed his company on the road for the last couple of days and it reminded me that solo riding has its downside. We pulled up just before the border crossing and Bill said,

"Well this is as far as I can go, I wish I was coming with you!"

"So do I!"

We promised to stay in touch by Skype and as I waved and rode the short distance to the crossing I felt very uneasy and a little anxious to say the least. My heart rate was increasing noticeably and knowing that from now on the whole journey was about to change, the intensity weighed heavily on me.

CHAPTER 18

"Bandit Paranoia" - Bienvenidos Mexico!

I crossed through the barrier and was officially in Mexico but had to get all the paperwork processed. This would be the first of many such crossings and I was led to believe that this was the easiest one. The process of getting my passport, driving licence and bike registration documents all photocopied, and my tourist card cleared was time consuming and very sweaty work. It entailed passing endlessly between departments, while each official tried to compete with each other for the title of "slowest worker of the year."

The final clearance was a temporary import permit for the bike. As I waited for the woman to process it I noted that if she worked any slower she`d be going in reverse and then had to remind myself to be patient! After much pouring over my passport and several phone calls it was clear there was a problem. She spoke no English but thankfully via an interpreter she said she couldn`t issue a permit on my passport! I was very confused and extremely worried,

"Why? Por que??"

"She says your passport has expired," the interpreter said.

"What!!?? But it`s nearly new!!!??" I exclaimed.

I felt a mild sense of panic hit me. Shit, have I missed something in the planning? That can`t be right? My immediate thought was what am I going to do? Is the trip over? That can`t be right? Once again my mind was over run with ANTS. I tried to remain as calm as possible as the queue behind me grew larger. In desperation I pulled out my old passport to prove a point,

"Look, it says 17! That means 2017!" jabbing the date with my finger.

"But it doesn`t say **2017**," pointed out the interpreter.

"But this is crazy! She must have seen lots of English passports like this!" I responded, trying to control the sense of desperation in my voice.

Several phone calls later and she seemed to be convinced, by that time, the sweat was pouring off me and pooling in my boots. Bloody hell! Mexico was supposed to be the easiest of all the borders to cross going south. What the hell will Guatemala be like?

I paid my money, finally got my passport stamped and quickly got out before she found something else wrong. With adrenaline pumping like crazy, I punched the co-ordinates of my next destination, Moctezuma into my GPS and headed into the border town of Agua Prieta aka bandit country.

Mexico

As I rode into Agua Prieta it was like I`d somehow found the missing portal to another world! The difference was extreme. I`d stumbled upon the real "wild west." Wild, stray dogs roamed the streets, cars that wouldn`t have been out of place in a British Banger race, kicked up clouds of dust. Groups of locals eyed me with suspicion or curiosity. All that was missing was tumbleweed blowing across the road. I felt like a latter day "Pale Rider", but without the machismo. Unlike Clint, I wasn't` gently sauntering through town, I was actually riding as quickly as I legally could to find my way out of town and on to the right road south, cursing the GPS as it struggled to orientate itself.

Eventually, the GPS got its act together and I headed south on the road to Moctezuma, which was a tiny little village 120 miles south of the border,

"Get through the border town quickly and get as far as you can before stopping. About one hundred miles should be safe enough." I was told by reliable sources.

Then followed a physically uneventful, but mentally, paranoia filled three hour ride. As it turned out, I had plenty of company on the road. My old friends, *fear, apprehension and anxiety* decided to join me for the whole trip. My head was still filled with stories of shootings, robberies, kidnappings, etc. The road was eerily quiet for most of the way, and every car or pick up truck that came into view in my mirrors was obviously following me for nefarious reasons. Each time a car passed me and sped into the distance I must admit to breathing sigh of relief. All was going well for about an hour when I passed a very beat up car parked by the side of the road. It had obviously seen much better days. The windscreen had a huge crack (clearly from a bullet) right across it. Thinking nothing of it I rode on. Several minutes later, I saw the same car in my rear view mirrors approaching fast. The road was a winding and narrow making passing difficult, so after being followed for several miles I slowed and waved the car on, but he slowed too and continued to follow close behind.

My paranoia was having the time of its life! I accelerated and so did he. This cat and mouse game went on for another few miles with my adrenaline levels at an all time high and mind racing through possible scenarios. Eventually the car passed me, accelerating dramatically and then proceeded to veer across the centre line, driving very erratically, finally disappearing into the distance never to be seen again.

After my heart rate had returned to some kind of normality, I then began to notice the actual scenery I was riding through. Mexico was a surprise in many respects. Rather than the dust and arid landscape I was expecting, I found lush, verdant rolling hills and many places reminiscent of Scotland. It was certainly a country of contrasts.

As I rode into my first small town, I was caught out by the "topes." I'd read about these beforehand and completely forgotten them. They are Mexican versions of "Sleeping Policeman." Speed bumps of a very vicious variety that are at the entry and exit point of every inhabited area. I hit the brakes hard at the last minute and just managed to slow enough to save my suspension. Cursing my lack of concentration, I crawled through the town remembering the Police love to catch anyone (especially Gringos breaking the speed limit) where they can then extract the "Mordida," an on the spot fine/bribe.

This kind of riding is extremely tiring with my senses operating on high alert all the time. My next challenge would be the Police/military checkpoints, and sure enough, thirty minutes later I was flagged down. I was asked for my papers, driving licence, where I was headed, what for, etc.

"Voy a Moctezuma!" I said to the soldier, trying to practice my Spanish.

When I discovered he understood a little English, I asked if the road was safe,

"Mas o menos," (more or less), he shrugged, but "be careful".

"Si, gracias... adios!"

I reached Moctezuma by early afternoon. I wasn't really sure what to expect, but Beverly Hills it certainly wasn't. I suppose it could be described as a typical small Mexican town, noticeably devoid of Gringos. Trying to find a cheap hotel that had been recommended I was riding around slowly, unavoidably attracting attention to myself. Remembering a piece of advice to head for the main Plaza if you're lost, I pulled up in the town square and stared at my basic map wondering what to do next. In less than a minute a local asked me where I wanted to go,

“Puede decir me donde esta Hotel San Antonio, por favor?”

Not bad, I thought, and he understood! I wish I could say the same about his rather long response! Luckily the town wasn`t that big, so I eventually found my first hotel in Mexico.

It seemed deserted and locked, but after ringing the bell a few times Jesus appeared. No, it wasn`t a vision. It was the owner. Here we go again,

“Tiene un habitacion para esta noche, por favor?”

“Yes!” It seemed Jesus could speak good English!

As you can imagine, it was basic, but perfectly acceptable and “muy importante” it had wifi!

After my ritual sorting of the bike I went on a recce of the town looking for an ATM and some food. Finding both, I headed back to my hotel armed with my lunch of bananas and water (my paranoia extended to what I could eat and drink too!)

So this was real, small town Mexico, off the tourist route. It certainly felt like it as I walked around that evening. Not surprisingly, everyone stared at the only Gringo in town. Desperate for some proper food, I asked Jesus and he directed me to a pizzeria. So pizza and beers it was. Strangely enough, I never had any problem ordering beer wherever I was.

CHAPTER 19

Searching for the Copper Canyon

That night I looked at my map, and having no real idea where to head for I decided on a bigger city, basically, something that looked and felt a bit more like civilisation. I felt I needed the minor comfort zone of a city. Hermasillo was just that, a modern city, several hours ride south west of Moctezuma. I think my initial taste of poor Mexican life had been a slight culture shock. I decided a couple of days with more amenities would ease me in a little more comfortably. As I neared the outskirts, the temperature rose markedly, and by the time I found a hotel it was already 100° with high humidity.

Stepping into what seemed like air conditioned luxury compared to the night before, I thought I might stay a couple of days to recover from the long ride and early mornings I`d been having recently. It would also give me time to do some work on the bike. But first things first, I needed to go out because I`d spotted a coffee shop on my ride in and was desperate for a decent cappuccino! Mexico isn`t noted for its coffee, but it wasn`t too bad and satisfied the desire for a kind of home comfort. It`s interesting what you miss on a trip like this, good coffee, chocolate, good wine, fruit and vegetables and of course, being English, I could have murdered a cup of tea!

My bike was parked securely in a sheltered car park out of the sun, so I thought I would be brave and change the front brake pads for the first time since Tony in England and recently Bill in Phoenix had shown me how simple it was. Bill had noticed how the pads seemed to be wearing unevenly so had told me to keep an eye on them. Now seemed to be a good time to do it. While I was busy sweating over the simple job I noticed the pistons were moving unequally and one seemed to be stuck, so having done the job and feeling quite proud of myself I decided to Skype Bill and see what he thought. He had just installed Skype but didn`t have a web cam or sound so we communicated by instant messaging.

To cut a long story short I spent the next few hours running up and down the three floors to the car park trying various strategies to resolve the problem and in the meantime, unbeknown to me, the Hermasillo mosquitos (633 Squadron) were having a feast day on my exposed Gringo flesh. I`d forgotten about the little bastards and only thought they appeared at dusk. That was clearly not the case.

After much placing, removing brake fluid, squeezing, sweating and test riding, it was decided to just keep an eye on them and see how it went. Once again, my lack of mechanical knowledge was causing me much unwanted anxiety

After an all too brief respite, the next day saw me up at dawn and heading off for the little town of Yecora. I was keen to find The Copper Canyon, which I'd heard so much about from other riders and I knew it was located near Yecora.

The canyon is much bigger than the Grand Canyon and yet few people have ever heard of it. The route took me inland and to higher ground. Although it was a relatively short ride of only 112 miles, it took me nearly five hours. The twisty, switchback roads up in the mountains demanded huge amounts of concentration and eventually brought me into an even smaller town than Moctezuma. It didn't take long to do a quick recce of the town and locate Hotel Las Brisas.

Compared to the previous night it was basic to say the least. Las Brisas was run a by a friendly owner who spoke no English, so we had an interesting conversation about restaurants and wifi connections. Internet connections and especially Skype connectivity were becoming more and more of a lifeline to me. My general emotional wellbeing and mood could be massively affected if I didn't manage to Skype Jane and it became clear that despite my insistence that I wanted to travel solo, I couldn't and didn't want to survive without my electronic umbilical cord.

He directed me to an internet café, but in reality, it was just a little shop that had a couple of old computers at the back. For some reason, the internet connection in the shop was intermittent and the signal kept dropping, which was no surprise considering I was in the middle of nowhere, but incidents like that served only to further test my attitude.

The truth is of course, the whole journey, had been, and always was going to be a huge test of attitude, given my lack of experience in everything I was attempting. There were times when I had real doubts and serious questions, and it was at times like those I had to keep reminding myself why I chose to do this, and I think it can be summed up perfectly in a quote my son Dan sent me,

"Twenty years from now you will be more disappointed by the things you didn't do than by the ones you did do. So throw off the bowlines, sail away from the safe harbour. Catch the trade winds in your sails. Explore. Dream. Discover." – Mark Twain

During the afternoon I had asked the owner if he could recommend anywhere for dinner that night as I had a brief wander around the small town and hadn't noticed any decent restaurants or cafes.

"Si, si," he replied, "a que hora?"

I told him around 7.00 pm would be good and he said he would drive me into town to a good place to eat.

"Muchas gracias!" I replied. Now that's what I call good customer service!

So at 7.00 pm that night I was driven the short distance to the restaurant he recommended. It wasn't actually a restaurant per se, rather someone`s front room with a few tables in it. With no menu except what was in her fridge, I was a bit stuck as to what to order so I thought I'd opt for a safe bet,

"Tiene enchiladas, por favor?"

Of course she could do enchiladas! It was staple food and so everyone cooked them. So with my order placed I said,

"Puedo una cerveza por favor"

No, they didn`t have any beer. And it was going so well. This was getting serious, but the night was saved when my driver indicated he would go to a nearby shop and get me one or two.

"Dos, por favor"

Well, I was thirsty! When I drained my last beer, my driver suddenly appeared and said,

"Vamos?"

"Si, gracias!"

And so we "vamosed" back to the hotel and I thanked him for his help and went to bed early ready for a dawn ride to the little town of Creel up in the mountains.

I`d read about Creel as a stopping off point for Copper Canyon and after an exhausting six hour ride to cover just one hundred and fifty miles of very windy, twisty roads, I finally rolled into the little town at about midday. I found a hotel on one of the main streets and noticed when I checked in that there was no air conditioning and no fan, just a gas fire. It just seemed a little odd at the time but I didn't give it a second thought until that night when I quickly realised that at 7,500 ft. you don`t need air conditioning. In fact the room temperature was refreshingly cool.

I was too exhausted to see the canyon when I arrived even though it was only thirty miles away. My body needed rest, beer and half a BBQ chicken, which was conveniently found just down the road at "Mr. Pollos" at a special cheap rate! I spent the rest of the day resting and working on my laptop.

The following morning, noticing dark and threatening storm clouds above I set off for a trip to the Canyon. For something so big, it was surprisingly difficult to find the vista point, until I found later that I had just ridden straight past it. Despite its huge size and geographical significance, it was distinctly under marketed and signposted. If it had been in the U.S. there would have been hundreds of signs posted for miles around indicating not only where it was but also where you needed to park for the shops selling the mandatory memorabilia. Mexico was clearly missing a trick here. Instead I ended up riding on to the runway of a deserted airfield and wandering around for a while before stumbling on the canyon!

The Copper Canyon

It was indeed huge, and at the same time for some reason not as awe inspiring as my first sight of the Grand Canyon. I savoured the environment for a while and then felt decidedly hungry, so I headed back for the other half of the chicken. After sating my hunger at "Mr. Pollos" (we were now amigos), I planned my route for the next day and opted to head for the town of Hidalgo Del Parral, which would be another five hour stretch but it seemed to be the only reasonably sized town on my chosen route.

At 5.00 am the next day I got up, packed the bike and set off just as the sun rose for more winding and twisting riding. I was continually reminded to keep my wits about me as I rounded a bend in the road to be confronted by several cows, wandering freely in the middle of the road. I immediately took evasive action I thought myself fortunate that I wasn't going too fast and most importantly there was nothing coming the opposite way. After the cattle incident, I treated every bend as if there was a hazard awaiting me, all of which stood me in good stead as I negotiated all manner of four legged beasts over the next few hours. God just give me a straight road for a change I thought as the interminable twistys continued.

Hidalgo Del Parral

Several hours later, after a mentally demanding and tiring ride avoiding potholes and wandering cattle, I finally arrived. Hidalgo's claim to fame was the fact that Pancho Villa was killed there, but I also discovered it was a town where it was possible to get a half decent cappuccino. After my usual routine of checking the bike and then checking out the town I happened across a pleasant little café where I sourced the aforementioned beverage. The owner spoke a little English so I asked her about my proposed route for the next day's journey.

"I was planning on taking this road," I said, pointing at the more direct looking route to Durango.

"It's unsafe," she said shaking her head, "it is very quiet and there are many bad people."

"Even during the daytime?"

"Yes. This is much safer," she added pointing to the more major of the two roads. I nodded quietly in response, mentally debating the two options. Take the longer, safer route or risk the shorter road. I felt sure the shorter route would be O.K. but knowing that night I would be Skyping Jane and we would be having the same conversation, it would be less of a concern for her if I opted for safety over speed.

"Thanks for your help" I smiled. She smiled back and busied herself cleaning tables leaving me with my map and my thoughts.

After checking in to the Hotel Turista I wandered around and found a nice little bar as it was past "beer o`clock," and it was here that I was introduced to the delights of Negra Modelo, which was soon to become my Mexican beer of choice. Mexico hasn't a clue when it comes to wine but there's no doubting their ability to produce a half decent bottled beer. Feeling a little more refreshed I headed for the Centro. Whenever I arrived in a new town the best way to get orientated was to head for the central Plaza, once you`re there you could easily find you`re way around most towns. As with every other town I`d visited in Mexico, Parral (as it`s known) had some beautiful churches and many other buildings of historical significance, so I whiled away an hour or two before heading back to the usual e mail/skype/ blog routine. Tomorrow would be another day on the road and another destination.

CHAPTER 20

"Kidnapping is big business in Mexico"

Up before first light, I programmed the GPS for the city of Durango and set off in the half light of a cloudy morning. It was going to be a about a six hour ride so I opted to spend some of it on the toll roads. In Mexico, as in much of Western Europe, there are many toll roads. These are usually faster, more direct and can be expensive if used often, or you can use the libre (free) roads. I was planning on taking a libre road initially, which looked fairly direct, but following the warning from the coffee shop manager the previous day, I'd opted for the safer toll road. There followed an incredibly dull several hours of riding where I was stopped on many occasions and money was extracted from me via countless toll booths, for the privilege of riding on the beautifully maintained and virtually empty roads! It seemed strange to have such beautiful roads when nobody was actually using them. God give me some twisty roads!

I'd planned to go to Durango because of a contact I'd made online. Stephen was an American who worked in Mexico as a geologist for a mining company and also rode a Kawasaki KLR 650. He'd offered to meet up with me and show me around if I had time. I was looking forward to a bit of company, but first I had to find my hotel.

I had been following a guide written by another member of the internet biking community. Sjoerd Bakker was an expert on Mexico and had ridden there for years. In that time, he had researched cheap hotel accommodation specifically for motorcyclists and had recorded them all in a little booklet, which he sold for a nominal sum on the internet. Each recommendation came with a rough sketch map of its location. This time however, my GPS looked confused! I was miles from where I should have been and had to resort to asking for directions.

"Perdon, puede decir me, donde esta La Hotel Bugambilias por favor?"

A couple of people scratched their heads, but a man on a bicycle seemed to know the hotel's location and agreed to lead me to it. So for the next fifteen minutes I followed him in 2nd gear as we crawled through many tiny streets wondering whether he knew where he was going. I`d built up quite a sweat by the time we pulled up outside an unnamed hotel. Amazingly he`d found it! I offered him some money but he refused, waved and peddled off. After checking room availability, wifi connections and secure parking, I was directed a ground floor room and was told I could park my bike right outside the door! I logged on to Skype and left a message for Stephen telling him where I was just before the hotel's internet crashed prompting me to go for a wander around the local neighbourhood. This was wandering with intent, as I really needed to find a reliable internet connection. I tried five places that were recommended none of which worked. I finally asked a policeman on duty in the plaza and located wifi in a local cafe where I spent several hours, eventually having to eat something I didn`t really want just to justify using their wifi!

I`d just arrived back and was chatting to a man in the car park who had noticed my bike, and was asking me about the journey, at the very same time, a Kawasaki pulled into the car park and came to a halt right next to my bike. The rider, cut his engine, dismounted and said,

Hi, you've got to be Brian!"

Stephen introduced himself and apologising for being late admitted to struggling to find the hotel. This made me feel much better. Even a local resident had difficulty finding the place!

"Shall we go and eat?"

"Sounds like a great idea, I'm starving!" I replied.

“What kind of place would you like to go to?” he asked, giving me various options.

“I’d like to sample a typical Mexican taco restaurant.”

“No problem. I know just the place!”

He took me downtown to a really good restaurant and very kindly treated me to dinner,

“Think of it as my contribution to your journey!”

Refusing nothing, I thanked him and accepted his offer. Over a few beers and superb tacos, he gave me a fascinating insight into the Mexican society he was now a part of.

“How safe do you feel? I asked, having seen quite a few armed “civilians” on my travels.

“Pretty safe,” he said, adding, “but the company has a security consultant who advises me not to take the same route to work on consecutive days but to vary the route and change cars regularly”.

“Really?” I said slightly incredulously, instantly thinking I couldn’t live like that.

“Yea, it’s not too bad. I’m not likely to be a prime target.”

“A target for what?”

“Kidnapping. It’s big business in Mexico”

“Why wouldn’t you be a likely target?” I asked with a kind of morbid fascination.

"They don't really go for Gringos. It would be bad for the tourist industry."

"How considerate of them!" I added.

"No, the real targets are wealthy Mexicans. They get kidnapped regularly and if the ransom isn't paid, body parts are sent to their family in the post," he said in a matter of fact way, "and that in turn has spawned a big business in negotiation specialists."

"Can't the police do anything about it?" I asked.

"Well that's kind of the problem," he said in a resigned way, "it's often the police who are behind the whole thing."

"In that case, there's no way out of it is there?" I replied as I drained my beer.

"Nope."

It was a fascinating insight into real life in Mexico and a really enjoyable evening. As we walked back to my hotel he asked me to drop into his office the next day for a coffee and he would help me with my route planning. Somehow, I kept bumping into extremely generous and helpful people. I went for coffee the next day and Stephen spent a good deal of time pouring over my map helping me plan the best route through the rest of Mexico. I filmed part of the conversation with him for my blog but he asked me not to name his company for security purposes. Mindful of his time as a busy manager I shook his hand warmly, thanked him for all his help and headed back to my hotel with a much clearer idea of the road ahead.

Stephen

CHAPTER 21

"They always show porn films tonight. Do you want to come with me?"

The next day feeling a little more rested after two days off the bike I headed for the town of Zacatecas. I'd heard it was a lovely city and it also had a nice sounding name! Up to now, although I was riding in the rainy season, I'd been fortunate to avoid any serious downpours because of my early starts. It tends to rain in the afternoon and evening. As I pulled into Zacatecas the skies looked very threatening, so I hurried to a hotel not wishing to spend too much time searching for a specific one.

"Tiene un habitacion para esta noche?"

"Si."

"Tiene internet – wifi?"

"Si."

Result!

I checked in, and after Skyping, sorting e mails and showering I suddenly felt totally drained. The strain of early starts and five to six hours riding everyday was beginning to show. What I really wanted to do was just lie down and rest for a few hours, but there was a city out there which needed exploring, so I dragged myself up grabbed a bite to eat and jumped in a taxi to the "Centro Historico."

Zacatecas is a World Heritage site and the streets of the old town are cobbled, narrow and full of fascinating little shops, bars and crowded markets. As I wandered around, not really knowing where I was, but still confident I could find my way back to the plaza, I noticed it suddenly going very dark. The storm that had been threatening all day was about to break. It started with gentle rainfall at first and then quickly became a torrential downpour with claps of thunder and bolts of lightning. I ducked into a small side street cafe and watched as the street turned into a river within minutes. Which was O.K. apart from the fact that I was wearing a T shirt not a raincoat and it didn`t look like it would be abating any time soon. As night fell, I decided it might be a good idea to get a taxi and head back. Unfortunately, half of Zacatecas decided the same thing. Struggling to hail a taxi where I was, I walked in the rain for about twenty minutes but with no sign of any available taxi I decided to shelter in the doorway of a shop and re-think my strategy. A short while later, I was joined by a young man also taking refuge from the deluge.

“Hi, where are you from? He asked me in good English.

“England,” I replied.

“I studied in Manchester for a year!” he said with a big smile.

“Where are you heading?”

“Just trying to get back to my hotel but having trouble getting a taxi.”

“Yes it will be difficult because of the rain. Everyone wants a taxi right now,” and then added, “maybe we should try to find one to share?”

“Sounds good to me,” I replied. Anything to get back and get into some dry clothes, I thought.

“Maybe you could come with me. I’m going to the cinema. I love the cinema.”

“Oh yea,” I replied, while scanning the streets in search of anything resembling a taxi.

“They always show porn films tonight. Do you want to come with me?”

“Porn?’ I replied, suddenly shocked out of my taxi search mode.

“Yes. There will be lots of people there,” he said, quickly adding, “do you like blow jobs?”

Before I could muster a witty response, he followed it with his coup de grace,

“A blow job’s the same whether it’s from a boy or a girl. Especially in the dark.”

Firmly pointing out my distinct preference, I headed back into the drizzling rain.

“The cinema is just down there,” he said, pointing across the road as he caught me up.

“Not tonight” I responded, ducking through some slow moving traffic before he could reply. By now I was soaked to the skin. I breathed a heavy sigh of relief as I spotted an empty taxi and flagged him down,

“Hotel Plaza, por favor.”

On the drive back I reflected on an interesting evening’s entertainment and wondered what kind of cinematic experience would be in store for a lone Englishman who decided on a foreign film night?

My reverie was broken as we pulled into the hotel car park and was replaced by the desire for a strong beer!

“Quisiera una cerveza, por favor!” I said to the receptionist.

He just shrugged and shook his head!

What! No beer? This hotel was clearly not all it looked on the outside. Not a good end to the night. I was too tired to go out again, so just collapsed into bed and decided I needed to stay another day to recover.

The following day I got into town early to beat the inevitable thunderstorm and had a better look at the town. I decided to treat myself to a nice meal that night as I`d seen what looked like an expensive Argentinian restaurant not far from my hotel and I had a real desire for a glass of red wine and just a change from the normal food I`d been eating. I was right, it was an expensive restaurant (relatively speaking), but I thought what the hell. A couple of beers, half a bottle of Cabernet Sauvignon and a lovely piece of salmon later, I felt distinctly more mellow and relaxed than I had been for a while! That night another huge thunderstorm woke me up, but I just hoped it would pass over before morning.

CHAPTER 22

"You can eat for free as long as you drink beer?"

The following day I woke up early and had packed up the bike before sunrise. As dawn broke and the last few drops of rain subsided, I rode south towards my first Mexican Couch Surfing experience. My host was Luis Nunez who lived in Leon about four hours ride away. Leon is one of Mexico`s biggest cities, so relying heavily on the GPS I was relieved when I finally arrived at the address he gave me. It would have been a very difficult place to find without the aid of technology. What on earth did we do before satellite navigation?

I pulled up outside the address he had given me and knocked on the door. A few seconds later the door creaked open and an elderly lady answered, well she didn't exactly answer, she just stood there as I faltered with my Spanish, eventually blurting out,

"Es Luis aqui?"

I obviously didn't make an impression as she just shrugged her shoulders and then closed the door!

Mmm, that didn't go very well, I thought. So there was nothing to do but wait until Luis showed up. About ten minutes later, a diminutive figure strolled down the road, and as he got closer a smile creased his face as he said,

"Brian?"

"Luis? Great to see you!"

Luckily Luis' English was very good so my overtaxed brain was given some respite.

"Is there somewhere safe I can store the bike?" I asked.

"Yes, of course" he replied pushing open a big, heavy metal door revealing a small space next to his dad's car.

"Perfect!" I said. I could now relax knowing the bike was safely tucked away.

After unpacking and a quick check of e mails, Luis decided to take me for a tour of his city. First stop was lunch. He`d told of this amazing place where you can eat for free as long as you drink! Sounded like Shangri La, so I told him to take me there with all speed.

As we headed for the bus to take us downtown I asked Luis about the Malaria situation,

Luis in Leon!

"It's not too bad in the city, but as you head further south it gets worse. But Malaria isn't the main problem," he said leaving me to ask the obvious question.

“What is then?”

“Dengue Fever,” he replied emphatically, “much worse, and there is no cure. I was very ill for a long time with Dengue Fever.”

Note to self – don’t catch Dengue Fever I thought, as we jumped on the bus for the short ride to town.

The restaurant turned out to be excellent and unsurprisingly, busy and vibrant. What a brilliant place. You could actually spend all day there and eat as much as you wanted as long as you just kept drinking beer. A few beers later and I was beginning to like Leon a lot, and my new mate Luis was really good company. I was eager to learn as much as I could about the history of the place and particularly the Mexican revolution and Luis was a mine of information, but time was moving on and we had a lot of places to visit.

We took another bus down into the centre where Luis had arranged to meet his friend Miguel and from there we went around all of the key historical sights, which of course is very thirsty work. Happily, Luis knew of another superb place to sample a beer or two (two as it happened). This was a bar themed on bullfighting which is extremely popular in Mexico. No sooner had we sat down when more food arrived! Gratis! I was really warming to this concept. We drank beer, ate food and listened to the Mariachis (bands who play typical Mexican music on request) for an hour or so when Luis suggested we go to another bar which had a good reputation and had live music until late. Who could refuse? A bus and taxi ride later we arrived at a very funky, lively and loud bar, filled with groups of young Mexicans, all of whom seemed to be on a mission to out drink each other with shots of Tequila.

More beer and snacks followed as the band took to the stage. I`d been so preoccupied with the day`s entertainment and Luis` company I`d forgotten how tired I was after so many days on the road, but by midnight I was beginning to wilt a little. Feeling the difference in the years between me, and the average person in the bar, I told Luis it was probably time for me to go, as I would have to be up early the next day. I felt slightly guilty as both Luis and Miguel would no doubt have partied until the early hours!

Only a few hours later and I was again, awoken by claps of thunder and torrential rain. Before 7.00 am I dragged myself out of bed and packed the bike. A light rain was falling as I thanked Luis for a fascinating Couch Surfing experience and rode off in heavy city traffic for the relatively short ride to San Miguel De Allende.

San Miguel De Allende

I`d read that San Miguel was a very beautiful town and I wasn`t disappointed as I arrived at midday, riding through a labyrinth of winding, cobbled streets. The beauty of the town was also reflected in the price of the hotels. It was obviously a popular tourist destination.

I found a suitable hotel just on the outskirts of the town and once I`d settled in and followed the usual wifi routine, I caught a taxi to the “centro historico.” Here I spent a pleasant, but very hot, couple of hours walking the streets and choosing which restaurant to have dinner in that night.

San Miguel is a beautiful town, filled with magnificent churches and is small enough to be able to see everything on foot. Having got my bearings, I came back to the hotel, worked on my blog and waited for the sun to go down before heading back to the centre. The centre piece of the town plaza is La Parroquia, a parish church famous for its Neo Gothic exterior which is lit up at night. When the sun sets, the town buzzes with activity as people congregate around the plaza and Mariachi bands wander the streets, serenading anyone with a few pesos to spare. It`s a place I`d like to have spent longer in, but the next day I was due in Mexico City.

CHAPTER 23

Viva Mexico! Viva Independencia!

Mexico City was never going to be on my route through the country, because it`s one of the world`s biggest cities, around twenty million people live there and I`d heard how difficult it was to ride through and how dangerous it could be. My plan had always been to circumnavigate it with a safer, simpler route. That is, until I saw a posting on "Horizons Unlimited" (a website for motorcycle travellers) from an Englishman called Garry, who offered to accommodate motorcyclists for free if they were brave enough to come and visit! I'd made contact with him while I was in San Miguel and he'd offered to meet me outside the city and guide me in.

It was too good an offer to pass up. I`d get to see a amazing city, a chance to change my tyres, service the bike, and spend some time in the company of a fellow Englishman and motorcyclist.

At the appointed time, I met up with Garry at a BMW dealership about forty minutes from the city. As is the norm, I arrived early (just to be on the safe side) and took the opportunity to pick up an oil filter, air filter and a change of oil. After finding somewhere to put all this new stuff on the bike I followed Garry for the "interesting" ride into the city.

The truth is, I would never have found his place by myself. Every little road seemed the same. Garry had warned me that the area was not the most salubrious and so when we entered what looked like "Graffiti City" I wasn`t too shocked. There wasn`t an inch of wall or garage door that escaped the aerosol. It was certainly a colourful environment. "Banksy," the king of street art, would have been right at home. By the time we`d negotiated heavy traffic through narrow streets and climbed impossibly steep twisty roads I was sweating heavily to say the least. When we pulled up outside Garry`s garage, I breathed a sigh of relief,

“I bet you could do with a cup of tea?” He asked.

“That would be fantastic!” I answered with enthusiasm, “I haven’t had a cup of tea since Canada!”

Perfect! An Englishman`s panacea! No matter what`s happened or happening, a good cup of tea always saves the day!

I was fascinated as to what brought an Englishman from Potters Bar to Mexico City? He`d met his Mexican wife Yvon back in England in the 70s and decided to move out to Mexico where they built the house they`re still living in.

“All this was just dirt roads” Garry said, “there were hardly any other properties except ours.”

Since which time, Mexico City has grown relentlessly in every direction and swallowed up their house, as more and more people flocked to the city hoping for a better life.

Garry

"Here's your room," Garry said, "I'll just get the kettle on."

I stowed my gear and Garry introduced me to his wife and son as I sipped my tea.

We chatted in English for a while and then Garry announced,

"Right. If you've finished your tea, we need to go and get your tyres sorted out!"

Tyres are expensive and difficult to get hold of in Mexico, but Garry had sourced some at a very reasonable price. Yvon drove us all the way across the city (and it`s a big city) to a little out of the way bike shop. It took over an hour through very heavy traffic to get there. I held on tightly as Yvon negotiated the traffic like a rally cross veteran. I quickly discovered there`s a real skill involved in driving around Mexico City!

Job done. Next stop was a quick sight seeing tour of downtown Mexico City and the Zocallo (main plaza) where everything was gearing up for the big Independence Day celebrations. There is a lot of talk about how dangerous the city is, but I have to say I found it a fascinating place and no more dangerous than London or any big city. Admittedly, it did help having Yvon as tour guide filling me in on the history of the place. Since arriving in Mexico, I`d become increasingly interested in the history and evolution of the country. I was particularly fascinated by the rich legacy of the Aztecs, Mayans, Zapotecs, and Teotihuacans. Also, I was under orders from Garry to learn as much as I could about the history behind Independence Day and the revolution,

"We have our annual Independence Day quiz. You'll need to be ready. Can't have you letting the side down!"

After a very cultural day in the city we headed back and I suddenly began to feel very weak. I guessed it must be dehydration, coupled with the altitude and humidity, or it just could be the stressful ride in. Either way, I was ready for my bed that night. It was nice not to have to worry about getting up early and hitting the road again for a couple of days.

Even the torrential downpours didn`t disturb my sleep that night. The following day was cloudy, overcast and humid. It was classic September weather, and just right for a visit to the Pyramids located outside the city. I admit to knowing nothing about the existence of Pyramids before my arrival in Mexico. The site is quite spectacular and justifiably a major tourist attraction. The Teotihuacans had created a huge city around 500 B.C. and most of it was still intact, including two major pyramids, one of which was the world`s third largest outside Egypt. My energy levels were still depleted and after climbing several pyramids I was feeling it. The three months on the bike and away from the gym were beginning to take their toll. Nevertheless, it was a real privilege to visit such an historical site.

I went to bed fairly early that night and prepared myself for a big day of bike maintenance the next day. First job was getting the tyres changed. Garry knew a little garage close by where we took both my wheels and the new tyres. I watched anxiously as a young boy (well he looked about fourteen years old) hammered and stamped on my precious wheels as he tried to remove the old tyre. Garry just stood their grinning!

“Don`t worry. He knows what he`s doing. They do this at the BMW garages, you just don`t see it,” he added, somewhat unconvincingly.

I must admit I felt like an expectant father waiting for a birth. After an agonising twenty minutes the job was done. Still expecting the inner tube to be pinched and flat by the morning, we bundled the tyres into Garry`s car and I paid the 150 pesos and said adios. Garry shared a private joke with the owner something along the lines of,

"Let`s hope they make it to Argentina!"

When we arrived back at Garry`s it was my turn to sweat some more. An oil and filter change isn`t normally a big deal but on the BMW 650 it`s a bit more complicated. Coupled with the fact it was only the second time I`d done the job on this trip it was going to be a long day! I had to be methodical, remembering what Tony, my mechanical mentor from home had told me about keeping everything in one place so as not to lose things. My biggest fear was what I call the "Ikea Syndrome" – you know the situation, you put together a flat pack piece of furniture and always have a couple of screws left over!

Garry watched with fascination as I sweated and cursed in the increasing temperature. I don't know whether he was inspired or what but he suddenly said,

"I think I`ll change my oil too!"

In twenty minutes he`d finished, while I was still struggling, this time with a stubborn air filter that seemed reluctant to fit in. After nearly a whole afternoon I was eventually finished. Feeling very hot and sweaty but quite proud, I wondered where I would be in another 6,000 miles when it would need doing again.

The following day I would be going back to school. Garry was the principal of a school teaching English as a foreign language, and as a former teacher, I was curious to see how it was done in Mexico. Garry had kindly agreed to let me accompany him for a day,

"Here she is!" He said pointing to a little Suzuki 125, "my commuting bike!"

"It's a perfect size for getting through the rush hour traffic," I said.

"Much cheaper too," he added, "about one hundred miles to the gallon!"

Early the next morning I stripped the bike of the unnecessary panniers to aid filtering through the traffic and headed into Mexico City's permanent rush hour, desperately trying to hang on to Garry's little Suzuki as we began a fifty minute commute, weaving in and out of the manic traffic. I must admit to being very relieved when he finally pulled into a secure underground car park, signalling our arrival at the school

Not wishing to spend an entire day observing the lessons, I spent the morning wandering around the shops looking for a new wrench (having broken my old one taking off the front wheel) and trying to find an external hard drive for my netbook, whilst dodging the now expected thunderstorms.

In the afternoon I sat in on three classes of different abilities. The students found me a bit of a novelty and some were eager to test out their English on me, which was pretty good, and tested my Spanish, which wasn't. It felt strange being back in an educational establishment after all these years, especially being in a foreign country, and once again reinforced how we English tend to be much lazier when it comes to learning a foreign language compared to most other nationalities who seem to embrace it.

The next day was the big Independencia celebrations which were scheduled to begin at 11.00 pm. Which would of course, be way past my normal bed time, so I mentally prepared myself for a late night and spent the morning in search of beer to celebrate the big night. This proved more difficult than you might think. If there was a major celebration in England, every off licence would be bending over backwards to relieve you of your money, but in Mexico it was different,

"It's illegal to sell alcohol today," Garry said.

"Are you kidding?" I asked, barely concealing my shock.

"No," he added, "They take it very seriously."

I felt sure, in this teeming metropolis, there would be some business savvy entrepreneur, and so set off to find them. Needless to say, Garry was proved to be right, as shop after shop refused to sell any alcohol. Having almost resigned myself to a very dry evening (being the only person in Mexico who didn't drink Tequila which was plentiful in Garry's house), when I happened upon a local shopkeeper who was willing to take the risk and oblige me with enough beer to keep me going through the night. I think she was touched by my heartfelt plea,

"Por favor! Lo necessito, para la celebracion de la Independencia!"

Now my only challenge was to stay awake long enough to enjoy the celebrations. Yvon had busied herself all day preparing the room and most importantly the food. Tonight we would eat traditional Mexican food and it didn`t matter how many people turned up there would be more than enough to go around.

People started arriving after 8.00 pm and Yvon insisted I blended in with the theme so I was daubed with the colours of the Mexican flag on my face and eventually succumbed to the sombrero. It seems I was an honorary Mexican for the night!

We watched the countdown to the official start of the celebrations. It felt just like New Year`s Eve, and when the poppers and foam spray appeared, the party had well and truly started. There followed many hours of eating, drinking and singing. Included in the celebrations was a birthday cake for Yvon whose birthday was the previous day.

There was also the traditional Mexican history quiz which was hosted by Garry and the judging of the fancy dress, which was won coincidentally by Garry himself dressed up as the father of the Independence movement – Miguel Hidalgo.

As with Luis in Leon, I turned out to be the lightweight of the group and had to go to bed at 2.00 am while the party was still in full swing. It wasn't like this in my university days at Loughborough, I mused while the sound of acoustic Mexican music played in the background and I fell into a slightly beer induced sleep.

The next day was a low key day of recovering for most people and I spent the day blogging and route planning for my early departure the following day to Oaxaca. It had been a real pleasure to spend time with Garry, Yvon and their family. They had been so incredibly kind and hospitable, and had given me a real feel for the authentic Mexico City. An experience I would never have had, and what a shame it would have been to miss one of the most vibrant and exciting cities in the world.

CHAPTER 24

Southern Mexico: "From culture to coast"

The following morning I packed the bike, programmed the GPS (hoping it wouldn't let me down navigating out of the city) thanked Garry for his hospitality and help and headed into the fray of the Mexico City early morning traffic. Having spent a few days there, I was a little more comfortable on the roads and very soon found the road which would take me eventually to my next destination which was the beautiful colonial city of Oaxaca.

While I was researching the trip in England, I had come across a brilliant website, brainrotting.com, which documents by superb video footage, the travels and exploits of Graham Styles who had been on the road riding through the Americas for two years. He very kindly responded to my request for help and advice before I left England. He recommended Oaxaca very highly and so that was good enough for me!

Needless to say, it was going to be another long day in the saddle.

About six hours later I rode into Oaxaca hoping that I could find a hotel quickly. After a long, arduous day's riding the last thing you want is to do endless circles around a new town/city trying to locate the right hotel. By right, the criteria had to be, cheap, wifi, secure parking and preferably within walking distance of the centre to save on taxi fares.

This time, the recommended Hotel Jimenez was easily located and fitted the criteria. Unfortunately, on many occasions, (this being one of them), the promised wifi failed to function in the bedroom and so any internet communication more often than not had to take place in the hotel reception area. Just another minor irritation, (or major one, depending upon how tired I was) that had to be endured on the road.

Oaxaca had an abundance of cultural influences and many activities were taking place around the central plaza. It was a great place to sit, sip on a beer and watch the world go by, which was pretty much my modus operandi for the day. The evening brought its inevitable thunderstorms and the following morning my planned excursion to the famous Zapotec ruins of Monte Alban were under threat, with even more rain and low cloud.

Monte Alban ("White Mountain"), was one of the main reasons for visiting Oaxaca and I wasn't prepared to come all this way and not go because of the weather, so I ran across the road and bought an umbrella (another article to be somehow strapped to the bike from here on in!) and joined a small group of tourists for the short bus ride up the mountain. As a group we hired a local guide so as to get the most out of the tour. The site itself was amazing. The Zapotecs had somehow managed to completely level the top of a mountain to build their sacred site. It would be a huge undertaking today with countless bulldozers, how on earth they completed it in 500 B.C. is a mystery. They were certainly extremely advanced and had worked out well before Galileo and Copernicus that the earth orbited the sun and not vice versa, without the aid of powerful telescopes. This was a fascinating place and once again, just like the pyramids of Mexico, raised far more questions than answers. How could such a highly developed civilisation just disappear?

That night I spent a pleasant couple of hours at my now favourite restaurant on the plaza and discovered a new Mexican beer, Bohemia Obscura! Not so obscure any more, and now my Mexican beer of choice! While sipping my beer I was contemplating my route from here. My two options were to head north towards the Yucatan and take in the famous ruins of Palenque or to head south and to one of the beach resorts of the Oaxacan coast. I was tiring of the constant rain and decided to head for the coast and either Puerto Escondido or the small fishing port of Puerto Angel.

The downside of heading south was the tortuous, winding mountain road. With seemingly never ending switchbacks and the constant danger of stray animals lurking around every bend, the demanding ride was taking its toll. I desperately wanted to stop for a break and something to eat, but there really wasn't anywhere suitable, so I just pushed on in ever increasing heat and humidity. By the time I arrived in Puerto Angel, I had been in the saddle for six hours without a break and I was too tired to ride another forty minutes to Puerto Escondido, so I settled for the sleepy fishing port instead. I quickly found a hotel right on the beach and despite the outrageous expense (£20 per night), I decided to treat myself and stay 3 nights to rest and recover and do nothing at all.

After nearly four weeks in Mexico, this was the first time I'd been to the coast. It actually felt like a brief holiday as I fell asleep that night to the sound of the waves lapping gently on the shore. However, my sleep was fitful, as often happens when I have something on my mind. The day I arrived I decided to have a quick check of the bike and discovered my rear brake pads were very worn. I concluded it was obviously too much trailing of the rear brake on those hours of mountainous roads. Shit! As much as I'd tried to control my speed through gear shifting, I'd clearly over used the rear brake.

Rather than getting too gloomy about it, I thought it would be a good opportunity to change the rear pads, having done the front ones in Hermasillo. I know that all this stuff is a piece of cake for anyone with a modicum of technical ability, but it just seemed to take on a task of bigger proportions in my imagination. I couldn't relax until I'd completed the task successfully, so giving up on further restless sleep, I was up as the sun rose and down in the hotel restaurant area (where they`d let me park my bike for security). Having re-checked the procedure in the bike`s manual, I set to the task as the hotel staff looked on with curiosity. It seemed to go pretty smoothly and I just hoped that the pads wouldn`t be binding on the disc when I came to leave the following day. But for now, I was satisfied and spent the day writing, video editing and watching the fishermen plying their trade.

On my walkabout the previous day looking for the cajero automatico (ATM), I`d noticed a tiny little bar on the beach which was obviously the haunt of the local fishermen from the port, so decided to have a quick beer there. The bar consisted of a few scattered white plastic tables and chairs (the kind of cheap garden furniture you`d get from B&Q). The barman had the mandatory dirty white vest and half smoked cigarette hanging from his mouth.

I settled in a chair opposite a group of five local fishermen who were involved in a loud, animated, and clearly drunken discussion, and ordered a beer. I nodded across to them and raised my beer (thought it wise to ingratiate myself with the locals) when one of them staggered over to me and offered his hand,

“Mi amigo!” he slurred, with one of those drunken smiles, you know the kind where their eyes are half closed like “Lord Charles,” the ventriloquist’s dummy!

“Si!”

“Mi amigo!” He said again, pumping my hand like a long lost friend.

One of his friends smiled at me making a drinking motion with his hand, as if I needed confirmation that he was drunk. One of the group spoke a little English and I spoke a little Spanish.

There followed an interesting half hour while we conversed about his fishing business, football, the price of lobster, child support in the U.S. my "Journey For Hope" and what I thought of Mexico. Somehow, I think we all managed to understand most of what was said, apart from the drunk who spent most of the time hiccupping and chuntering, "Mi amigo!" as he emptied yet more bottles of cerveza.

Having enjoyed practicing my Spanish and endeared myself with the locals with a few "Viva Mexico`s!" I waved goodbye to George, Jack, Raphael, Raymundo and the drunken one, and wandered back to my hotel to prepare for my early departure the following morning.

The next major destination was going to be San Cristobal de Las Casas, but it was too far to do in one day and so I planned on making it to the major industrial port of Salina Cruz about four hours ride along the coast where I would spend the night before the six hour ride to San Cristobal the next day.

Salina Cruz

As with my stay in Santa Cruz, California, Salina Cruz sounded a much nicer place than it turned out to be. I arrived in the heat of the day and had difficulty locating the hotel I was looking. Then I spent the next hour riding around in circles trying to find any hotel that was suitable, by which time I was losing a huge amount of fluids and was feeling very weak and dehydrated.

Eventually I had to pay over the odds for a place that was at best O.K. but by that time, I was just desperate for anything. I dragged my bags up to my room, got out of my sweat soaked gear, grabbed a quick shower and collapsed on the bed exhausted. After resting a while I took a quick walk around the centre and confirmed my suspicions that there really was nothing attractive or worth seeing in this most functional of towns. I headed back and busied myself with the incredibly tedious chore of editing and uploading video footage, this occupied the next three or so hours which were spent in the hotel`s restaurant as the promised in room wifi failed to function. That night, the now usual thunderstorms lit up the sky and I was hoping they would clear by the following day. After such a disappointing interlude I was eager to set off the following morning for what I hoped to be the beautiful old town of San Cristobal.

San Cristobal

I packed the bike in the half - light of a drizzly morning and set off for the long ride to San Cristobal. I opted for a long stint on the toll roads because I was just eager to get there and avoid the rain that was forecast for later that day. Sadly, I didn`t quite make it. About an hour from San Cristobal, as the road climbed steadily into the mountains, the now dark and brooding skies unleashed a torrent of rain and by the time I arrived it was raining very heavily, so I just headed straight for the centre and quickly found a cheap, little hotel with secure, dry parking a few blocks from the central plaza.

After a short while the rain abated and lulled me into a false sense of security so I went out to have a look around and find somewhere to eat. I`d been on the road early, and hadn`t eaten for over six hours. As I wandered the streets, it began to rain again, but this time I`d remembered to bring my trusty umbrella. I sat out the next deluge in a small cafe on the plaza and watched again as the street in front of me turned into a small river within a matter of minutes. Beginning to tire of the constant downpours, I made my way back to dry out my now sodden shoes and socks and decided to try again later in the day.

When I finally made it to the central plaza that night, it was all I expected it to be. San Cristobal was an attractive, bohemian type of town that attracted artists, musicians, and those seeking an alternative type of lifestyle. You could easily spend hours wandering around the many bars and cafes soaking up the rich cultural atmosphere, which is exactly what I did for a day or so. At the same time I was also feeling a little unwell. I thought maybe I'd eaten something that disagreed with me, but I'd been really careful with my food. Maybe it was a side effect of the anti malarial tablets I'd started taking, or maybe I was just totally worn out from the constant, long days travelling. Whatever it was, I was beginning to feel very rough.

I would have stayed another day to recover but I had been in contact with an American rider called Mark. He had replied to a post I had placed on one of the motorcycling websites. We had agreed to meet up the next day in the town of Comitan, so we could cross the border into Guatemala together. He had also been on the road for over three months and like me, was looking for a bit of company. Despite feeling under the weather, I was also looking forward to having a travelling companion for the more challenging leg of Central America. I had read of the notoriously difficult border crossings of the "Banana Republics" and was well aware that from now on, the challenge would ramp up considerably. I had somehow geared myself up for the culture shock of Mexico, but from here on in I had no real idea of what to expect.

CHAPTER 25

"Wanted: Conservative Englishman seeks crazy American for motorcycling adventures in Guatemala"

The next day I was on the road for the city of Comitan and my rendezvous with Mark. Comitan was just a short fifty mile ride from the Guatemalan border so it was a good place to stay and do some final checks and maintenance on the bike before the next big challenge of Central America.

Inevitably, it started to rain as I set off and by the time I arrived in Comitan I was thoroughly soaked. Mark had e mailed me some directions which enabled me to find the hotel very easily. Having set off early as usual, it was just past 9.00 am when I pulled into the hotel car park and parked next to a red Honda 650 motorcycle which, being the only bike there, was obviously Mark's. I was quite relieved to see it was a very nice hotel compared to the cheap and cheerful places I`d been recently staying in. The price reflected the quality, but it was worth it for the lovely hot shower, nice towels and wonderfully comfortable bed.

I checked in and was greeted by a very friendly and courteous receptionist,

"Good morning sir! Can I help you with your luggage?"

"No thank you, I can manage," I replied, slightly taken aback. I wasn't used to this kind of reception.

"Your English is very good!"

"Thank you sir," he replied with big beaming smile.

"I'm meeting with another motorcyclist. Mark. Do you know where he is?" I asked.

"Yes sir. He's in the room next to you. Shall I call him for you?"

"No it's O.K. thanks. I'll take a shower first."

After settling into my luxurious surroundings and relaxing in a beautiful hot shower for a while, I went to introduce myself to my new riding companion.

I knocked on his bedroom door and waited. I stood there for a couple of minutes and nothing stirred. I was just about to return to my room when the door slowly opened a fraction and bleary eyed figure blinked and stared at me.

"Mark?" I said. Wondering if I'd got the wrong room, "I'm Brian."

"Yea, yea. You're early," he muttered.

"Sorry about that. I set off earlier than expected," I replied, feeling somewhat awkward.

"Give me a few minutes," he said, closing the door.

"Sure. No problem," I replied heading back to my bedroom. Not quite the joyous meeting I was hoping for, I thought. Maybe he isn't too well. He certainly looked the worse for wear. A few minutes later there was a knock on my door. Mark had obviously roused himself!

"I'm sorry about that," I said ushering him into my room, "didn't mean to wake you."

"It's O.K. I'm sorry I wasn't a bit more communicative!" he added with a grin. "I had a very late night and had a "visitor." In fact, she was still there when you knocked!"

"A visitor?" I responded, waiting for the inevitable story. It transpires he had met a girl in a local bar and they had obviously hit it off. In fact, they hit it off several times according to Mark.

"She's gorgeous! She comes from Guatemala. We had a blast!" he said, hardly containing is enthusiasm.

"You hungry?" I asked.

"Starving!" he replied.

"Not surprising. You've worked up an appetite," I said with a smile, "Let's grab some breakfast."

We went out for breakfast and chatted about our experiences in Mexico. He had ridden down from New Jersey and was heading for Panama. It became clear that Mark`s experiences had been totally different from mine. Whereas I had ridden from Alaska to Mexico in three and a half months, he had spent the same amount of time just meandering around Mexico!

"Man, you need to slow down!" he said, "smell the coffee!"

"You're right," I agreed. "I think our meeting was no accident. I need to take a leaf out of your book and ease up." I then proceeded to relate my story of the journey so far and my failure to "go with the flow".

"Don't worry," he added with a smile, "we'll fix that!"

His virtually fluent grasp of Spanish had enabled him to immerse himself in the culture of the country, meet people and go to places I could never have experienced. It became immediately apparent to me that I had to slow down. I had been riding too hard for too long. No wonder I was feeling worn out and constantly tired.

"So what do you do back in New Jersey?" I asked. Mark was clearly an interesting character and since we were going to be riding together for a while I was keen to find out a bit more.

"I run a contract cleaning business. It's the third largest in the city." He replied, with a hint of pride.

"What made you want to do a trip like this?"

"I'm burning myself out." He said, "Because my teams work at night I have to be up to manage them but my clients operate during the day and I need to be available for them too. I'm getting a couple of hours sleep a night."

Mark was in his mid forties, with a moustache and jet-black hair, pulled back in a tight ponytail. He looked like a stereotypical middle-aged hippy, which was pretty much exactly what he was. Through sheer hard work and determination he had built a thriving business and because the majority of his workforce were Spanish speaking, he had picked up enough of the language to be almost fluent.

Over the next hour or so, he painted a very vivid picture of his world. We couldn't have been more different. He had been morbidly obese and in order to begin this trip he had lost a total of seventy pounds. At the same time he had just kicked a $3,000 a week cocaine habit.

"I needed it to keep me awake and productive," he insisted.

"I have everything I could ever want," he added, "cars, big house, boat. But no time to enjoy any of it."

"Mark, you're going to kill yourself if you carry on like that," I said, feeling like I was stating the obvious.

"I know," he said, gazing down at his half drunk coffee. "One of the reasons for doing this trip is to ride as far as Panama and check out the possibility of moving down there in a couple of years and maybe opening a little business somewhere, with less pressure."

"If I were you I wouldn't think of a couple of years," I added, "the sooner the better. The way you're working, you won't last a couple of years."

"Maybe you're right." He replied with a nod.

"God, this is a bit deep! And we've only just met!" I said, trying to lighten the mood, "tell me more about your young lady!"

He then proceeded to talk me through his travelling strategy. Speaking fluent Spanish, he had taken a leisurely route down through Mexico and at every stop had engaged the services of local taxi drivers to take him to where the "action" was. "Action" for Mark always meant girls, sex and plenty of it!

"I intend to enjoy myself to the full!" He added with a huge grin. "Before I set off, I subscribed to a sex website. It's fantastic!' he said with great relish. "It details all the places you can get laid. Even down to the actual names of the girls!" He continued, clearly warming to his theme.

"And that's basically your route map?" I observed. Slightly different from my GPS I mused.

"Yup!"

"Well, why not. You're not married. You've no steady relationship. Go for it, that's what I say!" While at the same time thinking it was going to be an interesting next few weeks on the road with my new friend!

We decided not to head for the border the next day but instead, take another day for me to rest and recover. That night Mark enlisted the services of Paco, a local taxi driver he had befriended, to take us to a couple of bars.

With the incessant rain hammering down on top of the taxi, we headed into what can only be described as a distinctly dodgy part of town and after a short drive turned off the main road and onto a potholed, dirt track. With total disregard for his taxi`s suspension, Paco bounced his way down the dirt road before pulling up outside a rather dubious looking bar. Mark and Paco exchanged a short conversation in Spanish and then turned to me,

"Here we are amigo!"

"Where exactly is "here"?" I asked, eyeing up the area somewhat anxiously.

"Paco says this is where we can find some action!" Mark said jumping out of the taxi.

"We?" I shouted, as we sprinted to the door avoiding a huge, water filled pothole by the kerb. Not for the first time on this trip did I feel completely out of place and not a little uncomfortable. A couple of stern looking characters stood by the entrance, doing a passable impression of burly doormen. The dark and dingy room was distinctly uncrowded, making our entrance even more noticeable. Maybe it was still early for any real "action." With the eyes of everyone boring into me, we sat at a little wooden table.

"Are you sure this place is O.K.?" I said to Mark, as I attempted a covert scan of the room.

"Sure! Relax! Have a beer," he said with a grin, clearly enjoying my obvious discomfort.

"Tres cervezas por favor!" He said to a scantily dressed and rather busty barmaid. She nodded and disappeared back into the gloom.

As my eyes grew accustomed to the half-light, I began to notice small groups of young girls huddled around several plastic tables, which were placed haphazardly around the room. The kind of cheap tables you would use on your patio at home.

“See anything you like?” Mark asked, as my eyes flitted around the bar.

“Not tonight,” I replied, downing my beer with unusual haste, “what about you?”

“Nah, I’m still a bit worn out from last night!” adding, “I think I’ll just make do with the beer tonight!”

I did my best to seem nonchalant and hoped he didn’t spot the huge sigh of relief I breathed when it appeared we wouldn’t be hanging around long. After a brief exchange between Mark and a more mature lady (obviously the “madam” of the establishment) we climbed back into the taxi and made our way back to the hotel. It was clearly going to be interesting travelling with my new companion for a while!

My new riding companion, Mark!

Apart from having some company, it would certainly be much easier crossing the border with Mark`s ability to speak the language. I had been getting by with my limited Spanish but often felt the frustration of not being able to converse in anything other than short, carefully thought out sentences. I was envious of Mark`s ability to talk to anyone and knew that in the days and weeks to come this would prove invaluable. I was also hoping that his "meandering philosophy" would rub off on me and slow me down.

CHAPTER 26

San Pedro: "Hangin' with the hippies"

The night before our border crossing I endured a disturbed sleep, happy I had company, but still apprehensive of what the next day would bring. My Mexican crossing hadn`t been as easy as it was supposed to be and all the Central American border crossings have notorious reputations for being at best, longwinded, bureaucratic nightmares and at worst full of corruption and extortion. We would have to be mentally switched on and totally prepared with all our paperwork in good order. Any mistakes made at the border could have serious ramifications later. After breakfast we loaded the bikes and with a final farewell to the hotel staff and photo call, rode towards the border.

Before leaving Mexico, we had to go to the Mexican customs near the border and cancel our temporary import visa for the bikes and get exit stamps in our passports. Failure to do so, could result in a hefty fine should we want to return to Mexico in the future. As my paperwork was being processed, the customs officer told us that due to the torrential rain Guatemala had been suffering (Tropical storm "Matthew" had been devastating Central America for days), there were many landslides and many of the roads in the area were blocked. If we were to cancel our permits, get stuck inside Guatemala and had to return to find another crossing, we would have to pay again. He suggested we take another border crossing four hours away, but we decided to chance our luck. If the roads were blocked we thought we`d have a better chance of getting through on our bikes. So with even more trepidation we headed for the Guatemalan border.

With almost no hold ups and a surprising lack of unnecessary bureaucracy, we negotiated customs, the banjercito (paperwork for importing the bikes), the mandatory fumigation of the bikes (just another opportunity to extract a small payment) and the money - changers (Pesos to Quetzals). The whole process was completed in less than an hour! Once again we were warned that the roads were blocked but we decided to go as far as we could. The other option was to find a hotel at the border town, but like all border towns it looked like bandit country, so that wasn`t an appealing thought.

Pleasantly surprised at the relative ease of the crossing we rode optimistically into Guatemala. As we passed through the many towns and small villages there appeared to be no flooding problems at all. It was all looking pleasantly normal. With each passing mile I was feeling more confident that we might reach our destination of Huehuetenango, then, as we rounded a bend we ran into backed up traffic. We overtook the stationary line of cars, trucks and buses until we could go no further. Mark asked several people what was happening. Sure enough, the road was completely blocked and had been for days. It wouldn`t be clear today, maybe tomorrow he was told. A couple of people had said there was an alternative route over the mountains on a dirt road. If I had been travelling alone there was no way I would have even considered such a route, but Mark was keen to try, as he would be, given his skill in off road riding and a much more suitable bike! I must admit, I was much more reluctant for obvious reasons. The spectre of the Dalton was playing on my mind and a steady drip of adrenaline started to build up in my system. I didn't like the sound of this at all.

"What do you think?" Mark asked.

We agreed to give it a go on the basis we could always turn back if it got too difficult and find a hotel for the night. With one final confirmation from another local that it was the right road, we headed up a steep, cobbled track which quickly turned to dirt (or mud, as it was by then).

After climbing for what seemed like a long time but was probably only twenty minutes, up a winding, twisting, often rutted dirt track, we eventually came to a fork in the road, in the middle of which stood a small wood built shop. What was a tiny convenience store doing here in the middle of nowhere? However, it was an obvious place to stop and re-assess. Besides which, neither of us had eaten all day and the nervous energy was beginning to sap my strength. A packet of Doritos and a coke later (Mark had to have caffeine on a regular basis) we asked the woman in the shop which was the right way. She unfortunately pointed back the way we had come.

“I didn`t notice passing any road back there?” I said, getting just a little worried.

“The only thing I saw was a track off to the right,” Mark replied.

It seemed certain we had missed the turn, and so eyeing the darkening sky with some concern, I suggested we head back and check it out fairly soon. Mark agreed, but was clearly relishing the adventure, whereas I was just keen to get off this mountain in one piece.

We reversed our route and soon enough we came upon a very steep, very muddy, rutted track.

As I was slowing down behind Mark, I lost control on the mud and ran in to the back of his bike, dropping mine and causing him to do the same. A passing driver helped us to pick up the bikes. There was no damage as it had been a very slow fall, but it brought home to me the situation we could easily get into if we were further up the hill and got into more serious problems. I was concerned about damaging the bike. It was just too heavily loaded for the kind of terrain we were attempting to ride through.

We stood for a while discussing the options. Mark was still fairly Gung Ho and would have headed up the track if I had said “Let`s do it!” I`m all in favour of stretching my comfort zone (I`d been doing it for nearly four months), but common sense told me this was not a good move.

“I just don’t feel good about this,” I said, gazing up the steep dirt track.

If something did occur further up, it would undoubtedly be much more difficult to reverse the route. In my own mind, I'd decided I wasn't going to do it. I was going with my gut feeling and wasn't going to be swayed. Thankfully, Mark didn't push the point although I could sense he was desperately disappointed to have his off road experience curtailed.

Having agreed the risk was too great we headed back down and it was with enormous relief we found a nice hotel a few miles away and settled down with a beer. Much the better option!

I asked the waiter how long it would take to clear the road,

"Posibliamente manana," he replied shrugging his shoulders.

So with the chance that it might be open the next day I was more than happy to sit it out in a hotel, rather than battle it out on the mountain.

The next day over breakfast we got the news that the road had indeed been cleared enough to allow traffic through, but that there was now another landslide on the road from the border. It looked like we had got through just in time. It was clear Guatemala was going to prove an interesting and challenging country.

We set off after a leisurely breakfast and made for Huehuetenango. The road was littered with debris and mud and was down to a single track in many areas, so it was slow going. As we approached the town it began to rain again and by the time we arrived there we were soaked. We rode into town in very heavy traffic and just opted for the first hotel that had secure parking. I was tiring of the ritual of putting on wet and by now smelly riding gear virtually every day. The rooms were functional and had the appearance of being relatively clean. It's amazing how quickly you can get used to the very basics. As long as it included a hot shower I could tolerate most deficiencies. I'd long ago accepted the badly wired "death shower" as par for the course.

CHAPTER 27

"That was the scariest riding I've ever done!"

Although Guatemala wasn`t a huge country, and the mileages were nothing like Mexico, the road systems and adverse weather made travel much more difficult. Our next destination was going to be the famous mountain market town of Chichicastenango and the following morning we set off accompanied by the now inevitable, tropical rains falling heavily.

Even sticking to the main roads, we passed many landslides and had to spend a good deal of time being diverted with makeshift signs to the other side of the dual carriageway which was pretty scary considering the average standard of driving in Guatemala. To compound the situation as we climbed higher we ran into thick cloud and visibility was now down to about ten metres. I couldn`t see Mark in front of me, I could only hear his exhaust. As we rounded a bend we saw ahead of us another line of stationary traffic. The road was blocked by an accident. A sobering reminder of just what a danger these roads, conditions and crazy driving were. Because we had bikes we managed to navigate around the crash and continue on our journey. When we finally arrived at the town, we both needed a beer and Mark admitted,

"You know what ..... I`ve been riding over thirty years and done some crazy things, but that was the scariest riding I`ve ever done!"

In some ways it was slightly comforting to hear that I wasn't the only person being terrified.

We were both looking forward to finding a place we could stay for a few days and get some much needed rest. Chichicastenango was primarily famous for its very colourful local market, which would be taking place the next day, so we decided to check out the market and then head for Lake Atitlan which was only an hours ride away. Mark was keen to see the lake and the three volcanoes around its shore, but that night it rained incessantly which didn`t bode well for the following day.

The market lived up to its reputation and was spectacularly colourful. Guatemalans certainly don`t dress down! By lunchtime and with the inevitable gathering storm clouds building, I suggested,

"I think we should pack up and go soon. I`d like to ride in dry conditions for once!"

Mark readily agreed and while he was packing his bike I was trying to get directions from the hotel owner of how to get out of the town. With tight, narrow and crowded streets it was impossible to know which direction to take and since my GPS had proved practically worthless since crossing the border we often had to resort to asking the locals. The hotel owner offered to jump on his bike and guide us out. On the way out, a tuk tuk driver shook his head at me and shouted something like,

"No paso!"

I didn`t think anything of it at the time but about thirty minutes later as we climbed an impossibly steep and winding road out of the town I knew what he was talking about. We ground to a halt in another stationary queue.

"Oh shit, not again!" I muttered inside my helmet.

This was getting ridiculous. Immediately thinking of one of my personal reasons for doing this trip. I wanted to learn patience and develop the ability to go with the flow. Guatemala was rapidly becoming my teacher, and I really didn`t like it one bit.

We turned off our engines, got off our bikes, assessed our

options and came to the conclusion that we didn`t have any.

“We could be here for quite a while,” observed Mark, as the rain steadily fell.

Yet another traffic jam in Guatemala

Resigning myself to the situation I was taking a few pictures when up ahead I could see some slow but discernible movement. The police had arrived and had somehow managed to unlock the tangled traffic, quickly donning our helmets and gloves, we fired up the bikes and joined the painfully slow procession up the twisty road. It was interesting to note that as soon as I had accepted it could be a long wait and relaxed with it, we suddenly started to move.

As the traffic thinned we were making good progress to our destination of Panajechal on the shores of Lake Atitlan. This was great I thought, we would be there by mid afternoon and settled in a nice hotel with a steaming hot shower. With these thoughts playing inside my head, we dropped down another steep and winding road right into another line of stationary traffic. I just shook my head in disbelief.

Overtaking the traffic we got to the head of the queue to be faced by a huge landslide completely blocking the road. People were picking their way over the rubble and a big group of men were attempting to remove what they could but it looked an impossible task with huge pieces of stone the size of a small car scattered across the road. Mark was talking to one of the men when a big shout went up. Almost as one, the group of men began to scatter looking up at the crumbling rock face.

“Bloody hell, it might be coming down again!” I said to myself.

This was not a good place to be right now. I gunned the engine, hit the horn to try to warn Mark and attempted to manoeuvre my bike out of the tight spot I was in. Seeing Mark was doing the same we headed fast back up the road. When it was safe to pull over we got off to discuss our options again.

“I had a plan B,” Mark said as we removed our helmets, “but you just shot off!”

“You`re damn right I did. Didn`t you see everyone running from the landslide?”

“Listen, this is what we should do. We go back and pay some of these men to carry our bikes across the rubble”

“Are you serious!!??

“Yea, why not? Give `em a 100 Quetzals and they`ll do it I`m sure.” He said matter of factly.

“Yea, and while they`re carrying the bikes over and another landslide hits, then what?”

I wasn`t convinced.

A couple of locals pointed us in the direction of an alternative route to another little town on the other side of the lake.

"We can take that route, stay in San Pedro for a couple of days and when they`ve cleared the road come back to Panajechal?" I suggested.

So with Plan C now in operation we rode in the rain towards the little town of San Pedro about an hour away. On the map, the road looked fairly straightforward. Never trust a map. The route took us down another long, circuitous dirt track, over huge potholes and fast running streams. It was the most demanding riding I`d done since the Dalton Highway. My fear and anxiety was matched in equal measure by Mark`s obvious delight in the appalling conditions. This man loved the dirt! He enjoyed every pothole and water crossing. When we finally arrived and got off our bikes his face had a permanent grin,

"Isn`t this just fantastic!"

"You must be bloody joking."

"Yea man, it must have been really hard on your bike. I kept looking in my mirror to check you were O.K. I was feeling sorry for you."

"Not half as sorry as I was feeling."

I was just so relieved to get down unscathed, and in the back of my mind was trying not to think of the return journey.

We found a hotel right on the shore and he was right, it was a fantastic place. I just wanted to be able to see it without the constant rain and low cloud. Maybe tomorrow would be better. That night we had a few beers in a local bar run by an Englishman,

"Hi, I`m Brian!"

"I`m Nick."

"Where are you from Nick?"

"Morecambe," he replied.

"Morecambe! Bloody hell!" I spent half my childhood on holiday in Morecambe!

"What on earth brought you to Guatemala?"

He had travelled the world, ended up in Central America and had put money into this bar, but because of the weather his business was in serious jeopardy.

"If it keeps raining, my bar will soon be under water," he said, his voice heavy with resignation.

He told us that Guatemala had been under a state of emergency for several months and this was the worst weather in sixty years. Hundreds of people had died because of the landslides. It was another very sobering conversation.

Tuk Tuks in San Pedro

“What`s the forecast like?”

“Another storm is coming through”

And with that comforting thought to dwell on, we headed off to bed.

The next day during a brief dry spell we went out to explore the town and in the process happened upon a great little cafe down by a very small harbour, which sold an excellent cappuccino. Over coffee we made a decision to base ourselves in San Pedro and take the boat across the lake to Panajachel. After the extremely demanding ride the previous day, I was more than happy to take a few days off.

San Pedro turned out to be a very chilled place with a couple of lively bars and brilliant food. It had attracted many ex pats who escaped the rat race and were clearly living a much less stressful life, a point that appealed to Mark in particular. In one little cafe, we got chatting to a Canadian,

“How long have you been here?”

“I moved down from Vancouver a couple of years ago”

He ran his own software business and regaled us with the usual stressful stories of self employment.

He just seemed amazingly happy and contented.

“Do you miss anything from your previous lifestyle?” I asked, pretty much knowing what his response would be.

“Hell no! I lost most of my money in the recession. Now I`ve got nothing but I`m happier than I ever was! I just chill out, smoke a joint a day, read lots of books, don`t wear a watch! What`s not to love!”

“I`m thinking of doing the same,” said Mark. Clearly feeling he was in the company of a kindred spirit.

“Do it man, check out as soon as you can. It`s crazy up there. Seriously, you don`t need the stress and it`s so much cheaper to live down here!”

We met several people who it seemed, had done just that and none of them seemed to be frowning, even in the worst weather for sixty years. It provided an ongoing topic of conversation between the two of us for several days.

San Pedro proved to be the perfect place for some much needed rest, but all too soon it was time to get back on the road.

CHAPTER 28

"This is definitely the wrong road!"

Antigua was to be our next destination and I was really looking forward to seeing this famous old colonial town. Before we left I enquired about the road conditions and an estimate of how long the ride would take. The roads were clear and on a bike should take no more than one to two hours I was told.

When we got up the next day, I couldn't believe the weather! The sun was shining and for the first time, we had a clear view of the volcanoes as we set off. It was hard to believe we had been staying in the midst of this magnificent backdrop and not been able to appreciate its beauty until we were leaving.

Finding our way back on to the main road, for some reason, proved amazingly difficult, as we attempted to navigate our way through several little villages. Every street looked the same and no signposts existed. It seemed ridiculous to be going around in circles in such a small group of villages, but it was critical that we got on the right road because the wrong one would take us in the opposite direction and straight into bandit country. The other side of the lake was notoriously dangerous with kidnapping a common occurrence.

After asking several locals, we did eventually get back on track and started to climb the twisty mountain roads. An hour into the ride and we were making good time on the main road when we the traffic ahead suddenly began to slow and eventually we ground to a halt. Not again! It surely couldn`t be another landslide, this was the Pan American highway! People were getting out of their cars and walking about trying to find out how far ahead the blockage was. I noticed intermittent traffic coming the other way so I guessed that at least there must be some way through. It was clear that there was only one lane open somewhere up the road and it would just be a matter of time when it was our turn. Sure enough, a few minutes later and we started to slowly make some progress. But the progress was indeed very slow and the hold up had set us back at least a couple of hours with a further traffic jam coming into the city of Chimaltenango delaying us even further. After we got moving, I spotted a sign for Antigua, turned out of the heavy traffic and headed down a much less crowded road. I had taken the lead from Mark, as despite his undoubted off road skill, my ability on the road to filter through heavy traffic was much better. The benefit of learning to ride in London.

I reckoned we were only about twenty minutes from Antigua when we passed through a little town, and without any signage to the contrary, I assumed the route just continued along the same road. This was to prove a costly and painful mistake. After a few miles the beautiful tarmac ran out and we hit a dirt road. I pulled up and knew instantly I had taken the wrong road. Looking at the map, it was clear that this dirt track would eventually take us to Antigua, but it would be much longer and obviously more demanding. Had I been riding solo, I would have just turned around and got back on the main road but Mark was clearly relishing the prospect of a another dirt adventure,

"It`ll be O.K. And you know what, it`s good practice. You can`t avoid dirt all the way to Tierra Del Fuego!" He said, his face beaming.

If I had my way, I`d ride paved roads all the way, I thought.

"O.K. let`s do it."

For the first few miles the track wasn`t too bad and then it turned a little rougher where they were carrying out some road maintenance, and it was at this point that I hit some heavier dirt, lost control and came off the bike. Cursing furiously at the stupidity, I had a quick check of the bike and with the help of some of the road workers picked up the bike and as I was about to get back on noticed a slight pain in my right ankle.

The anger and adrenaline masked the pain for a while but it was obvious I had sprained or twisted it and that was going to be a problem.

"Fucking dirt!" I screamed in my helmet. I hadn`t felt this angry in nearly four months on the road.

If only I hadn`t missed the turning. I was still pretty furious with myself twenty minutes later as we finally arrived in Antigua. Our one to two hours ride had become nearly six hours.

Antigua was indeed a beautiful old colonial town surrounded by three volcanoes, but every street was made of badly laid, heavy cobbles and I winced as we bounced over them sending a regular, painful reminder of my recent carelessness.

It was also clear that Antigua was very much on the tourist map as many of the expensive hotels advertised their rates in dollars. Passing up the very nice, but pricy $60 a night options, we found a much cheaper, but far more basic accommodation and settled there, negotiating a deal for the next six nights. I unpacked quickly and Mark went in search of some ice for my throbbing ankle.

An ice pack and two Ibuprofens later, we went out in search of food and a much needed beer.

Antigua is a lovely place to chill out, wander around, shop, eat good food and drink some of the best coffee anywhere in the world. All of the above we did for the next few days, hampered only by my lack of mobility and therefore, the unfortunate need to endure those awful bone shaking tuk tuks.

“Right I’ve found the place to go!” Mark said with a beaming smile.

“What place?” I asked. Knowing he either meant he’d found a great bar or more likely he’d been on his sex web site and located Antigua’s hidden denizens of lust.

“It’s about a mile from here. Let’s grab a tuk tuk and go and explore!”

We flagged down one that was passing and Mark gave the driver the street name.

“Are you sure about this?” I asked, as we turned down a particularly dodgy looking street. I got no reply. Mark was clearly in the zone and eager to indulge himself. A few minutes later the driver pulled up by the side of the road.

“Aqui!” he said pointing across the road, to a hole in the wall covered with some kind of curtain.

“You must be joking,” I blurted, “it’s a hole in the wall!”

“Come on!” Mark said as he disappeared through the curtain, followed by the driver. I didn’t have much choice so I ducked through the curtain behind them. The hole in the wall led to a courtyard, at the end of which was a metal staircase leading up to a nightclub. By the time I had climbed the stairs and entered the dark and dingy room, Mark and the driver had ordered some beer and were sitting at a table. I quickly joined them, and despite it being only 2.30 pm I felt in need of a beer.

The room was dominated by a raised platform, in the middle of which stood half a dozen girls in various states of undress. To the side stood a young man with tight jeans and bleached hair who began to bark some kind of orders in Spanish, as a rock song boomed out from the four huge speakers located in each corner. The girls then proceeded to perform a kind of dance. "Bleach Boy" was obviously their choreographer and from the look of it, was getting very frustrated with their lack of rhythm.

"She's nice," Mark said gesturing to one of the girls.

"Which one?" I asked. My cursory early glance had clearly missed the "nice" one.

"On the left," he replied.

"The young one?"

"Yea. I like her!" he said, simultaneously gesturing to the club's madam.

There then followed a protracted conversation in Spanish. Mark was clearly negotiating a deal. After several minutes, the madam shouted something to the girl and she broke off from her chorography practice and came to join us. She sat on Mark's lap while he finished his beer and seemed to be enjoying the conversation. Between them they had obviously struck a deal and were about to disappear to a nearby room,

"I hope you're not going to be long," I added hopefully.

"No, I only booked thirty minutes! And anyway, it looks like you've got your own entertainment!" He said, nodding behind me.

I turned round to see a huge TV, with a silent porn film in full flow and our driver fully engrossed in the performance. You couldn't make this up I thought, as I drained my beer and ordered a second. Exactly thirty minutes later, Mark and the girl emerged from the room.

"Great time management!" I said, "She's a good businesswoman."

"Yea, I wanted a bit longer but she wouldn't have any of it!" He said with a smile. I nodded at our driver and we headed back to the street.

"Feel better for that?" I asked.

"Fantastic!" he replied.

After all the appalling weather we had suffered since we entered Central America, we were blessed with a system of high pressure for our stay and every day we were greeted with beautiful sunshine, and pleasant breezes. My ankle gradually improved until I could dispense with my umbrella, which had been used as a makeshift walking stick. Sadly, Mark missed out on a couple of those days, for some reason preferring to indulge his love affair with Tequila! His penchant for the short drinks had surfaced while in the little bars in San Pedro.

"Southern Comfort!" he exclaimed as his eyes lit up, "my all time favourite drink!"

"Dos, por favor," he said to the barman.

"Not for me thanks. I don't drink shorts," I added quickly, "beer suits me fine."

"Go on you'll love it!" he replied, in that kind of way people do when they've had one too many and try to force it on others.

"Nope. I won't drink it"

He ordered two anyway and finished them both in quick succession. It became clear to me that although Mark had kicked his cocaine habit, he obviously needed "something" to enjoy life.

While in Antigua, and being a relative lightweight drinker in comparison, I had to abandon him on one of his attempts at all night partying. I could tell the signs. We had been out for a nice meal and had a couple of beers.

"Let's have one for the road!" he said.

"O.K. I'll have a beer"

I had a beer, and he decided he was in the mood for a couple of tequilas. A couple, led to couple more and the more he drank, the more garrulous he became and began engaging all the locals in a conversation, which would clearly be a long one. He was winding up as I was winding down. When it became obvious that he was in no mood for leaving any time soon, I made my excuses and left,

"See you for breakfast tomorrow," I said, knowing full well that it would be a minor miracle if he surfaced before noon.

He didn't. In fact I was getting quite worried the following day so I checked with the hotel owner and asked him if he had seen Mark get back,

"Si, si," he replied, "a las quatro!" he added with a smile.

"Gracias!" I said with a shake of the head. 4.00 am! Well, that's his day wiped out, I thought as I headed off for some breakfast.

We decided afterwards that it wasn`t good for either of us to be wandering back to our hotel alone, since much of Central America can be unsafe after dark, and as laid back as Antigua appears during the day, at night it can become a totally different proposition. Common sense needed to prevail.

After breakfast, I was in the mood for a conversation in English and so I made for Moto Café, a small café run by an Englishman. Dave had been in Guatemala for several years and organised motorcycle tours and was a good source of information. My next stop was going to be Guatemala City, which would be an altogether different proposition, so I popped in for a coffee and chat. While we chatting an American dropped by,

"Wow, what happened to you?' Dave asked, noticing a cut and black eye.

Antigua

"Last night," our American friend explained, "I was so drunk I could hardly walk in a straight line and as I came out of a bar, I was jumped by a couple of guys. They took my wallet."

"Did you go to the Police?" I asked.

"The Police were there. They watched it happen." He said with a shrug of the shoulders, "they've probably got my wallet."

I looked at Dave in astonishment.

"Yea, I wouldn't trust the Police. That kind of thing happens a lot," Dave added.

I made a mental note to have a word with Mark as soon as he had sobered up. In the state he would have been in last night, he would have been an easy target, despite his weapon of choice.

"You don't have a knife?" he'd asked with shock, when we arrived in Guatemala.

"No. I have no weapons at all!"

"You need protection," he said, "Here take this, I have a spare" he added, passing me a flick knife. "This is how you open it," he demonstrated with a deft flick of the wrist, "and this is how you close it," carefully folding it back. "Just keep it with you. You never know," he explained.

"Thanks," I said, wondering in what circumstances I would ever think of using it.

When I returned to our hotel and a bleary eyed Mark finally emerged from his room it was about noon.

"Good night then?" I enquired.

"Aw man, it was a blast!" He replied enthusiastically, "but I had a terrible night's sleep"

"I'm not surprised!" I added, with a hint of "I told you so" in my tone of voice.

"No, it wasn't the drink. It was these," he cried, taking off his T shirt to exhibit a back that looked like a peperami pizza.

"My God! What the hell's all that?"

"Bed bugs I think," he said rather disconsolately, "there goes my afternoon of fun."

"Oh yea," I added, "did you cancel them?"

The previous night we had ventured back into Antigua's dark side courtesy of another tuk tuk driver. This was a different bar but similar result. We had gone early in the evening on the basis that I fancied having a meal and nice bottle of wine later. This time the club at least had a proper door! It was however, locked. Obviously no riff raff allowed. Mark rapped on the door a couple of times and a few sliding bolts later we entered another dimly lit establishment. Déjà vu, I mused as we sat at a table and ordered a couple of beers. Within a minute we were joined by two young ladies. Mark immediately started his patter and homed in on the more attractive one. There followed a rather awkward few minutes as Mark and his girl snuggled closer to each other while I sat there smiling and attempting to make polite conversation in my poor Spanish with the other girl.

"Hey, guess what! They're sisters!" Mark suddenly exclaimed. Shortly after which he disappeared off to an upstairs room leaving me with older sister.

"How long?" I shouted.

"Only thirty minutes," came the reply.

Thank goodness for that I thought. A further minute's embarrassed silence ensued until I said,

"Usted es muy bonita, pero tengo una novia en Inglaterra." (You are very pretty but I have a girlfriend in England). At least now she knew there would be no business forthcoming tonight. I bought her a drink (it was the least I could do) and asked her where she was from,

"Honduras," she explained.

Being even poorer than Guatemala, many girls come over from Honduras to ply their trade. She then showed me photos of her children and became quite tearful when she explained the only reason she was doing this was to provide for her family back home. She might have been leading me on but I didn't think so, and I felt quite sorry for her and anyone else like her who had to resort to this way of making a living. Thankfully the thirty minutes seem to pass quite quickly and Mark and the sister returned to the table.

"They're coming to see us tomorrow afternoon," Mark said, his new girlfriend nodding excitedly, "before they start work."

Staring at Mark's spotty, red back, the following day, I could see why he decided to cancel the planned meeting. Not very sexy. Still, the attack of the bed bugs had got me out of another potentially awkward situation. Every cloud....

As much as I was enjoying my time in Antigua and the extended break from daily riding I was also looking forward with increasing anticipation to my visit to Costa Rica. When I originally planned the trip I was adamant that I needed to do it solo, having no idea at the time just how challenging it would be. Right now, having some company felt like a good idea and I had asked my girlfriend, Jane if she fancied meeting up with me somewhere along the road,

"Where will you be in mid October?" she had asked me.

"I'm not sure. Somewhere in Central America," I guess, "Maybe Costa Rica?"

So on that basis, Jane had booked some quality R+R resorts for a couple of weeks in Costa Rica. The difficulty was estimating the timing of the whole rendezvous. Here I was in Guatemala and having done some quick figures I believed it was possible to make the dates if I rode at a brisk pace through several countries, but that wasn't what I wanted to do so I decided to find a place to store my bike in Antigua and catch a short flight from Guatemala City to Costa Rica for a two week break with Jane and then fly back, pick up my bike and carry on in a more leisurely fashion. Satisfied with the plan, I had booked the flights and timed a final Couch Surfing session in Guatemala City to coincide with the visit. This new plan seemed to suit everyone and enabled Mark to fit his own trip into the city for another assignation with the girl he had spent the night with in Comitan.

CHAPTER 29

Welcome to one of the murder capitals of the world!

"Be very careful in Guatemala City," Marks's girlfriend had warned him, "it is a very dangerous place."

In fact, everything we had heard about the city was pretty frightening stuff with no go areas where gang warfare was rife with shootings, muggings and violence being commonplace.

"Watch out for the ones with tears tattooed on their faces!" We were warned.

"What do you mean?" I'd asked with some slight concern.

"For every person they kill, they have a teardrop tattooed on their cheeks," was the response.

It was clearly a city where it might well prove fatal to take a wrong turning. This had been preying on both our minds, so I was glad I had decided not to ride my bike into the city but instead jump on a "Chicken Bus" for the short forty minutes ride.

As has often been the case, people turn up at the right time to help you out. Dave from the Moto Café agreed to let me store my bike with him for the two weeks. Perfect! So now, I just had to get safely to Guatemala City for my Couch Surfing stay, get to the airport and get back again.

I must admit that I try not to over react to the many scare stories about dangerous countries and cities, but as I researched a hotel near the airport (just in case I needed a back up) it made pretty grim reading. The hotel was now part of a secure compound. In fact, this is an extract from the hotel's web site,

"VERY IMPORTANT - PLEASE READ

FOR SECURITY REASONS, THE NEIGHBORHOOD WHERE DOS LUNAS IS LOCATED (AURORA II) IS NOW GATED.

PEOPLE COMING IN A FLIGHT WILL BE MET BY OUR DRIVER AT THE AIRPORT. YOU CAN CALL US FROM THE TOURIST OFFICE AT THE AIRPORT IF YOU HAVE ANY DELAY OR PROBLEM.

TAXIS AND SHUTTLE DRIVERS THAT COME TO AURORA II, WILL BE REQUESTED TO SHOW THEIR VALID ID.

IF YOU PLAN TO WALK, PLEASE LET US KNOW, WE CAN MEET YOU AT THE AIRPORT. WE STRONGLY ENCOURAGE YOU **NOT** TO TAKE PUBLIC TRANSPORTATION BECAUSE THEY ARE NOT SAFE AT THE MOMENT.

ALSO FOR YOUR OWN SECURITY, PLEASE TRY TO MAKE YOUR BOOKING DIRECTLY AND IN ADVANCE IF IT IS POSSIBLE, YOU CAN CALL US OR EMAIL US.

TRY NOT TO USE OTHER PEOPLE TO DO IT, WE HAVE IMPORTANT INFORMATION TO SHARE WITH YOU

WE APOLOGIZE FOR THE INCONVINIENCE, BUT IT WILL BE A SAFER NEIGHBORHOOD FOR YOU, AND FOR ALL OF US."

Mmmm, it certainly provided food for thought as I packed my bag and jumped on a Chicken Bus for a very hair- raising ride to Guatemala City.

Guatemalan chicken bus drivers are fearless or reckless, depending upon your point of view; either way, they tear around bends at breakneck speeds in ex American school buses that have clearly seen much better days. They were universally called Chicken Buses from the days when they literally did carry chickens and all manner of livestock from the surrounding towns and villages to the cities to trade in the markets. The name just stuck.

Their motto must be "In God we trust," because each bus was packed with religious artifacts. Every journey was a leap of faith. Well it certainly was for me.

I`d arranged to meet my couch surfing host, Luis, at a big

shopping mall in the city. The plan was to spend a couple of days in the city and then catch a plane to Costa Rica. I arrived early for my rendezvous so I busied myself on my netbook at a nice café inside the huge mall. As with all my previous Couch Surfing experiences, the initial meeting is always interesting. For a start, although you will have seen their photos on the website, you never know how current they are, so I spent the time scanning the mall looking for someone who might look like the photo I had seen a few days previously! Eventually, my host arrived and did indeed look like his photo.

"Hello Brian!" he said with a big smile and a firm handshake.

Unfortunately, his English wasn't very good and combined with my still limited Spanish meant for extended periods of silence as I desperately racked my brain trying to compose coherent sentences to fill in the gaps. This was clearly going to be a more challenging Couch Surfing experience I thought, as we drove through the city. Before he took me back to his house he asked me if it was O.K. to drop in on his girlfriend who lived nearby.

"No problem!" I replied.

It would break up the silent interludes and maybe she could speak better English. Luis' girlfriend was an accountant so I was slightly surprised when we pulled up outside a rather run down, ramshackle building that turned out to be her house. I wasn't sure what to expect but assumed her profession would warrant more salubrious accommodation. I was even more shocked when we went inside. If this was the typical living standard of a professional person I wondered how "the other half lived". It was a sobering and salutary reminder of how privileged we are in the U.K. Sadly, Luis' girlfriend had even less English than he had, nevertheless, we all planned to meet up in the city that night for a drink.

Luis and his girlfriend

Having experienced his girlfriend's place I was curious to see where Luis lived, as I would be staying as his guest for a night. He explained to me in broken English that his area was quite nice and relatively safe. It certainly appeared so as we pulled up outside his compound. Most professionals in the city lived in gated compounds protected by armed guards and as we passed through security and the large heavy metal door clanked reassuringly shut, I admit to feeling a little more secure.

The house was pleasant enough and big enough to accommodate Luis and his two brothers, both of whom I would meet later. Grabbing my bag I followed Luis upstairs,

"This is your room," he said pointing at a small box room containing a single bed and pile of sheets and blankets stacked haphazardly on a dressing table.

"Gracias!" I said, as he disappeared off down the corridor. I dropped my bag and briefly took in my new surroundings. A slightly musty and damp smell permeated the room. I took a couple of the sheets made the bed as best I could and lay down. After what seemed like a reasonable amount of time settling in I got up and wandered downstairs. I had no idea where Luis was and indeed, I had no idea what, if any plan there was for the rest of the day. Luis had basically left me to my own devices in his house!

It was mid afternoon and because of our language difficulties we hadn't exactly discussed what was happening. It was all a little bit awkward. Did I go knocking on all the doors in the house to find him? Or did I just stay where I was and wait till he reappeared? I opted for the latter and busied myself writing up my blog for an hour or so, but eventually I couldn't stand it any longer and had to find Luis.

He'd disappeared to his room for a sleep! It seemed a bit strange. You invite a total stranger to your house and then leave them to their own devices? Nevertheless, I was very thankful to him for offering me a room instead of me trying to find a decent hotel in the city. By the time evening rolled around I was pretty desperate to get out and experience Guatemala City at night knowing that at least I wouldn't be wandering around the wrong areas by mistake.

We drove downtown to the Centro Historico and Luis took me to his favourite bar. "La Otra Puerta" was a very bohemian place, serving typical Guatemalan food, and an interesting line in DIY decoration. The entire place was covered from floor to ceiling with graffiti from all over the world. Here`s a place where you`re actually encouraged to write on the walls! Needless to say I obliged and my "Journey for Hope" is now recorded for posterity (or as long as the building lasts).

Afterwards we took a short walk around and although I didn't feel particularly intimidated by the city's violent reputation, I was glad I had Luis as a guide. On the drive back to the house I explained to Luis the plan for the following day. I would be heading to the airport for my flight to Costa Rica around midday. He said it would be O.K. because his brother would be home by then and he spoke good English and could organise a taxi to the airport. He emphasised the importance of booking a certain type of taxi,

"Not the white ones," he said shaking his head, "they are dangerous."

I made a mental note. Yellow **not** white.

I thanked him for his hospitality and said I would see him in a couple of weeks as I was staying with him one more night when I arrived back from Costa Rica. Making doubly sure he would be there to meet me at the airport in two weeks time I wrote all the flight details down for him and left them with his brother the following day.

That night I didn`t sleep well, with the anticipation of meeting up with Jane occupying my already active mind. I was up early. The house was empty apart from a maid, who came into clean twice a week,

"Buenos Dias!" I smiled. With several hours to kill before leaving I decided to go for a walkabout and risk life on the outside of the compound. Leaving any valuables at the house I waved a quick hello to the security guard and ventured outside.

It felt slightly eerie being on the outside of the compound and I tried not to look too much like the pale skinned Gringo that I was as I walked purposefully down the street heading for a little shopping mall I believed to be about half a mile away. Avoiding eye contact with locals hanging around on the street corners while still scanning the environment I shoved my hands in my pockets remembering I had left my "blade" back in my bag. I'd make a lousy gangster, I reflected as I hurried past a small group of men huddled round an old car, smoking cigarettes.

I reached the main road and took a left turn spotting what looked like shops in the distance. It was a relatively short walk and yet I was perspiring freely in the heat and high humidity of the city. The mall had nothing to commend it but at least it got me out of the house for a couple of hours and I found a cheap place for breakfast. Draining a very dismal coffee, I paid the bill and hurried back to the safety of the compound where I had an hour and half before my pre booked taxi was due to arrive. When I reached the house I met Luis' younger brother and so whiled away some time chatting to him about life in one of the world's most dangerous cities. He was an educated young man, who spoke good English and was studying at the local university,

"What is it like living behind these walls with armed guards?"

"You get used to it," he said, "I've always known it like this."

"Do you ever feel threatened?" I pressed him.

"Sometimes," he replied, "I was robbed at knifepoint two weeks ago."

"Where was that?" I asked with morbid fascination.

"Right across the street. In broad daylight," he said, as if it was a regular occurrence.

As I headed towards the airport (in the right colour taxi) I mulled over the previous twenty-four hours and concluded that my apprehension about Guatemala City was well founded. I wanted to spend as little time there as possible. Sadly, I was destined to visit it more than I would have liked in the weeks to come.

CHAPTER 30

"It was the best of times, it was the worst of times"

As I arrived at the airport I was relieved to see my flight was on time and so I settled down in the departure lounge, sipped on a coffee and updated my blog on my netbook using the airport's free WiFi. Every now and again my mind wandered with a rush of excited adrenaline to my imminent meeting with Jane. I was so excited at the prospect of seeing her I could hardly wait.

After the short flight I reached San Jose, Costa Rica, jumped in the first taxi I could find and directed them to the nearby hotel I had booked just for the night. The next day I planned on taking another taxi to the first resort Jane had booked, dropping off my luggage and then coming straight back to the airport to meet Jane's flight. That night I enjoyed a lovely meal, had a couple of beers and felt more relaxed than I had in weeks. It was a great comfort to me to know that Jane would be arriving the following day and we could spend some well earned quality time together. Needless to say, the excitement meant an unsettled night's sleep.

The resort was a perfect place to do nothing at all and just relax in the peaceful sanctuary, but I must confess to being far too eager to get a taxi back to the airport. When I have something pressing and important on my mind I can't rest until it is resolved. I booked one of the resort's own taxis and arrived well ahead of schedule. The English speaking driver arranged to return and pick us both up later. I thanked him and went to check the status of the flight. It was scheduled to be on time, and so with nothing to do for a while I went and sat out in the sunshine, full of anticipation.

I had been looking forward to this for weeks and had run and re-run the scenario in my mind over and over again. I couldn't remember the last time I had been this excited. It was like being a kid again and looking forward to Christmas. As I reflected upon how I felt, it reinforced just how much of a challenge it had been to do the trip solo and just how much Jane had come to mean to me. The journey had cemented my feelings towards her and had reminded me just what an amazing woman she was.

I walked back down to arrivals to check the flight status and as I did so I heard the sound of an incoming jet engine. Turning around I saw an Iberian flight touch down and immediately felt incredibly emotional. The intensity and spontaneity of this wave of emotion took me by surprise. I had a lump in my throat and was blinking back the tears as I took some deep breaths and attempted to compose myself. It seemed an eternity before people started to exit the arrivals area and several minutes before I spotted Jane. She was clearly as excited as I was as she rushed towards me and we gave each other a huge hug.

"Come on, I've got a cab waiting!" I said with a big smile, "let me show you what you've booked!"

The Xandari Resort was the perfect place for some real rest and relaxation. It was peaceful, tranquil and seemed to be an ideal place for us both to catch up after being apart for four months. Unfortunately, unbeknown to both of us, everything was about to change.

The next morning after a leisurely lie in, we were both keen to get up and explore the resort properly. As I was bending down to put on my shoe, someone shoved a red-hot poker right into my lower back. At least that's what it felt like as I let out a muffled scream,

"What's the matter? What's wrong?" Jane said, as she rushed in from the balcony.

"It's my back," I answered, wincing with the pain as I hobbled to the bed.

"It was the best of times, it was the worst of times"

"The worst of times….."

The spa centre manager was in a brief, but earnest conversation in Spanish with the physiotherapist while I lay in pain awaiting the prognosis.

"Do you want the good news or the bad news?" he asked.

"Give me the whole lot," I replied, not wanting to play games, but quietly steeling myself for the bad news.

"Well, she says you will get better, but it will take time and you should stay off the bike for at least three weeks"

"Three weeks!"

"She says your back is in bad condition and if you continue your journey, you could end up with permanent damage"

I lay there in silence as the words sank in.

"Your back isn`t in good enough shape to continue, and the roads further south will just get worse," he added.

"She says you need lots of rest and then exercises to build up the muscles"

His words became background noise as I struggled with a wave of emotions.

"Three weeks off the bike" -" permanent damage" - "can`t continue"

I`d always thought that if anything might jeopardise the trip it would be bike related and mechanical; I never imagined that my body might let me down, and here I was, faced with the distinct possibility that my journey might be over.

"I want it to be a memorable holiday!" Jane had told me on Skype weeks earlier.

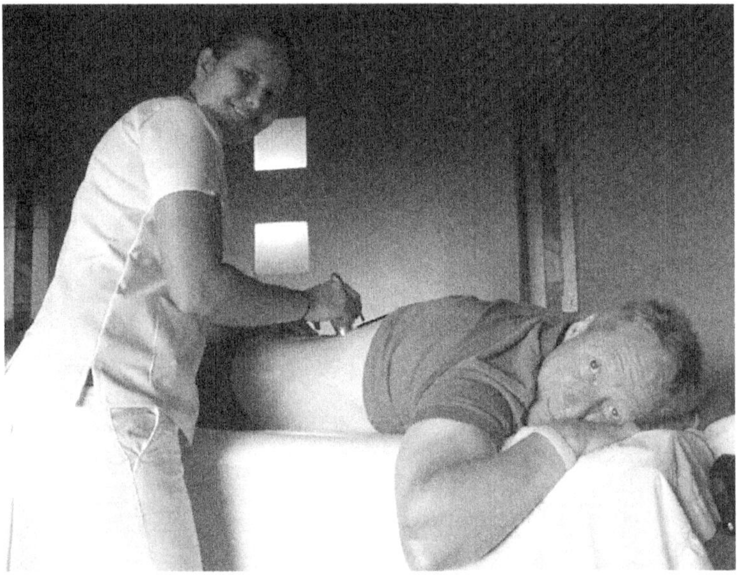

Emergency Physiotherapy

It was certainly turning out that way. I had trapped the sciatic nerve, and my back was in spasm. Two hours later, I was lying on the physiotherapists table listening to the spa centre manager translating words I didn`t want to hear.

Be very careful what goals you set for yourself, be very careful what you wish for. The Universe has a way of delivering everything to your door. Lying there, I reflected ruefully on my casual response back in England when people asked me about the journey,

"I want to challenge myself and step out of my comfort zone."

Now I was to face my biggest challenge so far, coming to terms with the possibility of failing to achieve my goal. I had always prided myself on being focused and determined in most things I do. If I commit to something, I invariably get it done. In 2007 I had an epic battle with Kilimanjaro. The mountain almost got the better of me but in the end I dug deep and reached the summit. My challenge now seemed even greater.

As Jane reminded me, the answer lay in letting go of my fixed idea of what the end result should be, and if necessary changing my goal. With that in mind, I focused for the moment, on enjoying our time in Costa Rica.

Two weeks later, back in Antigua, I would have an x ray on my back. The result of that would determine whether my journey was over, but for now I would have as much physiotherapy treatment I could get and try to enjoy the time with Jane.

For the first couple of days it was all I could do just to hobble around with a stick,

"I can't believe this," I kept repeating, "I've been looking forward to seeing you for so long and now this happens."

All the while, Jane was amazingly pragmatic about the whole situation and encouraged me to keep focused on enjoying the enforced rest. Her attitude was an object lesson in handling adversity and a constant reminder to me to stop wallowing in self pity and just get on and handle the situation. It wasn't as though I hadn't handled significant challenges already on the journey, but the time with Jane was so important to me I didn't want to ruin it for both of us.

"The best of times...."

Eventually, with Jane's help I managed to pull myself out of my little pity party and resolved to enjoy the time we had together and use it as well earned recovery time. The few days of physiotherapy treatment at the Xandari resort enabled me to become a little more mobile and then it was time to move on to the second of the four resorts Jane had organised.

She had arranged transport and a driver to take us to Arenal and the Los Iguanas resort in the north of the country and this entailed a rather bumpy several hour transit. The driver did the best he could to avoid the many potholes, as I lay out in the front seats supported by two big pillows, wincing if we passed over any little bump in the road. I was more than used to poor road conditions on the trip, but I'd heard that Costa Rica was the most affluent of all Central American countries and somehow expected their infrastructure to be of a higher calibre. Sadly, this was not to be the case. As with all the other countries where corruption was a way of life, the much need investment in the infrastructure failed to appear, so every year when the heavy rains came, many of the roads would be washed away causing traffic chaos, landslides and major delays.

The Los Iguana resort proved to be as good if not better than the Xandari, located in a beautiful rainforest setting nestling in the shadow of the Arenal volcano. After the arduous drive, I eased myself out of the transit van and straight into a little golf buggy for a short ride up to our apartment. It appeared we had been upgraded to what were termed "celebrity apartments" with stunning views of the volcano. We spent a delightfully relaxed few days during which time our biggest decisions were what to wear for dinner and especially for Jane, what cocktail to experiment with each night!

"The best of times..."

Being the super organised person she is, Jane had brought with her an appropriate set of clothes for me to wear, knowing that my by now tatty clothes wouldn't fit in with the environment of these luxury resorts. Each day ran blissfully into the next and our evening ritual became quite comforting. Jane would put on a stunning outfit and we would take a slow stroll down to the pool bar at a pace that wouldn't tax my back. The cicadas would provide the musical backdrop to the gentle warmth of another rainforest evening,

"Would madam prefer sex on the beach or maybe a slippery nipple?" I would enquire as we reached the bar.

"Mmm, difficult choice," Jane would reply, "let me have a cocktail first while I decide!"

Happy days.

I'm not usually comfortable with lounging around doing nothing as time tends to drag, but here I was more than happy to slow down to the pace of Costa Rican life, and yet all too soon, our time in Arenal came to an end and it was time to move on to our third resort. Jane had booked another beautiful resort by the sea at Arenas Del Mar where there was a lovely private beach. After checking in we climbed into the now familiar golf buggy for a short journey to our room. Our driver gave us a guided tour of the room and finally, sliding the door of the balcony back he pointed to a fridge to the left of the balcony,

"Unfortunately, we have had to lock your fridge," he said, pointing to a kind of makeshift padlock," the raccoons are very clever and in the evening would come and steal all the contents."

"Raccoons?" We echoed, almost simultaneously.

"Yes," he replied, "and we would ask you to make sure you lock the door every night before you go to sleep.'

"Of course," I acknowledged, as I caught Jane's look of mild consternation.

Here we followed our, by now well trodden routine, this time including a daily stint lying on the beach under palm trees. The tranquility only briefly disturbed by families of iguanas, slowly slithering through the undergrowth and chattering monkeys swinging high up in the canopy.

"I think I just want to stay here for a month or two!" I said as we lay on our beach beds sipping fresh fruit cocktails. Jane nodded in agreement and put her head back in her book. It was idyllic, and the perfect antidote to the gruelling hours in the saddle that had defined the previous four months of my journey.

I drained the last of my fruit cocktail and gazed out to sea with my thoughts being ever pulled towards the inevitable end of this idyll. I had to force myself to focus on the present moment. The

Buddhist concept of mindfulness was something I desperately needed to cultivate I thought, as I closed my eyes and listened to the gentle lapping of the waves.

The beauty and peace was shattered only once, when we were the subject of a failed, covert raccoon raiding party in the middle of the night. It must have been about 2.00 am when our sleep was disturbed by a massive crash. I shot straight up with an adrenaline fuelled cry of,

"What the fuck!" As I leaped out of bed wondering, where I was and what the hell was happening. I quickly pulled myself together to see Jane's suitcase on the floor. It had somehow dislodged itself from the chair it was secured on. There was no way it could have just fallen. It had to have been pulled off. It was then I noticed the glass doors, which we were warned to lock, were slightly open. Open enough for a Raccoon raiding party. My guess is, more than one had slipped in through the gap and were intent upon examining the contents of Jane's case. Needless to say, after that episode, Jane would jump out of her skin at the slightest noise. Each night after before we turned in, I was tasked with a quick and pointless room sweep to convince her it was a Raccoon Free Zone!

With each passing day my back was feeling slightly better and I could function without a stick to prop me up, but it was clear that as soon as I got back to Antigua I would have to get it checked out. Our brief time by the sea came to an end and it was with a feeling of sadness that we set off for our final resort, which would be a one night stopover closer to San Jose and the airport. We arrived at La Finca in the afternoon. Another exclusive resort based on a coffee plantation. We didn't have enough time to do it justice but nevertheless we were busying ourselves enjoying the outdoor Jacuzzi and strolling around the grounds when we happened upon a stable block,

"Let`s have a look," I said, knowing of Jane's love of horses.

The stable had a couple of horses, one of which was a beautiful big white one being put through his paces by his trainer.

"Muy grande!" I said to the trainer, commenting on the size of his charge.

"Si, si, mucho grande," he replied, subtly correcting my poor Spanish.

We watched with fascination for a couple of minutes.

"He's very well behaved," Jane observed. Having ridden for twenty years she could spot the tell tale signs of good and bad behaviour.

The trainer then motioned to Jane to climb in the saddle and before I could say anything she already had one foot in the stirrup! She was obviously destined for test ride and so they duly went off down the leafy lane leaving me waving from the stables! That night would be our last night together. The following day we were both due to take our separate flights, Jane back home to the U.K. and me back to Guatemala City. Despite the initial trauma with my back, it had been such a fantastic time. It was a time of re-connection for both of us and much needed rest and recovery for me.

I had purposely booked my flight back to Guatemala as close as I could to Jane's flight to the U.K. so that I wouldn't be hanging around the airport after she had gone. It's always a difficult time saying goodbyes at airports and as I waved her off I reflected on our precious time together and wondered when I would see her again. Thankfully, I didn't have much time for introspection as my flight was called shortly afterwards and I boarded on time for the short flight back to spend one more night Couch Surfing with Luis.

CHAPTER 31

"Healing Hands and Hope"

We'd arranged for Luis to meet my evening flight, as I didn't want the stress of finding the bona fide taxis at the airport at night. As I came out of the arrivals hall into the warm and humid air of the city, I scanned the throngs of people jostling for places to spot their friends and loved ones. There was no sign of Luis, so I dropped my heavy bag and waited for a while in a place where I hoped he would spot me amidst the busy nightlife of the airport. After ten minutes I decided to walk around to see if I could see him. Maybe he'd forgotten I thought, as another ten minutes passed. I was concerned that it might be the case, and started to plan for such a contingency by asking a uniformed official if there was a local hotel he could recommend. At that moment I saw Luis in the distance waving frantically. It looked like we had got our exits mixed up and he had been waiting somewhere else.

"I'm glad to see you!" I said with a smile as I climbed into the back seat of Luis' car.

Luis had brought his girlfriend and together we spent a pleasant evening back at his favourite bar, although I did begin to feel rather jaded as the night wore on. I was probably feeling the strain of coming back to the reality of my journey after my oasis with Jane, coupled with my back problem and the pressure of trying to converse in my limited Spanish. The following morning Luis dropped me off at the bus station to catch the bus back to Antigua.

I arrived back in Antigua early in the morning after another bone shaking ride in the Chicken Bus. The bus station in Antigua was vibrant, noisy and awash with people going about their daily business. I hurried to get out of the throngs of people, sidestepping the ever present street beggars and made my way to a hotel I had checked out before I left. The previous one I had shared with Mark was basic to say the least and so I had a decided an upgrade was called for. The plan was to book in for a couple of nights until Mark arrived back from his sojourn in the city and we could decide our next move. I checked in and went online to drop Mark an e mail and let him know where I was before heading out for a much needed coffee and time to reflect on what to do next about my back problem.

Before I`d left for the city I`d noticed a painted sign for X rays and ultra sound above a slightly dilapidated building. It seemed so incongruous at the time which made it stand out in my mind, although I never dreamed for a minute that I would have need of it, so after my coffee I made my way down there and enquired as to how I could go about organising a X ray. It did smack of some dodgy back street operation but at least it was a place to start. I was informed that first I would have to see a doctor and then if they agreed it was necessary I could have the X ray. Later that day I returned and proceeded to wait for over two hours, until at last I got to see the doctor, who of course spoke no English.

I managed to explain in Spanish what the problem was and she agreed to sign off the X ray. Forty minutes later I sat in her office as she interpreted what she saw. It didn`t sound good and it certainly didn`t look good. She pointed out that the gap between the first and second vertebrae was very small. If it got smaller due to more impact and punishment on my back it could be very serious. I got the message.

Before sending it back to England for a second (and third) opinion, I`d discovered a physiotherapist in Antigua who came highly recommended, so I took it to Micky Morrison of "Healing Hands" who basically confirmed in English what the doctor had said.

"Can you fix it?" I asked, desperately hoping for a positive answer.

"We need to re-align your pelvis and then work on strengthening your core muscles. Yes, I think we can definitely help."

Those few positive words gave me some hope, and if there is one thing I've learned on this journey, it's that you've got to hang on to hope, when you lose that, you lose everything.

When I decided to call this trip the Journey for Hope, I had no idea how significant it was going to become.

Whether I could rehab to a sufficient level to finish the journey was still an unknown factor. I was hoping a further analysis back in the U.K. would give me a better idea. With that in mind I went straight to the DHL branch in Antigua and sent the X rays back home. The whole process would take three working days and then several more days before I could get the feedback I needed.

Rather than sit around with my thoughts in turmoil and major decisions to be made, I decided the best course of action was to stay in Antigua for a while, besides which, I still hadn't heard anything from Mark and I was getting a little concerned. We both knew how potentially dangerous Guatemala City was and the last I knew that's where he was with his latest girlfriend. I went back to our previous hotel and made enquiries to see if they had seen or heard from him and then checked out the Moto Café,

"No, I haven't seen him since you were both here a couple of weeks ago," Dave said.

I was getting a very strange feeling about the whole situation. Surely he would have replied to my e mail? Well there was nothing I could do but wait to see if he showed up, and I also had the rather pressing issue of my back to sort out. After my initial meeting with Micky, it became clear that I would need at least a couple of weeks to rehab my back and so I looked for a more suitable hotel that had secure parking for my bike and negotiated a better rate for a longer stay. I then embarked upon an intensive rehabilitation programme of physiotherapy and exercise in the mornings, and in the afternoon I signed up for intensive Spanish lessons. I decided I might as well get some benefit from my enforced sojourn.

The news from the U.K. was inconclusive.

"He says you really need an MRI scan because the X ray wasn`t clear enough," Jane told me after having sweet talked her way into seeing Northampton`s best back specialist.

Back at Healing Hands, I asked Micky where I could get an MRI scan done,

"In Guatemala City. Let me call a doctor I know and arrange for an appointment."

And so, the next day I was on my way to the city for a consultation with another back specialist with an MRI scan lined up for an hour later. With my bike secured back at my hotel I had booked a recommended taxi for the journey into the city. The driver spoke good English, which made conversation much easier and I was curious about the political scene and particularly the amount of gun crime and corruption in the city,

"Why don't the police do more about it?" I asked.

"The police are part of the problem," he replied with that all too familiar resignation. As with Mexico, corruption was rife and the police were so poorly paid they tended to attract many people with limited education. We arrived at my destination and I arranged to meet my driver thirty minutes later after my consultation. I was thankful I didn't have to negotiate through the city by bike and now just needed to concentrate on making myself understood. The consulting rooms were thankfully bright and modern, a far cry from the run down place back in Antigua, and after a brief wait I was ushered into the office of Dr. Luis Cruz Sanchez,

“Buenas Dias!” I said shaking his hand.

“Buenas Dias,” he replied, “Hablas Espanol?”

“Si. Un poco,” I said with a smile. I then proceeded to attempt an explanation of the problem in my best Spanish, which seemed to make sense to him as he then decided to dispense with the services of his receptionist who had been drafted in as an informal interpreter. The plan was for me to return the following day with a copy of my MRI scan for him to give me a proper diagnosis, so feeling quite pleased with the way I had managed to communicate, I headed back to meet my driver and make for the MRI department a few minutes drive away. Agreeing another rendezvous and not really knowing how long this procedure might take I pushed through the swinging doors of the hospital and looked for any meaningful signs, hoping that a “MRI scan this way” sign might magically appear. It didn’t, so it was back to my best Spanish,

“Donde esta la resonancia magnetica, por favor?” I enquired at the desk and was pointed in the direction of a corridor where I would practice the same question again, eventually being directed to a seat where I would await my turn. In the midst of all this, I hadn’t given any thought to what having an MRI scan would entail, but as I was directed into the room and was shown the MRI equipment it seemed scarily like loading a human torpedo. It all happened so quickly I had no time to think about what was taking place.

What did the nurse say, forty minutes? Bloody hell! Forty minutes buried alive in this metal coffin. A wave of anxiety suddenly rolled over me. I'm not particularly claustrophobic, but I had to consciously work hard to control my breathing and heart rate, besides which the noise was so loud, if I had panicked and shouted, no one could have heard me. After a couple of minutes with my eyes closed and my breathing under control, I managed to focus my mind and concentrate on more positive thoughts. My strategy seemed to do the trick as the time passed incredibly quickly and I was soon being "unloaded." I was informed the results would be ready the following day and all I needed to do was pay my bill.

The following day I was back in the doctor's office as he explained to me, half in English and half in Spanish, that I had a degenerative disease, which he said, was not uncommon and I should exercise everyday.

"You should continue with your activities, but if the pain gets very high you will have to stop and have surgery"

Continue with your activities......?

This all sounded very positive but I wasn`t sure whether he really understood what my "activities" entailed on this journey. But again, there was a ray of hope that all was not lost.

Maybe I could finish the journey after all?

On the drive back, my mind was racing through all the possible scenarios.

If I continue and risk it, what happens if I have a similar problem in Bolivia or Peru miles from good medical back up?

And will my back take the constant punishment from poor roads even if I exercise every day?

If I have another fall from the bike, how will that affect my already weakened back?

Over the past two weeks I had been on an emotional rollercoaster as I tried to come to terms with my predicament and had prepared myself to accept the possibility that it was all over. Now, maybe it wasn`t?

With so many questions and no concrete answers I posted my scan back to the U.K. for Nick the back specialist to analyse. I decided I would trust his prognosis and follow whatever advice he was going to give. This would give me another week of deep thought and contemplation. My options were clear:

1. I nurse myself and the bike to Panama and fly home
2. I`m given the green light to head for Argentina

In one week I would know.

CHAPTER 32

"It's not over till the fat lady sings!"

During this period I busied myself with my routine of rehab in the morning and Spanish in the afternoon, interspersed with regular visits to my favourite coffee shops where I would sit and watch the daily Antiguan life unfold, all the while mulling over the ramifications of the decisions I would be making in the next week or so.

In the evenings I generally patronised one or two local restaurants where I would often sit in the same place at the bar, order the same drink. Very quickly, the waiters knew my routine and I didn't need to order my beer. It would just magically arrive as I sat down! It's amazing how quickly we can generate routines and I suppose with all the massive uncertainty surrounding the next weeks, the routine gave me some comfort.

One of my favourite bars was Las Palmas, which even had a tiny cinema in a back room. Well, not exactly a cinema, just a small room with a few comfy chairs where you could watch a film chosen from a large selection of DVDs the owner had collected. Every night I would walk in and check out which film was being shown. If no one was in the room (which was often the case) I would ask if I could choose a different film than the one advertised for the evening and so I got to watch one of my favourite films, "The Bucket List" for the third time. As I sat sipping my beer and watching Morgan Freeman and Jack Nicholson compiling their respective Bucket Lists, I reflected once again on the reason I had embarked upon this journey and concluded that whatever the outcome, I was glad I had at least tried. I would hate to reach the end of my life and be left wondering, what if?

The following night, still uncertain as to what was going to be the outcome of my back specialist's advice, I sat at the bar with a beer and my notebook and made two lists. One entitled **Panama** and the other **Argentina**. On each list I recorded my thoughts on how I would feel if I had to cut the trip short and return from Panama against how I would feel if I could continue to Argentina. Whichever way I looked at it, the Argentina list was always much longer, and it was clear that I needed to move. The weeks of introspection were beginning to wear me down,

12.11.10 Diary

"Sitting in the bar of Las Palmas thinking it really is time to move on. Been very tired today. Not sleeping well at all. Too tired to do my rehab exercises tonight. Been in Antigua two weeks now. I need to get back on the bike. I need to move. Waiting for feedback from Nick my back specialist. Going back early wouldn't be a good thing – back to winter – no work/money.... I really need to finish this trip otherwise I'll regret not trying hard enough. I have one shot at this...."

The uncertainty was becoming very draining and beginning to affect my already disturbed sleep patterns. The next day I was having a coffee in the Moto Café talking to Dave about the strange disappearance of my former riding friend Mark, when he said,

"You should contact Lenny. He's riding a Kawasaki 650 and going the same route."

"Lenny who?"

"He's an American rider. He was here a couple of days ago. We sorted a problem for him."

"O.K. that would be great. Have you got his e mail address?"

That night I e mailed Lenny and suggested it might be worthwhile riding together for a while especially on the crossing into

Honduras which could be notoriously difficult. Two pairs of eyes keeping a check on the bikes would benefit the both of us. We agreed to meet up in the little town of Flores in a few days time, because regardless of the outcome of the MRI assessment, I still had to ride my bike at least as far as Panama City.

After a long week's wait I finally got the feedback from the U.K.

"The possible risks of continuing your journey are, recurrence of pain, and needing more treatment in countries where that might be difficult to access. The worst case is that the problem, i.e. your pain, doesn't settle and that the trip is then effectively over. I would suggest that to begin with, you ride less hours a day and take regular breaks to stretch your back.

. ... you won't cause any further actual damage to your spine by continuing to ride, although you might get a recurrence of symptoms because of the ordinary wear and tear changes in your back being irritated by bouncing along rutted roads. "

So that was it. "The Journey for Hope" was back on the road! With a commitment to exercise religiously every day, I decided I would just keep going and see how far I could go. Anything after Panama was going to be a bonus.

Getting back on the bike after a break of nearly five weeks was a strange experience. As desperate as I was to get back in the saddle, I'd grown quite fond of Antigua. It had provided a safe haven for me and so it was with a combination of considerable trepidation and nervous excitement that I loaded the bike and said my goodbyes to the hotel staff before heading out of town towards Guatemala City.

I had planned to ride north from Antigua and head for the small island town of Flores. From there I could take the short trip to Tikal, the site of the biggest Mayan ruins in Central America. I decided to break the journey in the small town of Rio Dulce which was still a longer ride than I would have liked and by the time I arrived there I was tired and my back was aching. Rio Dulce was a favourite stopover for the affluent, yachting set, so obviously I fitted in perfectly.

I was up early the following day for the relatively short three hour ride to Flores, there I was due to meet up with Lenny who was riding his Kawasaki 650 all the way to Tierra Del Fuego. Flores was a beautiful island town reached along a narrow causeway and a delightful place to spend a couple of days. Whilst out exploring on the second day I was apprehended by a Guatemalan TV crew who wanted to interview me (there was obviously no one else around!) about my views on Flores. The interview was brief. I think "Muy bonita" (very pretty) figured heavily, nevertheless, the interviewer seemed happy. The next day I'd arranged to get a bus to Tikal and check out the famous Mayan ruins, as I didn't want to spend a day walking around in my cumbersome riding gear. The driver doubled as a guide and we spent a fascinating few hours exploring the site. The ruins had become completely overgrown over time and the jungle now dominated them, with only a few of the highest pyramids breaking the canopy covering. I climbed the tallest one to get a better perspective of the scale of the site and by the time I reached the top I was noticeably and uncomfortably out of breath. The months of riding and lack of exercise had definitely taken its toll. I felt completely out of condition and silently vowed to make it a priority to get back into shape on my return. On the way down from the pyramid the air was torn with a horrendous growl which resonated throughout the jungle and seemed to bounce of the trees,

"What was that?" I exclaimed to our guide.

"Howler monkey," he replied, showing no concern.

"A monkey?" I said incredulously, "it sounds like something from Jurassic park!"

Once again the canopy reverberated with this awful sound,

"I'd hate to be stuck here at night," I said to no one in particular, still not believing such a blood curdling howl could be made by a monkey. Just then the heavens opened and the ominously grey clouds unleashed their daily deluge. Time to head back and rendezvous with Lenny I thought.

Shortly after my return, Lenny arrived. A totally different character to Mark, he was an IT specialist who had given up his job, sold everything he possessed and took off on this trip of a lifetime. He was also au fait with all things technical, including fixing mechanical problems, which would briefly alleviate my ever present anxieties about my lack of expertise in that area. That night as we discussed our past experiences and future plans over a beer or two it was clear that Belize was in Lenny`s plans.

Belize wasn`t even on my original route, but when he said he was going there, I thought, why not, a short hop across the border and another border crossing would be good practice.

Belize is a strange country. The only Central American country where everything is written in English and everyone speaks English, they even have the Queen on all their bank notes. The border crossing was easy and marred only by Christmas songs blasting out of the two little speakers on the customs desk. It seemed rather incongruous until I realised that we were well into November, and back in the U.K. this would have been happening in every store throughout the country for weeks.

Twenty minutes from the border we arrived in the town of San Ignacio. Within minutes someone approached us and guided us to "Nefry`s Retreat" which turned out to be a cheap and clean (well, only one dead cockroach under my bed) hotel.

The following day Lenny took off to the islands and I decided to spend a couple of days resting, exercising and attempting to fix an electrical problem. The recurring issue with the horn not working had returned and was further compounded by the headlight not working. Both of which were pretty critical to safe riding. They had to be fixed. I stripped off the panels and did what I always did in these situations, poked around a little and scratched my head a lot. It`s never really been the best strategy and this time proved equally fruitless. I was still debating what to do as I sipped on my beer in a local bar. A lively group of people beckoned me to join them. The rest of the night was spent in the company of Phil and Maria.

Phil was from the U.S. and was involved in real estate, spending his time developing land in Belize and commuting back to the U.S. Maria, was a Russian accountant who now lived in New York and had travelled extensively. Both had fascinating stories to tell. When I explained what I was doing there and my electrical problem, Phil said,

"You should try Mad Dog."

"Mad Dog?"

"Yea, he`s the best mechanic in town. Everyone calls him Mad Dog."

The Mad Dog and the Englishman

And so the next day, in the mid day sun, the Englishman went to find Mad Dog.

"Hi, I`m looking for Mad Dog," I said to the man under the bonnet of a car.

"You`ve found him."

It turned out that Nat (aka Mad Dog) had ridden from Alaska with his son two years before, but ran out of money in Guyana where his bike still remains. I explained my situation to him.

"Yea, that'll be no problem. Bring it by this afternoon and I'll take a look."

I rode the bike up that afternoon and left feeling confident that it would be fixed by the next day. In the evening I headed back to my favourite bar to meet up with my new friends Maria and Phil for a farewell drink (to be honest, several farewell drinks). The following day Phil was off back to the States for Thanksgiving and Maria was going to the islands.

"Mad Dog!"

True to his word, the following day, my bike was ready and waiting. Mad Dog had worked his magic and found the faulty relay. His wife Debbie gave me a card with contact details saying,

"If you get into trouble anywhere just call us or e mail and I'm sure he can help you."

I rode off reflecting on how comforting it must be for someone like Nat to know that whatever goes wrong with the bike he could fix it or at least confidently diagnose the problem. Not for the first time I wished I had more technical competence instead of relying on others to help me out.

But, *"it is what it is,"* I reminded myself as I headed for more help with my other priority – my body.

Shortly after arriving in San Ignacio I came across a sign for a massage therapist and decided my back could do with some attention. Gretel turned out to be an excellent masseuse who gave my back a thorough deep tissue (and painful) going over.

"What are you doing in Belize?" she enquired.

I explained about the Journey for Hope and my recent problems.

"When are you leaving?"

"In a day or two."

"Come and see me before you go and I'll give you a complimentary back massage."

So now my bike was fixed, I made my way to see Gretel and get my body fixed.

CHAPTER 33

"Even if it is only $10, I still expect a toilet seat!"

We left Belize the following morning and headed back to Flores. The idea was to retrace our steps from Flores to Rio Dulce, stay there one night and then make the run to the El Salvador border the next day which would hopefully give us enough time to put a good two hours ride down through El Salvador to the coast and the little town of Acajutla.

The border crossing was very quiet and uneventful. In fact there was only Lenny, two nuns and myself, but it still took one and a half hours.

We`d looked on the map and found this little town right on the coast and thought a little sojourn by the sea would be pleasant. When we arrived in Acajutla it was disappointingly drab and run down, but nevertheless there were several "hotels" right on the beach. The first one we looked at wanted $15 which seemed a little on the high side so I suggested we check out another one.

"Tiene una habitacion por una noche?"

"Si"

Cuanta questa por favor?"

"Diez"

$10? That sounded much better, so I asked to see the room. I followed as we ducked under three washing lines full of clothes drying in the evening sun,

"Aqui!" He said, pointing towards a room. Call me old fashioned, but even for $10 I still expect a toilet seat. The bedding looked like it had never seen the inside of a washing machine. It was the kind of room that makes your skin crawl, so it was back to the first one again. We rode back to the first place, went into the courtyard and asked to see the room. The good news was at least it had a toilet seat, the bad news was the whole room stank like a toilet. There was more sand and dirt in the bedroom than on the beach and again the bedding looked disgusting. With the light beginning to fade we had to make a decision quickly. We`d passed a couple of places on the way in, one was a "Love Hotel." These places were incredibly popular in the Americas. They are very secure, private and clean (apparently) but tend to be booked by the hour and not by the night! However, Lenny had spotted what looked like a truckers' hotel, which had a restaurant so we opted for that. A ridiculously expensive $26 bought us basic rooms but at least we could get some food. El Salvador was proving much more expensive than either of us thought.

Still not giving up on the idea of a beachside stay, we set off the next morning for the town of La Libertad, around which were supposed to be lots of surfer type accommodation. We rode around for a while trying to find suitable accommodation and it became clear that we both had different ideas of what suitable meant, so we decided to go our separate ways for the evening and source our own accommodation. Travelling with virtual strangers can sometimes be like that. It wasn't a big deal; we just needed to do our own thing. We agreed to meet up the next morning for the biggest challenge of Honduras.

The next day was going to be interesting. This was the day we would cross into Honduras. Of all the Central American countries, Honduras is the one with the reputation of being the most corrupt, bureaucratic and time consuming crossing. We`d both read many internet postings so we were as prepared as we could be for what was likely to come. Our strategy was to be as patient as possible and not be hurried or hassled by the gang of "helpers" we would encounter at the border. Nor would we hire any of the aforementioned helpers to navigate our way through the mound of complex paperwork. If we were patient and methodical, we believed we could do it alone.

Dante`s Inferno aka The Honduras Border crossing....

About a mile or so from the border itself we had to slow down as several men rushed onto the road waving us down and offering their help. This was an obvious precursor to what was about to come. As soon as we had pulled up at the El Salvador side to process the paperwork to exit the country, we were inundated by a crowd of people offering their services,

"Hey amigo, I can help you. I speak good English."

"No thanks, we`re O.K."

"I`m his brother. We will help you with the paperwork."

"No thanks, we don`t need any help."

And so it went on. Like piranhas sensing blood.

Lenny just pointed at each one of them and said calmly,

"No, no, no, no, no!"

The one with good English said, "If you need anyone I can help you."

"Thanks. If we need anyone we`ll let you know."

And this was just to get out of El Salvador! Before we crossed to the Honduran side, we had to get photocopies of our exit papers. Lenny watched the bikes while I was directed to a small office to get the copies.

"Dos copias por favor," I said to the woman behind the desk. With a look of total disdain she dragged herself from behind the desk, copied the paperwork and said,

"Vente cinco."

I wasn`t sure I heard her right, so I asked again,

"Vente cinco," she repeated.

"$25 dollars! Are you kidding? For two photocopies?" I exclaimed in English. My Spanish wasn`t good enough to formulate, "you`re taking the piss."

She just shrugged her shoulders and repeated the amount, but I could tell from her body language that this was just another scam, so I just shook my head and started to walk away, refusing to give her anything at all.

The crossing into Honduras was certainly living up (or down) to its reputation.

Once again we were hassled by “helpers” who insisted on trying to guide us through the totally ridiculous process, which is basically a simple 3 step, process.

Step 1 Migracion - Get your passport stamped and officially enter the country

Step 2 Aduana – Import your bike on a temporary import permit

Step 3 Fumigacion – Pay for someone to spray your bike (for no apparent reason)

That 3 step process took between two to three hours. We were sent to various offices were we had to provide our passports, vehicle documentation, drivers licence and exit paperwork from the previous country. At each stage we had to get multiple photocopies of each document at a different building. All down the line, the unhired “helpers” were insistent we gave them all our paperwork and they would expedite the whole thing much quicker (for a fee of course). Having been scammed for a fictitious $35 “road tax” early on in the process, I then had to go to the bank and pay 700 Lempiras (about thirty seven dollars) for the official paperwork, but it was closed.

“It`s closed for lunch and won`t be open for one and half hours,” my helper said, “but I can help if you give me the money and paperwork I can go to another window and get it done sooner for you.”

“Great. Let`s go to the other window.”

On the way there he insisted I give him my paperwork.

“No. I`ll come with you,” I replied. At which he thrust my

paperwork back in my hand and stormed off! Not surprisingly, the bank was now open and I processed the whole thing by myself and it cost 636 Lempiras! And so the whole fiasco went on and on as the temperature pushed into the high 90s.

Rarely have I witnessed such a blatant process designed specifically to relieve the Gringo from his money and create mounds of pointless paperwork and meaningless bureaucracy. The Honduras border crossing must contribute massively to Rank Xerox and Canon`s bottom line.

We eventually did give our "helper`s" two dollars because at least they steered us in the right direction, but we managed to limit the damage by doing most of the leg work ourselves. It`s a shame because that experience leaves a distinctly unfavourable impression of the country before you even cross the border. Having had our paperwork checked several times by officials in the first few miles we were also stopped at a police check point within the first ten minutes. The officer attempted to give us a ticket because we hadn`t got reflective stickers!

"Yo tengo dos!" I said, as I climbed off the bike and pointed to the two yellow, smiley faces I had stuck on my panniers. Lenny did likewise and the policeman just shrugged and waved us on. It was yet another blatant attempt to extract more money.

We rode quickly across country and headed for the town of Choloteca, which was about halfway across Honduras. Our plan was to spend one night there and exit the country as fast as possible and cross into Nicaragua the next day.

Less than an hour`s run the next morning brought us to the border of Nicaragua, which would be our sixth border crossing, so by now we were getting the hang of it.

"This time, we`re not paying that road tax," said Lenny, still mightily pissed off for being stung in Honduras. Lenny was a real man of principle. He would rather camp out at the border and refuse to pay than line the pockets of the corrupt officials.

The Nicaraguan crossing was much easier and less bureaucratic, although the Honduran “helpers” offering their services still repeated,

“You`ll need $35 for the road tax!” But we just rode passed waving them away.

“No we don`t pay road tax!” Lenny shouted.

Strangely enough, because we didn`t need the helpers this time, we didn`t get asked for the “road tax”. You live and learn.

CHAPTER 34

"Lazy Bones and Bearded Monkeys"

As we rode into Nicaragua, I was surprised by the quality of the roads. I had heard that this was the poorest of all the Central American countries and yet the roads seemed as good as anywhere else and maybe even better. Apart from the random potholes that appeared occasionally for brief stretches. Dave, a Canadian rider we`d met on the road described some of them as "coffin sized!" A salutary thought.

Lenny

The first stop in Nicaragua was the small colonial town of Leon where we stayed for a couple of nights in the "Lazybones" hostel. A single room, shared bathroom and no hot water for $16. I decided that having spent so much money on physiotherapy,

I had to be careful with the budget otherwise I would run out of money before I reached Argentina.

Our next stop was Granada, where we`d had a recommendation of a good hostel and thought it wouldn`t be too hard to find. If in doubt, just stop and ask. We stopped, we asked and still couldn`t find it, which was a pity as it turned out to be infinitely nicer than "The Bearded Monkey" hostel we eventually ended up in. For three nights I felt like Papillon in my dark cell and had to pay $12 for the privilege.

Granada was another example of old, colonial splendour, sitting on the shores of Lake Nicaragua. Very much like a bigger version of Antigua, it had plenty to offer in the way of great cafes and restaurants at affordable prices. It`s interesting how travelling in this part of the world makes you re evaluate the cost of things. One of the things I learned is that the U.K. is ridiculously expensive. Of course everyone living at home is aware of the fact but being here brought it into stark contrast.

After a couple of days savouring Granada`s colonial style I decided it was time to head further south. Lenny was planning on signing up for another week`s Spanish school, so I wished him all the best and set off for the beach resort of San Juan Del Sur about an hour`s ride south. Lenny had heard good reports about the place and it wasn`t far from the next border crossing. I thought a couple of days by the beach relaxing and reading would be a good way to prepare for the solo crossing into Costa Rica.

San Juan Del Sur

As soon as I rode into town I got a good feeling. It just felt right. Finding the right accommodation however wasn`t so easy. The prices were higher (as you`d expect by the beach) but there was a distinct lack of places with secure parking. After about my third lap around the town someone stopped me,

"Are you looking for a place to stay?" he enquired in perfect English.

"Yes, but I need secure parking for my bike."

"No problem. I have a friend who has a good hotel up there on the hill. Very clean rooms, cheap and your bike will be safe."

"How much?" was the obvious next question.

"$10 a night"

That`ll do nicely I thought. Two minutes later his friend rolled up in a 4x4 and escorted me up a steep hill to a little hotel/ hostel. He was right. $10 for a nice, clean room and it even had a kitchen! Perfect.

The town was a hangout for backpackers and the bleached, tanned surfing community. It had plenty of wifi spots and a very funky café/book shop called *El Gato Negro* which rapidly became my favourite place to relax, read and check e mails. This place was as trendy as anything you`d find in Crouch End, Hampstead or Notting Hill (except half the price). They ground their own organic coffee and baked some of the best chocolate muffins I`ve ever tasted. I could easily have spent a few days in San Juan, but I was eager to push on to Panama City and organise my bike`s transport across the Darien Gap to Colombia before Christmas. So that meant the small matter of crossing Costa Rica.

"It`s like Déjà vu all over again" – Yogi Berra

I was up early on the day of the border crossing because you just never know how long these things will take. I didn`t expect it to be as bad as Honduras but I didn`t want to be complacent.

This would be my first solo crossing since Mexico (it seemed a long time ago now), but with the experience of Guatemala, Belize, El Salvador, Honduras and Nicaragua behind me I felt confident in the process. Apart from the ability to speak even a little Spanish, the key to border crossings is huge amounts of patience. With enough time, you can figure out most things. Never attempt to cross a border if you are pushed for time. The Piranhas (aka helpers) will sense that, and basically you'll get screwed.

As I approached the border I passed what seemed like several miles of queuing, stationary trucks. There must have been hundreds of them and by the look the hammocks slung between the wheels they had obviously been there for a while. This could be a busier crossing than I thought, I mused as I weaved past them to the front. There was certainly less pressure than Honduras but the whole process still took over two hours of being shunted from building to building getting the mandatory photocopies and stamped paperwork. Considering my previous struggle with anything involving queuing, this process would have driven me crazy, but now I just took it in my stride. What a transformation! I wondered if it would last?

With all the paperwork complete and sweat pouring from me, I fired up the engine and crossed into Costa Rica for the second time. It seemed very strange to be riding the same roads Jane and I had driven down only six weeks previously, and at the same time it was reassuring. It felt familiar and comfortable. The key difference this time would be I would be roughing it instead of enjoying the good life!

I made for the coastal town of Jaco which I'd noticed six weeks earlier. It was another surfer type town with Costa Rican type prices. Nicaraguan value for money seemed like another world. Costa Rica is well known for being the most developed and expensive of all the Central American countries. I wouldn't be spending too much time here although I really like the place. The people are nice, language isn't a problem, they are very geared up for tourism and they have great coffee.

I spent a couple of nights in Jaco mainly to recover from the ride. My back was feeling the strain so I thought it best to give it an extra night and try to book a massage to speed up the recovery time.

From Jaco I followed the coast road and was trying to get as near the border as I could to make it a quicker crossing the following day, but every likely town I came across looked depressingly run down so I just kept on riding. I noticed a large town on the map and decided that Ciudad Neilly would definitely be my stopover point as it was only twenty minutes from the border and I was bound to find somewhere decent to stay.

The town was much smaller than it appeared on the map and after riding around for a while I was drawing a blank. As I pulled over to ask for help, a man on a little 125 cc motorcycle rode up to me and asked if I was looking for a hotel.

"Follow me. I'll show you," he said, and so a few minutes and couple of dirt tracks later we pulled up in front of what appeared to be a decent place, with air conditioning and internet. Perfect! The only drawback being they were full.

"Can you recommend anywhere else?" I asked hopefully.

"Everywhere is full," was the reply.

"Everywhere? But there must be a room somewhere?" I added, trying to mask the mounting frustration. After a long ride, with sweat pouring off you and rain now looking imminent, this was not the situation I wanted.

"Everywhere is full because of the festival."

"Festival?"

"Si, Festival de La Luces."

Apparently I`d arrived at a bad time. "The Festival of the Lights" was a huge celebration in parts of Costa Rica and people from miles around had descended on this little town to celebrate it.

I sat in a local restaurant, ordered some food and thought through my options. I could wait for a couple of hours to see if they had any cancellations or push on further. As I drank my coffee, the threatened rain appeared. That was it. I wasn't riding anywhere today. There must be a room somewhere. As I drained the coffee and finished my chicken sandwich the man on the 125 appeared again,

"I have found a place with one room left. It`s very nice and just around the corner, but they want $50 for the night."

"$50!" I exclaimed, "That`s crazy!"

He shrugged his shoulders in agreement. They were obviously cashing in on the situation. With no other options available and with heavy rain falling I found the hospedaje (guest house) and was determined not to pay their asking price,

"Estoy recaudar fondos para la gente sin hogares y no tengo mucho dinero. Si es posible lo hacer mas barato por favor?"

I told them I was fundraising for homeless people and didn't have much money, but I could offer $30 (which was still over the odds) and we had an agreement.

That night I went to a bar and watched the huge celebrations on TV from the capital, San Jose before heading out into the streets for what was the longest parade I`d seen in years. Very colourful and very loud, but after one and a half hours I was beginning to tire somewhat. Still, now I knew what “La Festival de la Luces” was all about.

The next day I was up early for another border crossing into Panama. Surely this would be a simple affair compared to the others. Either way, armed with my new “laid back” philosophy, I was optimistic and confident.

Exiting Costa Rica was fairly straightforward and so when I arrived at migracion to get my passport stamped into Panama I expected it to be equally simple. Even the long queue didn`t phase me (initially). I waited in line for well over an hour, pouring with sweat, and the queue didn`t move an inch. NOT AN INCH!! And nobody bothered! I`ve come to the conclusion that Central Americans are either born with an exceptional “laid back gene” or they`re just resigned to the bumbling incompetence and pointless red tape that their countries’ thrive on. One thing`s for sure, no border official will EVER die of stress related illness.

Whilst watching this fiasco of ineptitude unfold, I noticed another bike pull up behind me. It had U.S. plates so I naturally assumed Andy was American. He was in fact from Grimsby (!) but now lived and worked in New York. He too was heading south. I was on my way to stay with an ex pat from England in a town not far away, so I suggested he join me and maybe we could both stay with Norman.

CHAPTER 35

"Stormin' Norman and the Crazy Monkey"

Norman had responded to a post I'd put on the net offering me a place to stay for the night, and since I never refuse offers of help I readily accepted. When we eventually found his place in the country it certainly wasn't what I was expecting. *Villa Paula* was a huge sprawling place. We rode in and pulled up in front of several bikes with a party seemingly in full swing. A tall bearded man in combat trousers greeted us with,

"You must be Brian, help yourself to a beer!"

"You must be Norman, thanks I will!"

"This is Andy. We met at the border. I hope you don't mind both of us staying?"

"No problem. We have plenty of room."

There must have been nearly twenty people, Brits, Americans and Panamanians having a BBQ and drinking beer. Norman introduced us to everyone and as we relaxed and chatted over several beers it transpired that all of the Brits and Americans had moved to Panama after years of disillusionment with their respective countries. A theme I had heard many times during my journey. I asked Billy from the U.S.,

"Yes, but what do you do all day?"

"Drink beer and fuck women," he replied.

"Yes, but are you happy?"

He didn't answer, just gave me one of those looks. And with that $1,000,000 question left hanging in the air I went to talk to

Norman. On the way I was accosted by a monkey. One of six that seemed to live with Norman, only this one was a relative baby and was free to roam and terrorise. He had clearly taken a liking to me.

"The Crazy Monkey!"

"It`s the colour of your hair. He`s attracted to fair haired people. I think it reminds him of his mother!"

"Thanks Norman. None taken!"

From that moment on, the bloody monkey wouldn`t leave me alone. I had my very own simian stalker.

Later in the afternoon, most of the bikers headed off and things quietened down (apart from the monkey).

"Is it like this every Sunday?"

"More or less" Norman replied.

Not surprising then that many bikers on their way south call in and sample Norman`s legendary hospitality.

"This reminds me of Apocalypse Now," I said, "You`re Marlon Brando. You`ve gone native and set up a biker commune."

He threw his head back and roared with laughter at the image.

That night we went to the nearest village for a beer and something to eat. It literally was a one saloon town and over a couple of beers I chatted to one of Norman's friends who was out visiting from the U.K.

"So what do you do back in England?"

"I'm a freelance television producer for Channel 4."

"How's it going?"

"It's O.K. but what I really want to do is move out here as soon as I can."

"Really? Won't it be a bit too quiet for you?" He was only in his early 20s and I felt sure it would drive him crazy after a few months.

"No, it'll be great! Just drinking beer and chilling!" He said with real enthusiasm.

I continued to sip my beer, reflecting on his comments as I gazed around the tiny bar and imagined what it would be like to live here permanently. I quickly concluded that it was great for a short break, but there was only so much chilling I could stand.

The next morning we set off early (though not early enough to avoid the monkey) to get as close to Panama City as possible. As the sky turned dark and began to rain I was leading the way along a dual carriageway when up ahead I spotted a policeman by the roadside waving me down. Not another check, I thought as I switched off my engine,

“Como esta?” He enquired (very politely I thought)

“Muy bien, gracias.”

It was then I saw the speed gun in his hand and with a smile he mentioned several numbers in Spanish and then pointed to the readout on the radar gun,

“96 kph,” he said.

Apparently the speed limit was 50 kph. Which is crazy. That`s just 25mph. On a dual carriageway?

Bugger, for the first time on the whole trip I’d been caught speeding. It was almost funny. Me, speeding? On my bike?

Nevertheless, I was guilty as charged. I pointed out the Journey for Hope sticker on my windshield and what I was doing it for, hoping it would make a difference. He said something I didn`t understand and then mentioned “bolleto” and in English “ticket” which I did understand, followed by “*pero*”……

In essence, he said he should give me a ticket *but* this time he won`t. With profuse apologies, thanks and not a little relief, we waved an adios and rode off sticking to the ridiculous speed limits from then on.

By midday I had ridden enough and decided I would find a hotel while Andy decided to push on and find somewhere by a beach.

"Ride safe. Maybe we'll catch up somewhere in Panama City?" I said.

"Yea, we'll stay in touch by e mail." Andy replied, and waving a goodbye, headed off to check out the coast road. The benefit of solo riding is the ability to be able to do your own thing without worrying whether the other person is in agreement. I liked Andy but it was also refreshing to be on my own again. So firing up the engine again, I clicked it into gear, turned the bike around back down the road we had just ridden along. I'd noticed a decent looking hotel in the town of Penonome and checked in just as the rain began to fall again. The room was clean and had a/c and when I enquired about the bike's safety,

"Tiene estaciamento segurro para mi moto por favor?"

"Si, aqui!" she said, pointing to the lobby.

That's great I thought, now I have to just negotiate the slight incline and narrow doorway and position the bike as close as possible to the wall without dropping it in front of the staff and guests. After removing the panniers and the rest of my luggage, I managed to manhandle it into the beautifully marbled lobby and just prayed I wouldn't have a re-occurrence of my oil leak on their lovely polished floor.

The bike was now sorted, but sadly the promised wifi didn't work, and after a tiring and fruitless search through the town I called it a day and had an early night.

Another early start saw me on the road to Panama City. I wanted to get there with plenty of time to find The Mamallena Hostel which had been recommended to me. I'd managed to locate it on my GPS which although not very detailed, was proving useful enough to navigate around and through cities and towns.

Panama City I had been told, looked remarkably like Miami and as I approached, I noticed the skyline from a distance full of high rise buildings and sky scrapers. After negotiating heavy traffic I knew I was very close to the hostel but unfortunately, the GPS didn't seem to recognise the city`s one way system and so there followed a very frustrating forty five minutes riding in circles trying to get into the road I needed. After asking a couple of locals I eventually managed to find the right road. The hostel was obviously the main backpacker`s destination in the city. It was almost full with the only bed available in a dorm with seven other people. Still, any port in a storm, and it was only $12. As I checked in I was told,

"Unfortunately, we don`t have any water. The water`s been off since yesterday. Panama has had too much rain."

"No water! No shower and no toilet?"

She just shrugged and said, "Hopefully it will be back on tonight."

The sweat was pouring off me and my clothes were probably capable of standing up by themselves. But judging by the squalor in my dorm, everyone else stank just as much as me. And as the saying goes, "Pigs don`t know that pigs stink".

For the next few hours I sat around in my sweaty clothes and caught up with my e mails. I heard a whisper around the hostel that the water was back on, so I rushed (in a very dignified way of course) for my towel and found the showers. There was indeed water, but just a trickle of cold water. Nevertheless it was water and I did my best to shower as the trickle downgraded itself to a few drips. Feeling strangely refreshed from the shower, I reflected on how the very basic things in life can raise your spirits.

The next morning I had planned to ride to the cargo terminal of the airport where I had to find Girag, the shipping company. The only way to get to Colombia from Panama was to go by sea or air, because the two countries are separated by a one hundred and twenty mile stretch of virtually impassable jungle populated only by bandits and drug gangs. This area of jungle is known as The Darien Gap and is the only break in the Pan American highway. I had corresponded with the shipping company by e mail and according to my contact there, all I had to do was take my bike in the day before I wanted it shipped and it would all be very straightforward. Feeling skeptical about anything being straightforward in Central America I set off early and arrived just after 9.00 am I had been in touch with Andy to see when he was planning to ship his bike, and since our itineraries' matched up, we agreed to meet up at the cargo terminal and try and get it done together, on the basis that it would be more difficult for them to lose two bikes than one! As I pulled into the cargo area of the airport, I noticed Andy's bike.

"How`s it going?" I asked.

"No problem. They just inspected the bike and didn`t even ask about the petrol."

When shipping a bike, most companies insist on the tank being virtually empty and often you also need to disconnect the battery. My bike was processed in the same way. Nobody mentioned fuel, battery or anything for that matter. A couple of hours later, and having both been relieved of $901 cash, we were sitting in a taxi on our way back to the city. Andy would be flying out in a couple of days to meet up with his American girlfriend for a romantic week in Bogota, while I had to wait for another four days. We both agreed that there was nothing in Panama City to tempt us to stay a day longer than necessary.

When I arrived back at the hostel I enquired as to the possibility of upgrading to a private room,

"Don't like the dorm life?" the manager asked with a wry smile.

“I just can`t get any sleep,” I replied.

The previous night just reinforced the fact that I`m not cut out for the backpacker`s life. Every few minutes someone would be getting up, going to the toilet, opening doors, closing doors, tossing and turning, snoring. How the hell can people sleep through that stuff? I knew I`d been spoilt in Cost Rica with Jane but this was the sublime to the ridiculous.

“Well there are a couple of hotels around the corner for about $25-30.”

“Thanks. I`ll check out in an hour.”

I found a reasonable hotel a couple of blocks away and now with no bike to worry about I didn’t have to specify secure parking which was fortunate as most of the city hotels didn’t have any. The next few days were spent in the relative luxury of a single room, comfortable bed and a noisy generator outside my window. Still, at least it didn`t make snoring noises. On my second night, I was having a quiet beer at the bar, immersed in my own thoughts when a man who was clearly another resident, sat on the barstool next to me and ordered a whisky,

“Hi, d’ya mind if I join you?” he asked.

“Not at all” I lied, slightly disappointed that my peace had been disturbed.

“I’m Sandy,” he said as we shook hands,

“Brian,” I responded.

“What are you doing here?” he asked, clearly wanting to engage in a conversation.

As I explained my situation, I became fascinated by Sandy’s

uncanny resemblance to Phil Silvers in Sgt. Bilko (an old American sitcom of the 60s). It was an image I couldn't shake off from then onwards. It transpired that Sandy was a sixty two year old retired business man who was staying in Panama City for a few weeks while his accountant organised his investments. He'd been advised to move his money into Panama for tax reasons. I suppose when you have a spare $2 million, it did make sense to look after it.

"God I can't stand this place," he volunteered, after taking a long swig of his drink.

"So why are you still here?" I asked. Thinking I might aswell engage in the conversation since I had nothing better to do that evening.

"My accountant says I need to spend a certain amount of time here each year to qualify for the tax breaks."

"How long?" I enquired.

"Six weeks a year," he replied somewhat dolefully, "I've got two weeks left."

"I can understand. I don't think I'd want to spend six weeks here either."

"You'd better believe it," he said draining his beer, "Want another one?" he asked, pointing at my by now empty glass.

"Sure, why not. Thanks!"

We chatted for a while and in the course of our conversation I mentioned my back problem,

"I could really do with a massage," I said.

"There's a place a couple of blocks away that does massage."

"Really?"

"Yea, why don't we go tomorrow? I think I might book one myself."

"Sounds like a plan," I said. We arranged a time to meet up the next day and I retired to my bed.

The following day I spent the morning wandering around the local area but there was little of interest within walking distance so I came back to the hotel for my meeting with Sandy. I was really looking forward to getting a decent massage as my back was still in need of attention. In my short walk I hadn't seen any sign of the place Sandy was talking about. Maybe he'd made a mistake.

"Are you sure you saw a sign?" I asked him as we made our way through the busy streets.

"Absolutely! It's just down here," he said, pointing down the next turning. As we got closer, there was indeed a small sign, which I would never have found. As we arrived at the door I had the distinct feeling that this was not exactly the kind of massage I had in mind. The glass window was blacked out and as I tried the door it was locked.

"Oh well, maybe another time," I said to Sandy as I turned away. Just then we heard bolts being pulled back and the door opened. I looked at Sandy,

"Maybe it is open after all," I said, as I pushed the door further open and went in. The room was dark, which was strange considering it was the middle of the day, and as the door closed behind us and my eyes became accustomed to the half -light, I glanced around the room. To the left of the doorway was a small glass kiosk in which stood a man looking like someone you need to buy a ticket from. Sat around the room were a bevy of young women in various states of undress, all of them staring at the two of us. Feeling slightly awkward, I did the only thing I could think of,

"Quanto cuesta para un masage, por favor?" I enquired of the little man in the dimly lit kiosk,

"$65 para todo," he replied. $65 for fully inclusive?

"Muchas gracias!" I said, and with a final glance around the room, we both turned and left, shielding our eyes in the bright Panamanian sunlight.

"Fuck! Did you see that!" Sandy exclaimed, hardly containing his excitement, "I'm going back there later when I get some money. Did you see the girl in the corner? What a fuckin' beauty!"

With Sandy's walking pace noticeably increasing, we seemed to get back to the hotel in double quick time. On the way we discussed the Sandy's forthcoming assignation,

"Listen," he said, "I'm sixty two, and I've got more money than I can spend. Where would I ever get the chance with a beautiful young girl like that?"

"I can't argue with that," I replied, not that I would ever argue. It was his money and his life.

"I bet you're glad I suggested checking out this massage place?"

"You bet! He said, his face beaming, "We're gonna have a good night!"

I left Sandy to his daydream and asked the hotel receptionist to organise me a taxi to the Miraflores locks of the Panama

Canal, the country's most famous landmark. It proved to be a fascinating place, especially the politics surrounding it`s transference from U.S. rule to Panama in 1999. It was easy to understand the U.S.'s reluctance to part with this stretch of water when you consider the cost of passing through it could run to hundreds of thousands of dollars, it was almost a licence to print money. I stayed to watch a couple of huge container ships passing through and then headed by taxi back to the hotel and a quiet evening to myself. On the ride back I asked the taxi driver how the people had benefitted when Panama reclaimed the canal for itself.

"We don't see any money," he said with disgust, "it's in the pockets of corrupt officials."

No change there then I thought, and yet Panama was the most thriving of all Central American countries. Clearly, the poor people in the street would remain poor while the few at the top became progressively richer.

That evening as I caught up with my blog and e mails, I reflected upon Sandy's anticipation and wondered what his night would bring. Mine was more predictable, catching up with my blog and looking forward to my flight to Bogota and the prospect of setting foot on South American soil, for the third and final leg of my Journey for Hope. I met up with Sandy for a drink on my last night and I must admit to being eager to hear all about his nocturnal adventures!

"Man, she was amazing!" he told me later over a beer. "I've never met anyone like her. It's like she really understands me!" he continued to gush.

"That's great. I'm glad you both had a good time," I responded, thinking I bet she *really understands him*. I pushed aside my cynicism and was genuinely pleased for him. He seemed much more cheerful than he had done when I first met him. Mind you, he would be wouldn't he?

"I'm taking her shopping tomorrow," he added, snapping me out of my cynical thoughts.

"Shopping?" I said, with just a hint of incredulity.

"Yea, I asked her what she enjoyed doing, and she said shopping."

"Of course," I responded, obviously neglecting to hide my cynical intonation.

"No, I know what you're thinking," he replied, "listen," he added, leaning forward and putting his beer down, "I'm not stupid. I know the score. I'm sixty two she's twenty five. I know what she wants, and as long as I get what I want, it's O.K."

"Just as long as you're O.K. with it, good luck" I said as we clinked glasses.

"I want to take her back to Montana with me."

I said nothing, but I suppose my raised eyebrows spoke volumes. I knew he had a huge ranch there sitting empty, maybe it was time to enjoy it?

"Well, I just figured why not enjoy myself while I can. If she's going to use me to get a better life, why not give it to her? I'm going to enjoy it for as long as it lasts."

I didn't respond. I didn't need to. We just raised our glasses in unison and drained them. I put my empty glass on the bar and easing myself off the bar stool I said,

"It's been great to meet you Sandy and I hope it all works out for you."

We shook hands and I was about to go back to my room when I remembered my small backpack I'd been carrying.

"Oh, by the way, can you use this?" I asked, thrusting my hand into the bag and retrieving the gold canister I'd been carrying for the last three months.

"Bear spray?" he said with a bemused look on his face.

"Well it's kept me safe through eight countries and I can't take it on the plane. I wondered if you might find a use for it?" I said with a smile.

"Sure, why not!"

"Take care."

"You too!"

CHAPTER 36

"Bogged down in Bogota"

Leaving Panama City proved as difficult by plane as previous border crossings had been by bike. I booked my flight online and the following day received an e mail cancelling my reservation because they didn't accept international credit cards for flights booked with less than three days notice. So I re-booked with another company and secured the last seat on a direct flight to Bogota. It was with some relief that I organised my luggage for an early departure the next day. I was eager to leave Panama City after nearly five days of waiting and in the meantime I had somehow picked up what I thought was a bad cold. You know, the usual stuff, painfully sore throat, streaming nose and eyes, hot sweats. By the time I arrived at the airport the next day, I felt a whole lot worse, only to be greeted by an extremely long queue to check in, which snaked it's way around the concourse. By the time I made the check in desk I was sweating profusely and my mood was not helped when I was informed,

"The flight is overbooked and we have put you on standby."

"Standby?"

"Yes. Maybe you can stay in Panama one more night and we give you a hotel....."

"I don't want to stay in Panama. I need to get to Bogota today," I said, not allowing him to finish his sales pitch.

He finally gave me a boarding pass with no seat number and told me to speak to the person at the departure gates. He obviously didn't want to get involved in an argument and decided to pass me on to someone else.

Another huge queue to get through security finally got me flight side where I could sit down and get some food inside me. While really not relishing the prospect of another day in Panama, there was nothing I could do except "go with the flow" and see what would happen as we began to board. It`s amazing how much more difficult everything becomes when you are physically below par, but this was yet again something to test my resolve and attitude. It was beginning to wear thin.

At the departure gate I noticed a young girl waiting at the desk and I guessed she was in the same situation. I guessed right. She was Colombian and was returning for Christmas and was eager not to miss her family reunion, and so we both put our best pleading case forwards (well she interpreted for me). They must have liked her smile because minutes before departure we had our seats allocated.

"What about our luggage?" I asked her.

"That`s a good point," she said, "I`ll ask them."

She was assured there would be no problem and so we could finally relax safe in the knowledge that we would soon be on South American soil.

"The best laid plans..............."

I arrived on schedule in Bogota, but sadly my luggage didn`t. So sneezing and sweating my way through the lost luggage process, I was finally assured that my luggage would be delivered to my hostel that night at 9.00 pm.

Needless to say, it didn`t arrive that night and to compound things my bike not only didn`t arrive either but hadn`t even left Panama. Having paid for next day shipping, it still wasn't there five days later. But at that stage I was feeling so ill I couldn`t get worked up about anything. The temperature in Bogota was considerably lower than Panama and I had no warm clothes to wear (all being still in Panama) so I borrowed a jacket from the hostel manager and went to bed fully clothed, with three blankets and was still shivering uncontrollably. I`d gone to a 24hr pharmacy and got some over the counter antibiotics and just hoped they would do the trick because I was feeling like shit. I couldn't decide whether I had the flu, swine flu, malaria or maybe even dengue fever. With no one to talk to about it, I was falling into the trap of dwelling on the negative. The only thing worse than feeling ill, is feeling ill thousands of miles from home and being alone and isolated.

As I lay in my bed feeling sorry for myself and sweating heavily, I flicked on the TV to try and distract myself from the trough of despond I felt myself sinking into. I don't remember exactly what I watched but something must have touched a nerve because the next thing I knew I was sobbing and wondering what the hell I was doing there. The minor breakdown clearly released a lot of tension and I pulled myself together and snapped out of my self pity, nevertheless, my plan of spending New Year in Quito, Ecuador with my friends from New Zealand, Tim and Kris was looking less and less likely.

There were still some huge bureaucratic mountains to climb to get the necessary insurance and clear the bike through customs (whenever it might arrive in the country) then find a BMW garage to get the service done, and all before Christmas in a week`s time. It would prove challenging but I decided to take it one stage at a time.

I decided to move from my hostel to a hotel in downtown Bogota in the Candalaria district which is the old part of town and also a little more dangerous, but the hotel had been recommended to me by Juan, a rider Andy had met while trying to sort out the air freight problems. Juan was an Argentinian who was now living in Costa Rica and was on a trip south back to Argentina. It also made sense to work together to get the bikes through customs and Juan`s Spanish would prove invaluable.

On the day of the move I was still feeling extremely unwell, the antibiotics made me feel nauseous and upset my stomach every time I took them, but I had to drag myself up and get on with it.

When I checked in and opened my e mail I discovered that the bikes had arrived at last and we had a cab ordered for 11.30 am that day to all go down and sort out the paperwork. I had a feeling it was going to be a long day.

Girag Air Cargo was as laid back at Bogota as it had been in Panama. Everything happened at Latin American pace. There was no sense of urgency. Each stage of the process operated at a snail`s pace. After the mandatory paperwork, photocopies, and long walk to the customs and back again, we eventually got to see our bikes. I was anxious to see what, if any damage had been done. To my relief, there was only a slight break in the windscreen. So within two hours we had liberated our bikes! While Andy went straight to the BMW garage for a long overdue service, I said to Juan,

“What about asking them for some compensation for the delay?”

“Yes, I think we should. If you watch the bikes I will go and see what we can get.”

There followed a three hour wait while Juan negotiated with the man who could make the necessary decisions. More paperwork followed, but we eventually rode away with the princely sum of $100 each. At least that will cover three day`s accommodation I thought. Better than nothing and as Juan said, there was a principle at stake.

With that major hurdle overcome, the next step was to find the BMW garage and get them to do some basic work on the bike.

The truth is, I could have done most of it but it would have taken just too much energy. Each day after taking the antibiotics, I feel nauseous and generally worse for several hours.

The garage turned out to be eight miles away in the north of the city, but at least they were extremely friendly and helpful. Enrique, the service manager spoke good enough English and promised to have all the work done by the next day, which was good because the next day would be Christmas Eve, and if it couldn't be completed by then it would mean waiting in Bogota until after Christmas.

I had decided to set off on Christmas day with Andy no matter how I was feeling. Maybe being back on the bike would help me re-focus my attention on something other than how shit I was feeling.

Christmas Eve in Bogota with Andy and Lenny

So it looked like Christmas Day would be spent on six to seven hour ride to Cali. In the meantime, Lenny, who I had last seen in Nicaragua, had also arrived in Bogota and was planning on visiting Medellin and Cartagena in the northwest of the country. We had been in e mail contact and I had suggested he stay at the same hotel. So Christmas Eve was celebrated in Bogota with Lenny, Andy and myself wandering the back streets of the city trying desperately to find a place, any place to eat. It appeared that on Christmas Eve in Bogota everything closes early. We eventually found a solitary shop and bought a few cans of beer and persuaded a small pizzeria to sell us a couple of pizzas, making the transaction through a locked metal gate. The owner was obviously not taking any chances.

Merry Christmas!

Cali

Lenny headed off to explore eastern Colombia and Andy and I spent Christmas Day on an eight hour ride through the twisty mountain roads towards Cali. As with many of the countries I had ridden through, I wasn't really sure what to expect and Colombia offered some beautiful and surprising scenery. I hadn't really expected rolling green hills and mountains. At times it felt like we were riding through the Alps and at other times we could have been in England. The roads were some of the best I`d ridden in Latin America. Nevertheless, it was a long day. Longer than I would have liked having been off the bike for a while and my back was definitely complaining as we pulled up outside our next hostel, strangely located in the middle of a quiet residential district.

That night we went out in search of food and more importantly, a cold beer, hoping we would have more luck than we had on Christmas Eve. We found a lively strip and several beers and some BBQ`d chicken later I was ready for an early night! The hectic scene and thumping drum and bass music were taking their toll. As Andy pointed out,

“You know you`re getting old when the music is too loud to have a conversation!”

Cali may be a party town, but we both agreed it wasn`t a place to hang around in for long, in fact Andy was setting off in the morning to head for Pasto and then into Ecuador. Lenny had decide to explore eastern Colombia and I`d decided to stay one more day to allow my back to recover. So the following day, after waving him off I went back to my room and hoped to catch up on e mails, the blog and Skype, only to find the internet had gone down. I was a little irritated, in fact so irritated, I packed the bike and an hour after Andy had left, I too was on the road. I’d checked the map and decided to head for the little colonial town of Popayan, which was only a couple of hours ride. Hopefully my back would be able to manage that.

Popayan was a much nicer place, and like all colonial towns had some beautiful buildings and lovely central plaza which was decorated with Christmas lights and at night looked amazingly festive, which was more than could be said of me! The joy of Christmas had definitely passed me by, mainly because of being on the road, and also I still prefer Christmas in a cold climate.

I arrived in Popayan on Boxing Day and of course everything was closed, so I decided to stay another day, and the following day set off for Pasto, the last big town before the border. This proved to be another long day of about six hours riding. The main road between Popayan and Pasto had been closed for several days due to landslides, but Andy had e mailed me to say it was now open. Nevertheless, there were many hold ups where the road was being repaired.

On the road I also experienced an interesting Colombian tradition. It appears that on this day for some reason, the local population of all the towns and villages had decided that it would be a good idea to throw buckets of water and water filled balloons on to all passing traffic. As I approached even the tiniest enclave of civilization, there would be groups of mainly young people lining both sides of the road, their hands filled with buckets, balloons and basically any receptacle that would hold water. As the unfortunate driver or rider got within striking distance, the crowd would unleash a torrent of the water on the passing vehicles. It would be irritating enough in a car, but on two wheels it was downright dangerous. I got a complete soaking. What a great idea. I`m still laughing about it now.

Eventually I arrived in Pasto, very wet and irritated but I just didn`t like the place so I kept on riding and ended up in the little town of Ipiales quite near the border where my back told me to stop.

The town was much closer to the border than I realized and the next day I arrived at the border within five minutes. The crossing into Ecuador was the easiest I`d experienced. No hassle and friendly, it was the complete antithesis of Honduras.

CHAPTER 37

"La Mitad Del Mundo!" – The Middle of the World

As with Colombia, I didn`t really know what to expect of Ecuador, but I was again surprised. The quality of the roads was excellent, much better than England. In fact most of the roads seemed to be virtually new, probably as a result of the massive investment in the infrastructure paid for by huge loans from the U.S, which the Ecuadorian government will never be able to repay. This is of course is exactly what the U.S wants (see "Confessions of an Economic Hit Man" by John Perkins for the real story). Anyway, enough of the politics.

After an hour or so of riding great roads with only my own thoughts for company, I passed a rider coming the opposite way on exactly the same bike as mine, and as I gave him the customary wave it occurred to me that I hadn`t seen any other biker for such a long time and that thought was occupying my mind when a few minutes later I checked in my mirror and saw the same bike right behind me approaching at speed and signalling for me to stop. I pulled over and cut the engine,

"Do you speak English?" the lone rider asked.

"A little," I replied with a grin.

"I noticed you were riding the same bike and I was on my way to find a garage," said Yaneev, an Israeli who had been riding with his girlfriend.

"My girlfriend has had a fall off road and broken her clutch lever. I don`t suppose you have a spare?"

"As a matter of fact I do!" I replied, rummaging through my

spares and tool pannier.

What are the chances of that? In the mountains of Ecuador, looking for a spare clutch lever for a BMW Dakar and you just ride by another rider on exactly the same bike who just happens to have a spare? After all the help I`d been offered on the road, it was a real pleasure to help somebody else in need. Thanking me profusely, he gave me his card, and because he was heading the same way, we felt sure we would meet up again on the road somewhere.

I didn`t want to push my body too hard, but wanted to get close to Quito, so as I arrived in the town of Cayambe, it seemed a good place to stay for the night and Quito was only an hour`s ride away the next day.

I was excited about the prospect of spending New Year with my friends Tim and Kris who were stopping in Quito en route back home to New Zealand. I was really looking forward to seeing them as the planned rendezvous had been under threat many times in the previous few months and as I got closer to Quito, I realised just how important it had become to see friendly, familiar faces again. I had met up with Tony and Claire in Carlsbad, and of course Jane in Costa Rica. This would be the last of the planned rendezvous and I wanted to make sure it happened.

The next morning I was up early and on the road with plenty of time in hand so I decided to visit the Equator Monument as it was on the way.

Le Mitad del Mundo

As I arrived at the Real Equator (not sure where the false one is) I felt strangely emotional and had a lump in my throat as it just occurred to me that I had ridden from the Arctic Ocean to the Equator, and it was with some sense of pride I had my picture taken in front of the monument.

Reaching the Equator

My moment of reflection over, I pressed on to Quito. The GPS maps I had been using were often hit and miss in terms of accuracy so I hoped it would manage to navigate through what was a pretty big city.

CHAPTER 38

"Cappuccinos and the Meaning of Life!"

The GPS did its job and got me within "asking distance" and a few minutes later I pulled up outside Casa Encalada, an apartment that Kris had rented for the few days over New Year. Quito is situated high up in the mountains and the apartment was located near the top of a very steep hill. Coming to a halt, I clicked the bike into neutral and with my foot on the rear brake I lifted my visor and to check if this was indeed the correct address.

"Hola!" I said to a man stood smoking a cigarette by the door of the apartment, "Casa Encalada?" I enquired.

"Si," he replied with a warm smile.

Great, I thought, at least I found the right place. Now my challenge was where to park the bike. Kris had informed me there would be some secure parking space, so the best thing would be to park the bike safely and unload before I decided where to leave it for the duration of my stay. The steep, cobbled street proved very difficult to negotiate, but I eventually turned the bike sideways to find a spot as near to a level surface as I could. By this time two other men had arrived which was very fortunate as it saved some potential damage and not a little amount of embarrassment from occurring! I'd angled the bike as best I could, cut the engine and kicked down the sidestand. As I dismounted, the sheer weight of the fully loaded bike was too much for the side stand and it began to topple over in what appeared to be slow motion. I threw my whole body weight behind it as the men rushed to my aid and we managed to right it and man handle it into safer ground,

"Muchas gracias!" I repeated several time to my helpers. If they hadn't have been there it would undoubtedly have caused some damage to the bike and I would have had to strip all the luggage off to make it light enough to pick up singlehandedly. With the adrenaline settled, the safe parking space located and my gear safely stowed in the apartment, I decided I was in need of a coffee,

"Hay un café aqui cerca?" I asked the security guard.

"Si," he answered pointing down the steep hill.

"Gracias!" I said and wandered down the street. Being on the outskirts of the city itself, there were few local places within walking distance and as I made my way down the street it looked mainly residential properties and I couldn't recognise anything that resembled a café, but then I came across a small, hand painted sign hanging outside what looked remarkably like a house. I tried the door and despite the "Open" sign the door appeared to be locked. I turned away to continue my search for caffeine and then heard the rattling of bolts and I glanced back at the door as a bleary eyed, black face blinked at me,

"Tiene café?" I enquired, not really sure if this was indeed a café or not.

"Momento," he responded and disappeared for a minute before re-opening the door in a rather grubby dressing gown. I checked my watch to confirm to myself that it was indeed well into the afternoon. They must have had some party, I thought as he motioned me to a rickety staircase, which took me to a dirty looking room with a wooden balcony. The sturdy wooden table was covered in detritus. I felt like I'd stumbled upon a crack den and felt distinctly uncomfortable and yet it would have felt even more uncomfortable to make an excuse and suddenly leave.

"Café, grande?" he asked placing a hastily emptied ashtray in my direction.

"Si, gracias," I answered, wishing I hadn't knocked on the door in the first place. A few minutes later he reappeared carrying a big mug of coffee.

"Muchas gracias," I said, wondering how clean the mug was and just how quickly I could dispose of its contents without seeming too hasty. He clip clopped back down the staircase and I sipped the coffee. One taste confirmed my earlier fears and I looked around for a suitable place to deposit the hot coloured water. A tatty looking plant pot balanced precariously on the edge of the balcony caught my attention. Perfect! I poured the coffee into the pot and waited for a couple of minutes before making my exit. As I turned the corner at the bottom of the staircase I now counted four dishevelled men hunched around a table smoking rather long, hand rolled cigarettes. I nodded to them saying, "adios" as I opened the door to the street. Welcome to Quito, I mused as I made the trek up the steep cobbled street back to the apartment, I sincerely hope tomorrow's coffee will be slightly better quality.

By the time I reached the apartment I found myself breathing heavily, then I remembered that Quito is over 9,000 ft. up in the mountains and made a mental note that it was important to keep hydrated. Tim and Kris were due to arrive that evening so it gave me time to sort my gear and wash my disgusting riding suit, which I had worn virtually everyday since I started six months previously.

New Year in Quito

As the clock ticked down to their arrival time I found my anticipation and excitement building. I was really looking forward to seeing some friendly faces and Tim and Kris had always been hugely supportive of me and what I was attempting to do and had even offered to come and rescue me if I got into trouble,

"We've decided that if you get kidnapped by bandits in Mexico or Colombia we are going to pay the ransom," Tim had reassuringly told me on Skype, "but if it's more than $10,000 you're on your own!" he added.

"Thanks!" I replied, "it's great to know who you can rely upon!"

They arrived pretty much on time that night and we had a great time catching up and drinking beer. Kris had also e mailed me previously to ask what special treats I would like and so obviously turned up bearing gifts of chocolate and tea bags!

New Year`s Eve was spent in traditional fashion, dinner, a few beers and into bed at 10.30 p.m. In fairness, they had been up very early and crossed a few time zones in the previous few days and wanted to catch up on the sleep they`d missed. Sadly it was to no avail. Down in the valley, several miles away, a renegade DJ was determined to see in the New Year his own way, playing non stop music from 10.00 p.m. to 10.00 a.m. The wind carried the sound up the mountain and it felt like he was right next door. Even with my motorcycle ear plugs I hardly slept a wink. Happy New Year Quito!

The next few days were spent wandering around Quito old town, searching for cappuccinos and the meaning of life. Whenever I'm with Tim and Kris we always get involved in deep and meaningful discussions, usually over a good cup of coffee and later over a beer or two. We've done it all over the world and Quito was no exception. It was on such a quest that I decided to get myself a much needed haircut, so while Kris was shopping, I found a local hairdresser. I had an uneasy feeling as soon as I sat down, it all smacked of "Sweeney Todd," I bet if I`d have looked closer I would have seen traces of blood around the place.

Happy New Year! Tim and Kris in Quito

It was undoubtedly the worst haircut I've had since going to the barbers in Blackburn when I was about ten years old. I'd always assumed with age goes wisdom and experience. My barber was well over seventy years old and maybe a little blind and unsteady, but by the time I'd thought it all through it was too late, I was committed, as big chunks of hair fell to the floor, much to the amusement of Kris as she dropped by to take photos. Still, I thought, it doesn't matter, it'll have plenty of time to grow again.

I paid the $3.50 for the "haircut" and left quickly.

"You're bleeding!" Kris pointed out as she rummaged through her bag for a paper handkerchief.

Never trust a blind man with a cut throat razor, I reflected as I stemmed the blood flow from my cut ear.

"Did Van Gogh ever come to Quito?"

Whilst wandering the streets of Quito we must have strayed away from the beaten track as we turned a corner and suddenly the atmosphere changed. Where before we had been greeted with smiling faces and helpful people, now the mood of the people in the street changed markedly. The men hanging around the street corners held eye contact just a little too long for comfort. I was feeling distinctly uncomfortable as a man approached us wearing something resembling a uniform,

"Are you English?" he asked us with a look of concern on his face.

"Yes," I replied.

"You need to leave here now," he said indicating a sense of urgency, "this is not a safe place for you."

I didn't need a second request as I motioned to Tim and Kris explaining as we retraced our steps why we needed to move on quickly. It just served to highlight the need for constant awareness when travelling and how easy it is to become complacent. Getting back to a safer neighbourhood, and continuing to wander, we noticed an interesting Ecuadorian tradition, outside many shops and houses were life size dummies (very much like the Guy Fawkes tradition in England) which are ritually burned at midnight along with a last will pinned to the dummy, symbolically getting rid of everything you didn`t like about the year gone by. I thought it was a pretty good idea – one way of exorcising the past.

We did find the cappuccino and we were still working on the meaning of life when all too soon it was time for Tim and Kris to head home to New Zealand. They were up at 5.00 a.m. for an early flight, and after waving them off, I packed up the bike and set off for the town of Riobamba, a four hour ride across the mountains.

With my GPS no longer playing ball, it was down to the old fashioned way to navigate my way out of Quito. At every junction I would ask locals and taxi drivers and eventually found the main Pan Americana. The temperature had certainly taken a steep dive since crossing into Ecuador and now I was glad of the ice breaker, merino wool layers I had bought back home. At this rate I would be digging out my heated jacket I hadn`t worn since Alaska.

Riobamba was a pleasant place. I arrived in bright sunshine and spent another thirty minutes riding around looking for the "right" hotel. Luckily because I`d set off early enough, the weather stayed warm and comfortable while I unpacked and sorted the bike out before the ominous black cloud that had followed me over the mountains finally unleashed its contents. Time to break out the umbrella again. It seemed I`d entered another rainy season.

The next stop was the city of Cuenca. This proved to be a more demanding day than I`d expected. More mountainous roads and high altitude riding through dense clouds and where the beautiful paved roads I`d become used to suddenly ran out. Nevertheless, I still arrived in plenty of time to find a reasonable hotel in the centre. Again, the temperature climbed as I arrived in the city only to cloud over and rain heavily later in the afternoon.

Cuenca was a nice city and I decided a two day break from the bike would be good for my back. My stay also coincided with yet another festival. Latin Americans really love to party. Another huge parade with many floats carrying pointed political messages, most of which were aimed at the Gringos` greedy exploitation of Ecuador`s oil and natural resources (again see "Confessions of an Economic Hitman" for the real explanation).

I reckoned I had another two days ride over the mountains to the border of Peru so the next day I made for the city of Loja which would put me within striking distance of Peru if I rode hard all day. I was conscious of not overdoing it but at the same time was eager to cross into Peru. For some reason Peru was a key milestone for me. I`m not sure why, maybe because I`d heard so much about it – the beautiful scenery, the Andes, Machu Picchu, Lake Titicaca, the beaches, whatever it was, I was excited about crossing the border.

As with all my riding in Ecuador, the ride from Loja to the border proved to be much longer and harder than it looked on the map. The beautiful paved roads suddenly ran out and I was back on dirt and mud. As I climbed up the mountain road and rounded a bend I came upon a long line of stationary traffic reminiscent of the many long lines of traffic in Central America during the rainy season waiting for landslides to be cleared. I rode to the head of the line and pulled over. Cutting my engine I was aware of the relative quiet and stillness. It was clear the traffic had been waiting there for some time and in the distance I could see diggers and trucks working on the road up ahead. I took off my gloves and helmet and walked to the nearest waiting driver to find out more,

"Cuánto tiempo está cerrado?" I enquired.

"Posiblemente 20 o 30 minutos," he said with a shrug of the shoulders.

Could be worse I thought, preparing myself for a thirty minute wait and since I had started early it was still only 7.30 am so I had plenty of time. It was unusual to see roads in this condition in Ecuador. I had become used to the high quality and made a mental note not to get too complacent in future. Happily, within only a few minutes, the flashing orange light of the pilot vehicle came into view and with the sound of dozens of engines being fired up, I quickly gloved up, put on my helmet and slowly began leading the huge convoy through the dirt and mud of the half constructed road. Relieved to be on my way, I also secretly hope it wouldn't continue like this for miles. The scars of the Dalton were still with me.

These were obviously the last roads to be constructed, and so the journey to the border took nearly six hours. The mountain sections were really cold and I was glad I'd remembered to put my thermals on before setting off. Nevertheless, as soon as I started to drop down into the valleys the temperature soared back to the highs of Mexico and I was soon stripping off the layers. Maybe this would be a precursor to the climate I would face in Peru I thought, as flat, straight roads took me ever closer to the border.

CHAPTER 39

"Barren deserts and bent cops" – Welcome to Peru

As I approached the border town there was a clear sign pointing towards the Peruvian border, so I naturally took it and was pleasantly surprised to find myself on a beautiful, brand new two lane highway. All was going well until I passed under a sign saying,

"Gracias por su visita," followed quickly by another one saying "Bienvenidos a Peru."

Bugger! I was now in Peru and hadn`t passed through Ecuadorian migracion to get my passport stamped and aduana to cancel my temporary import permit for the bike. How the hell did that happen? Pulling up at the Peruvian control I asked,

"Donde esta migracion de Ecuador?"

The border guard pointed back down the road. Somehow I must have missed it. With the temperature rising I climbed back on the bike and headed back two miles and asked again, this time I was directed to Ecuador`s migracion on a completely different road. I got my passport duly stamped and looked around for the customs office,

"Donde esta la aduana?" I enquired.

I was directed another two miles down the road I`d originally ridden! The simple border crossing was becoming unnecessarily complicated. Eventually I arrived back at the Peruvian migracion which was unnervingly quiet after the fiascos of Central America, in fact, there was only me and two other bikes, ridden by two Colombians who were riding down to the town of Mancora before heading back home to work. We had a brief chat about our respective journeys and one of them asked if I wanted any help with the paperwork. I thanked him for his offer and said I had everything I needed and it occurred to me just how much I had learned along the way. The process went fairly smoothly and I was soon on the road in Peru, my thirteenth country.

What a complete change to Ecuador. The mountainous, verdant landscape had now changed to hot, flat desert conditions reminiscent of Arizona. Even though I'd been on the road for several hours I was keen to push on to Mancora which was another one and a half hours away. Juan, my Argentinian friend had recommended it and as the Colombian riders were going there too, it seemed like a good idea.

The road followed the coast and it was refreshing to be by the sea again. It reminded me of riding the Pacific Coast highway in California, but I was beginning to tire and I was pleased to see the outskirts of Mancora appear ahead. After a fruitless ride around the town searching for accommodation I came across The Grand Hotel (not so Grand in reality). The cost of a room was more than wanted to pay but I'd had enough of trawling around in the heat so, given that I got a discount for staying more than one night and they had a secure garage, it was a done deal.

I stayed for three nights, got some much needed washing done and enjoyed some time walking on the beach and watching the surfers drain the last drop out of the surf before the sun went down. I even found a little café that managed a half decent cup of coffee which is saying something because most of the time you just get a cup of hot water or milk and a jar of instant powdered coffee.

After three nights I was ready to move on and make some headway south as I still had a long way to go to get to Lima, the capital and more long rides to reach Machu Picchu, one of my original goals.

I decided to make the journey as comfortable as possible for my back by riding only three to four hours a day, so my plan was to set off straight after breakfast and reach my destination late morning, which would give me a full afternoon to find a hotel and look around the city/town. The first stop was the colonial city of Piura which wasn`t as picturesque as I was expecting but across from the hotel was the city`s best Chinese restaurant, so naturally it had to be tried. Chinese cuisine, Peruvian style, washed down with a couple of beers. The locals seem to be very keen on their local drink "Inca Kola" (yes, that`s what it`s called), I would have been tempted to try it if it hadn`t look remarkably like a bottle of urine. Call me unadventurous, but anything that colour is unlikely to tempt me away from a decent cerveza. In fairness, the meal itself was pretty good. As ever, I had a huge plate and felt like another one within an hour.

With nothing really tempting me further, I left Piura early the next day and made for the bigger city of Chiclayo. The main Pan American Highway hugs the coast on the way through Northern Peru and then deviates inland and carves its way through mile upon mile of barren desert. It reminded me of the Arizona desert without the blistering, intense heat. Straight, flat roads with nothing on the horizon but sand and more sand.

One night in Chiclayo was also enough and the next day I was on the road to the more attractive Trujillo. Another three hours of desert to cross. It`s interesting how even on a motorbike your mind can wander and even dip into a minor trance while riding in a straight line for hours on end. I had to consciously pay attention and focus to keep my senses on high alert and my mind occupied to avoid being run off the road by reckless truck and bus drivers attempting suicidal overtakes. In the mean time, I occupied my brain by singing all the back catalogue of Simon and Garfunkel, Jackson Browne and as many Beatles songs as

I could remember (yes, it was a long road). With the final chorus of Lady Madonna ringing in my helmet, I rolled into Trujillo. With my GPS unit out of action, I adopted the same strategy in every town; I stopped and ask the locals.

"Donde esta el centro por favor?"

I make for the centre and try to get accommodation as close to it as possible. So, following the directions from a local, I headed for Trujillo`s central plaza and then tracked around looking for a suitable hotel. The first one wanted the equivalent of $80! I had been warned by Andy that Peru wasn`t as cheap as you might think and so it was proving. So sadly, it was back to the "hostel experience", or to be more accurate the "hostal experience", which is not a backpackers hostel but a more basic kind of hotel.

One night was enough, and the next day saw me on the road to Chimbote about a hundred mile ride away, although I had been warned by the hotel manager in Mancora that Chimbote wasn`t a particularly nice place and had an unpleasant smell! It was on the route and I thought it would be a convenient place to stay a night, but as I approached the city the stench wasn`t just unpleasant it was almost making me gag. There was some kind of fish processing plant located there which produced a stench that seemed to permeate the very landscape. I fuelled up, looked at the map and decided that I would push on to the next likely looking town which was Barranca, which meant a further hundred miles or so across the desert.

The desert road snaked its way southwards occasionally touching the Pacific Coast, with a continual onshore wind blowing sufficiently strongly for me to maintain my course only by leaning into it at a 50° angle which made the going very tiring. Mile after mile of barren flat desert, intermittently broken by mile after mile of barren hilly desert eventually brought me into the town of Barranca. It had been a long day in the saddle so I didn`t waste much time searching for a hotel but basically stopped at the first place that looked O.K. and so I found myself at the door of Hotel Chavin (you could probably lose the "in"), but it was comfortable and had wifi and a nice hot shower. Oh for the simple pleasures!

One night with the "chavs" made me eager to get to Lima which was now only a short two and a half hour ride. I had decided to find the one BMW garage in Peru (located in Lima) and possibly get a tyre change and maybe chain and sprockets too, as it would be another 2,600 miles to the next BMW garage in Santiago, Chile and I wasn`t sure whether both would last that long.

The last few miles heading into Lima were littered with multi coloured shanty towns, clinging precariously to the hills. The noise, the heat and the traffic congestion ramped up considerably. The tranquil trance of endless desert miles evaporated quickly. But unfortunately, not quickly enough.

The road into Lima is a dual carriageway and across the other side of the carriageway I saw a group of Police, but only as one of them waved me down and it wasn`t to have a polite chat and admire my bike. I heard the words,

"Quarente cinco," - "infraccion," as he pointed to the speedo. Then he took out a little book and jabbed his finger at paragraph b, subsection c,

"Infraccion," he repeated. Of course I had no way of knowing whether I was "speeding" or not. Then he wrote down on his pad S100 (100 Nuevo Soles, about £22). He wanted to give me an on the spot fine under the guise of motoring infringements. This was a common method of extracting money from passing foreigners. I was taken so unawares that I actually paid it! I didn`t even offer less, for which I berated myself for several minutes afterwards. As I rode away from the mugging, I tried to console myself with the fact that it was the first time I had been a victim of this literal highway robbery in the whole journey and vowed to pay much more attention in future.

These thoughts were still in the background of my mind as the traffic intensity and heat increased, as I got closer to the city. Vowing not to get mugged again, it was with almost total disbelief that I saw a police car in my mirrors and then heard the siren right behind me signalling me to pull over. "You`ve got to be joking" I said out loud to myself. This was turning into an interesting day. So what was it going to be this time, more speeding? You`ve guessed it.

"Quarente cinco," – blah blah – "infraccion," – blah blah.........

"No es possible............yo vie.....45kph.......la misma...... todo trafico......"

This time I was putting up a defence saying I was going the same speed as all the other traffic. Then he pulled his ace and said that I passed a radar trap some kilometres back. Whether I did or not is a moot point as he wanted his bonus too. Clearly he had been informed by his mate that a "meal ticket" was riding his way and I was an easy target. This time the "fine" had gone up,

"S150," he demanded, and he had my paperwork for the bike.

"No es possible. No tengo mucho dinero," (you scum bag, I added under my breath).

"Quanto tienes?" (how much do you have)

"Quanto tienes?" he repeated

I rummaged in my pockets for a smaller denomination knowing I had a couple of S20 and a couple of S100 notes and just hoped that I pulled out the right ones. The offer of S20 saw him wrinkle his nose up with disgust, eventually the bribe cost me S44 and he returned my precious paperwork.

Welcome to Lima! Apart from a decent cup of tea and coffee, I`m even missing the good old English bobby.

I subsequently found the copy of my paperwork that would have given me more leverage if I had it at the time. You live and learn I concluded, but it was still a bitter pill to swallow and the injustice stayed with me for some time.

Another thirty minutes careful riding brought me into the seething, cacophony and chaos that is Lima. My next challenge was finding my way to the BMW garage and then to a hotel in a completely different part of the city without my GPS. This all took another two hours. I finally arrived at the garage only to discover they didn't have any tyres and they couldn`t check whether they had a chain and sprocket set because the service department was closed. This was all relayed to me by a very helpful Peruvian biker who spoke good English. Carlos gave me the address of a shop that sold tyres,

"Here`s my e mail address and phone number. Give me a call if I can be of any more help."

Faith in human nature restored again, I thanked him and set off to find a hotel in the Miraflores district of Lima about thirty minutes away. After asking the way several times I finally arrived at 2.00 pm. My short two and a half hour ride to Lima had now become six hours. I discovered that all the cheap accommodation was full but negotiated a three night deal at reasonable hotel with an interesting name Hotel Esperanza (The Hope Hotel!)

After showering and collapsing on my bed, I contemplated the challenges of the day and how remarkably calm I felt considering how that would have affected me a few months ago.

I spent the rest of the weekend wandering around Miraflores and on Monday morning set off to find the garage that could supply me with tyres, luckily it was located very close to my hotel and even better, when I arrived they had the correct ones in stock. Result! Strapping them to the bike I rode to the BMW garage to get them fitted and also change my chain and sprockets if they had a set available. They did! The plan was coming together. It seemed strangely sad to change the chain I had so lovingly tended every day since Alaska, and maybe it could have lasted the course? But it would have been right at the end of its life and why take the chance? Tomorrow I would be back on the road south heading for the town of Pisco, (presumably the home of the sour?) then Nasca and across the Andes to Cusco.

For my last night in the city I had decided to head into the centre and buy myself a really nice meal to celebrate getting the bike sorted and toast my final night. During my days there I had checked out all the local eateries for the best value and had spent a long time pouring over menus posted outside all the restaurants. Tonight, I had decided upon Italian. The restaurant looked clean, homely and not too expensive and so I entered,

"Tabla de uno y una cerveza, por favor."

Sipping on my beer I perused the menu. Not that I'm a creature of habit and routine, but I like to have beer before I eat and a glass of wine with the meal. My little table was opposite the windows looking out onto the street and afforded me an interesting vantage point to observe the passing Lima nightlife. I'd drained my beer and ordered another while I waited for my pasta dish to arrive when I glanced up at the window and noticed an attractive girl staring at me. Catching my glance she smiled and naturally I returned the smile, desperately trying to place her in my memory. It was clear she had recognised me from somewhere. Where the hell have I seen her before? My brain was racing, working overtime to get the answer. Maybe she worked at the hotel? I just wasn't sure and didn't want to appear ignorant so obviously I smiled back. Still smiling, she waved and kept eye contact as she slowly walked down the street catching my gaze at each window pane. She then pointed at herself and then pointed inside the restaurant. She was clearly indicating that she wanted to join me. This was all getting a little bizarre, so with a slightly embarrassed smile I shook my head and pretended to become engrossed in my pasta while keeping an eye on her with my peripheral vision. As soon as I noticed her disappear from view I reflected with some amusement and curiosity on what had occurred. My memory is too good for me not to have remembered someone as striking as her, so the only other conclusion was that she was a very high - class hooker, who had spotted a gringo and thought she would try a different approach. I was mentally congratulating her on her original approach when she suddenly reappeared at the window with a big beaming smile. I just shook my head slowly and pushing my finished plate to one side sipped my glass of red wine. Maybe she was stalking me I considered.

"La cuenta, por favor," I motioned to the waiter as I pulled out a handful of Pesos. Settling my bill I left the restaurant and as I stepped outside I saw her standing by the wall. This should be interesting I mused, as I approached her.

"Hi!" she said, in good English and still smiling.

"Hi," I responded as I drew level with her.

"My name is Angela!" she said, simultaneously linking my arm and walking along with me.

"How are you tonight?"

"I'm good," I replied, "how are you?" I asked, wondering where this conversation would lead.

"Would you like to go to your place," she asked, "I can give you a very good massage!"

"I don't have much money," I added without really thinking what I was saying.

"Who said anything about money," she replied with that smile again, "Why don't we go back to your place?"

"I don't think they would allow guests," I replied, still talking rubbish but not really knowing what to say and by this time actually beginning to enjoy this unexpected encounter.

"Well we could go back to mine," she countered.

"Angela, you're a very attractive woman and thanks for the offer, but maybe not tonight!" I said, unlinking my arm, "have a good night".

She just smiled as I blew her a kiss and walked off back to my hotel. I was still mulling the whole thing over as I reached my room. I pulled the covers back, dropped into bed and thought, boy, I could really do with a massage right now.

CHAPTER 40

"These are the days that must happen to you" – Walt Whitman

The following morning I loaded the bike up and headed south. Feeling more confident now the work was done on the bike I navigated my way out of the teeming metropolis of Lima and headed down the coast to the town of Pisco about one hundred and fifty miles away. An uneventful ride brought me into the town at around mid day. As the temperature began to soar I happened upon a convenient and affordable hostal right next to the town`s central plaza. Pisco was an uninspiring place and made more so because they were completely resurfacing all the roads around the plaza adding to the general unattractiveness of the town which, like many other Latin American towns, seemed permanently in the process of being built. Each street had several houses and buildings in various stages of construction. It appeared that halfway through the construction, the builder's became bored and moved on to something else.

The next day I set off for Nasca, a world heritage site famous for the "Nasca Lines". I was about forty miles into the journey and just leaving the town of Ica when I heard a strange noise and felt a slight jerk on the back wheel, pulling over immediately, I got off and a cursory inspection saw the chain flopping around. That doesn`t look good, I thought, but it came out as, "oh fuck, what the hell...."

I quickly found the right hand, rear chain tensioner had completely exploded (or imploded – either way it had disintegrated). I unloaded the bike and got out my tools in a pointless attempt to put some tension back into the chain. To be honest, I didn`t know what else to do. It was clear I wasn`t going any distance with the chain as it was. At that point, a local tuk tuk driver, who had been parked at the side of the road exactly where I stopped, came over to see what had happened,

"Necessito un mecanico," I said. "Hay un mecanico acqui cerca?"

He said there was a mechanic back in Ica a few minutes away and offered to guide me there.

"Muchas gracias!" I said as I fired up the engine and turned the bike around. I then proceeded to follow his tuk tuk so slowly I was barely getting out of first gear. He took me first to a Honda dealer which I knew was a long shot as the part I required was specific to BMWs. After a brief conversation between the tuk tuk driver and the Honda mechanic I heard the word, Repuestos. He was suggesting we find garage that sells spares. I was still doubtful we could just pick up that kind of part, in fact I was certain we couldn`t. My mind was racing ahead with possible scenarios. I would either have to get one shipped in from The U.K. or maybe even go back to Lima and pick one up from the BMW garage as it would probably be quicker than getting one sent, and how would I describe which part I needed? All these thoughts were racing around my head when we pulled up outside a spares garage. Alonso, the tuk tuk driver ran over to the garage and came out a few minutes later and pointed to another one down the road. Eventually we found a man who insisted he could make me a part,

"Si es posible?" I asked desperately hoping he would confirm what he said.

"Si, Si!" He seemed very confident which is just what I was looking for.

"Puede hacerlo hoy?" (Can you do it today?)

"Si, si, tres horas."

A part made in 3 hours!

Three hours? That would be great! So, with a possible fix, I said I would come back that afternoon. In the meantime, I asked Alonso if there was a local hotel with internet that I could stay at, having decided that whatever happened I wouldn`t be riding further that day. He raced off and came back a couple of minutes later. He`d found one just down the road and helped me unload the bike and took me with all my baggage to the hotel. I thanked him profusely and paid him for his troubles. With sweat pouring off me I dumped my stuff in the room and grabbed a quick shower. When I`d recovered I thought back over the last few hours. It had finally happened, I reflected. Ever since I began this journey, one of my biggest fears had always been breaking down and not being able to fix the problem. It had been at the back of my mind virtually every day. Even with a limited knowledge of quantum physics, the notion that "thoughts become things" and whatever you continually focus on will manifest eventually, has been proven time and again. I finally got what I`d been focusing on. What was interesting though was how I was much calmer than I thought I would be, probably helped by the synchronicities that surrounded the day. How convenient to break down right next to that tuk tuk driver?

The hotel I was staying in unfortunately had no garage or secure parking, but there was a garage I could use at night about a block away. Not ideal, but never mind. At the appointed hour I went back to see if he had managed to fashion a replacement part. It cost me an arm and a leg but amazingly he had done the job! From possibly being stranded in the town for several days I was now in a position to get back on the bike the next day! As I rode back to the hotel my mind was still puzzled by how the problem had occurred in the first place and also, when I checked the chain, I noticed it had a tight spot which shouldn`t occur in a brand new chain. Something wasn`t quite right and I didn`t know what. It was just a gut feeling.

That night I rode slowly up to the garage and enquired what the cost would be to store my bike for the night,

"Cuanta cuesta por una noche?"

"Tres soles," he replied with a smile.

Well that was reasonable, three soles for parking overnight. We had a brief conversation as I was locking the bike up and in the course of our chat it transpired that he was a bike mechanic! Synchronicity number 2. I asked if he would look at my lights and horn as they had suddenly decided to stop working, strangely, just after the BMW garage had finished working on the bike.

"Si, no problema!" he replied, "manana a las ocho."

The following day I was at the garage for the appointed time of 8.00 am and sure enough the mechanic turned up on the dot at 9.00 am Peruvian time! For some reason, before we even looked at the lights, I asked him to take a look at the chain. When he took off the front sprocket cover, I couldn`t believe my eyes. There should have been a huge nut and washer holding on the front sprocket. It wasn`t there! Nothing. Nada. The BMW mechanics had forgotten to put it back on! I had ridden nearly two hundred miles with nothing stopping the front sprocket from coming off and taking the chain with it. If that had happened at high speed it could have been extremely serious. I didn't even want to contemplate it.

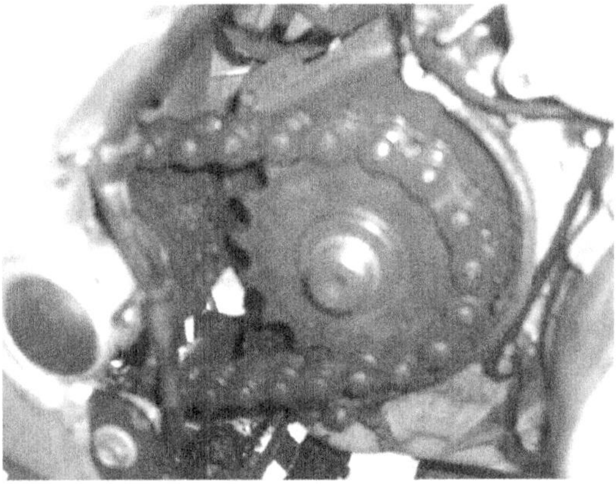

The missing nut.....

The mechanic asked if the BMW mechanics were German or Peruvian. When I said Peruvian, he just shrugged his shoulders.

My next problem was where could we possibly get the right size nut as it wasn`t a standard size. Asking him if he knew somewhere, he nodded confidently, jumped on his bike and took off, reappearing ten minutes later with an exact match. Was I glad I bumped into this man the night before.

He spent a good three hours working on my bike and finished off by testing and cleaning the rear sprocket also, before declaring it ready.

“Cuanto cuesta por su ayuda?” I asked him.

Job done!

He asked for 40 soles (about £9), which was a fraction of the amount I was charged by the plush BMW garage that caused the problem in the first place. I think he was quietly pleased to be given the opportunity to work on something other than the usual small, 125 cc Chinese bikes that everyone rides in Peru. A BMW was a rare bike in South America, which is probably why he insisted on having several photos of himself posing next to the bike. I thanked him and rode back to the hotel to pack the bike and head off, finally for Nasca. While I was packing, I reflected on the last 24 hrs and considered the lessons I had learned:-

1. Always trust your gut feeling
2. Be mindful of what you focus on
3. Never trust Peruvian BMW mechanics

The ride to Nasca was thankfully a short one. The Nasca Lines are the world famous drawings in the desert around Nasca. They are thousands of years old and are of such a scale they can only be viewed in their entirety from the air. Which of course begs the question how were they created by people who hadn`t the wherewithal to view them from the sky? It was all very interesting to ponder on as I rolled into the town and found some accommodation right on the main plaza. Sadly my budget didn`t allow for the popular flight over the lines themselves. Instead I had to make do with wandering around the exhibition of photos in the plaza. Despite not viewing the phenomenon from the air, it was still fascinating, especially if you remember Eric Von Daniken`s 70s best seller, *Chariots of the Gods*, where he poses the interesting question "Was God an astronaut?" Many people believe the Nasca Lines were ancient landing strips for extra terrestrial spacecraft. Why not? It seems like a pretty coherent theory to me.

While in Nasca I had to make one of the most difficult decisions of the whole journey. My original plan when I set off all those months previously was to visit Machu Picchu when I got to Peru. It had been one of the key sights I wanted to see and yet the situation with my back and the recent troubles with the bike had forced me to re-evaluate my original plans. If I wanted to take in Machu Picchu I would need to cut across the Andes and ride up to Cusco, from there I would need to do some walking to reach the ruins and I must admit my confidence in my back, and now also the bike itself had been shaken. After much soul searching I finally decided taking care of my back was a greater priority than visiting Machu Picchu. I rationalised that I could always come back another time if it was that important to me.

The following day I was on the coast road south heading for Arequipa which was going to be too far to ride in one day, so after several hours in the saddle I reached the small town of Camana which would put me within a couple of hours ride of Arequipa the next day. Camana had little going for it apart from a bikini contest being held in a hotel on the main square. With nothing else to tempt me I thought I might drop in and check it out that night. Whilst in Camana, I also noticed with concern, a disturbing trend developing. It would appear there was at large a "Phantom Peruvian toilet seat thief."

The last hotel I had stayed in had no toilet seat forcing me to go to the reception and actually request one! The manager had disappeared (obviously to his toilet seat cache somewhere in the basement) and magically dug one out. No doubt when I checked out he would remove it again for "safe keeping". Maybe I should buy one and strap it to the back of my bike? This time when I dropped my bags off in my hotel room, I did my now mandatory toilet seat check, noticed the missing seat and came straight down to reception and said,

"No tengo una asiento en mi banos?"

The manageress just looked at me with one of those looks that clearly said,

"Yes, and your point is.......?"

Having explained my preference for the necessary seating, she disappeared into one of the unoccupied bedrooms and reappeared several moments later brandishing the seat and handed it to me without a word, probably thinking I was a fussy Gringo. Clutching my prized possession, I hurried back to my room and had it fitted in no time. Feeling satisfied with my handiwork I wondered whether I had a mild dose of OCD. Of course not, I chided myself, I just wanted a toilet seat in the toilet!

For the record, I didn`t actually make the bikini contest that had originally tempted me into the plaza. It started at 10.00 pm and I was such a lightweight after over seven months on the road, I`d eaten, had a couple of beers and was in bed by then.

The benefit of retiring early was it bought me extra time in the morning when I would get up early and complete my rehab exercises and still be down for breakfast by 7.30 am I sat outside in the plaza and was just finishing my breakfast with my bike already packed and ready to go when I risked yet again asking for a coffee. The standard of the coffee throughout my journey had been inconsistent to put it mildly. Ever the optimist I decided to try again,

"Café con leche por favor?" I enquired.

"Si signor," the little waiter acknowledged, hurrying off to the kitchen to return minutes later carrying a cup of hot water and a rather large tin of powdered Nescafe.

"Bollocks," I exclaimed to no one I particular, "I'm just not going to bother ever again," I continued with my one way conversation. I didn't even attempt to drink the coffee and thought it was definitely time to hit the road.

I arrived in the city of Arequipa at around midday and made for the historical centre of the city hoping to find a decent hotel and stay for a couple of days. After the usual ride around the central plaza in ever increasing circles, I came across a good hotel (with toilet seats included, obviously more geared up for tourists!). It was more than I wanted to pay and whilst negotiating a better deal, an older lady at reception (maybe the owner`s mother, I thought) said to me in broken English,

"Que paix? Where are you from?"

"Inglaterra."

“Inglaterra! I am poor, you are rich!”

In other words, pay the going rate you stingy bastard! I must admit I didn`t look rich, stood there in my filthy riding gear, but I suppose my second hand bike was worth more than some would make in a year. A salutary thought, but I didn`t have the Spanish to say,

“Yes, but I borrowed the money from a good friend and now it`s running out and I`m on a tight budget.”

The historical centre of Arequipa is very attractive and at its heart is the large main plaza, where, as with every town and city I`ve visited, everyone comes out in the evening to walk and socialise.

From Arequipa I headed south for the border and stayed in the little town of Moquegua which would leave me a short ride to the Chilean border the following day.

CHAPTER 41

"Long, Thin and Very Expensive!"

My last night in Peru was celebrated in fine fashion with three cans of beer and a bag of peanuts in my hotel room, as I had dismally failed to find even a half decent restaurant anywhere within walking distance. The next day I crossed into Chile, my fourteenth country. The border crossing was reasonably straightforward apart from their insistence that I take off my bag and put it through an x ray machine – the first time that had happened. The customs offices and aduana looked very new and modern compared to many of the others I had passed through and I somehow expected Chile to be a more modern version of Peru. What I hadn't factored in was the cost of living being so much higher than any other country I had visited in South America.

My destination was the city of Arica only fifteen miles down the road, where I was pleasantly surprised to find a half decent cappuccino and a healthy salad. My hotel was also of a reasonable standard and although the Chilean currency was officially the Peso, all the tariffs of the good hotels advertised their rates in US Dollars. It seemed to me that Chile could cost me more money than I would like to spend so I would have to keep a tight check on my fast dwindling finances. The financial situation had been further complicated by some anomalies that had started to appear on my debit card account. As part of my research and planning for the trip I had investigated the best credit and debit cards to use and had opted for two that had the least amount of charges levied against travellers who use them abroad.

Whilst checking my account one day I'd noticed some withdrawals for an amount of Pesos that I just couldn't recollect. The figures didn't seem to add up when I did the currency conversion. Shit!

Maybe someone had cloned my card? Concerned about my fast diminishing resources I contacted my bank back in the U.K. and cancelled my debit card, which would now make withdrawing cash more difficult and potentially more expensive. Still, it was worth it to stop those low life thieves from draining my accounts I thought. It seemed the right thing to do, right up until the time I did the maths again and found out who was syphoning money from my account. The culprit was me. I had miscalculated a couple of withdrawals. What an idiot! Now I had no debit card for the rest of the journey. I put it down to being worn down and fatigued and maybe just a little travel weary.

I remember having a conversation with my friend Tim on Skype where he had told me of friends of his who had toured the whole of Africa for a year in a 4x4. He had asked them at what stage of their one year journey had they felt ready to go home. Apparently, at the nine months stage it got to them. I think I was going through that stage now at seven months. Maybe, travelling solo exacerbated the feeling?

Before leaving Arica I had another ritual to complete and so I made my way to the local market where I scoured the stalls for a Chile sticker for my panniers. I had bought my tough, "metal mule" panniers from a friend who had ridden throughout Europe and had covered the panniers with stickers and decals of all the countries he had visited. Before this trip I had been riding around England with all these stickers feeling somewhat of a fraud. My goal had always been to remove them all and replace them with stickers from every country I passed through on my Pan American adventure. They would be a lasting memory and reminder of my journey. I had become obsessed with tracking the stickers down and had often gone to great lengths in order to acquire them. Happily, in Arica this was to prove the easiest of them all and within five minutes I returned to the hotel and proudly stuck the fourteenth decal onto my pannier.

After Arica, my plan was to follow the coast line all the way down and ultimately reach Santiago about 1,300 miles away. I exchanged the long desert days of Peru for the equally long desert days of Chile. My next stop was Iquique which was a city by the sea and I made the mistake of heading for the beach front hoping to find a cheapish hotel.

Sunset over Iquique

After a fruitless hour checking out every hotel and hostal in the area I was forced to pay an extortionate amount for two nights in an apartment block with no wifi and no cable TV Apparently I had arrived at peak summer time. Iquique was not a great experience and so I was very keen to get back on the road after my enforced sojourn and make my way further down the coast to the small seaport of Tacopilla.

Tacopilla was a working seaport and to be honest a little rough around the edges, in fact, parts of it were completely disgusting and yet the hotels had the audacity to charge almost $60!! Certain things were becoming apparent, if South American countries were supermodels, Chile would be Elle McPherson – long, thin and very expensive. At this rate, I was doubtful whether my funds would get me as far as Buenos Aires.

One night in Tacopilla was certainly enough, and the next day saw me following the coast down to the city of Antofagasta for another $60 room. I had planned to possibly take a couple of days off the bike and rest up but I couldn`t really justify the expense, and also none of the places I`d been to so far really captured my imagination, so I decided to keep moving.

The following day I was heading for a little seaside town of TalTal, which meant the small matter of riding through the famous Atacama Desert. Famous at least for being officially the driest place on the planet. There are parts of the Atacama that haven`t seen rain for over four hundred years. Looking at the map, I had two possible routes to take. I could follow the main Pan American highway or taker a shorter, more direct road right through the middle of the desert. I was debating the issue on the road the following day when I came across a long stationary queue of traffic, riding to the front of it I found another rider on a BMW 1200.

Mattie was a German who was riding through South America in stages, and in between flying home to work. We discussed our routes south and he told me the direct route through the desert was actually a good, paved road and not a dirt track as I first thought. Perfect! That was obviously the road to take. I waved my thanks to him as he disappeared into the distance (I couldn`t have kept up with him if I`d wanted to!) and settled into my 60 mph rhythm. At the next fork in the road I took "the road less travelled" cutting through the beautiful Atacama Desert. Beautiful, and very cold. Much of the Atacama extends into the Andes and as I climbed to about 2,600m I started to shiver and had to pull over and put on extra clothing.

The terrain was unlike any of the other deserts I'd crossed during my journey. It seemed vaguely familiar in a strange way. Then I realised where I'd seen something similar before – on Mars! Apparently, soil samples taken from Mars by several NASA probes are similar to samples taken from the Atacama. NASA even uses this desert to test instruments for future missions to the Red Planet. It was also the home to one of the most powerful telescopes in the world and I recalled a couple of documentaries I had watched where they had filmed from this famous observatory and here I now was riding my motorbike right past it! One of the key reasons for placing the observatory in this area was the clarity and lack of air pollution and it occurred to me it would be a great place to film me riding along the desert road in the middle of the Atacama. Sadly, unlike Ewan McGregor and Charley Boorman, I had no back up film crew so I rigged up my camera and placed it on a tiny tripod by the side of the road, ran back to my bike, rode off into the distance and after about half a mile I turned round and rode back straight past the camera to get the shots from both angles. There was no one around to question my odd behavior and I was pleased to get the shots!

At the same time I'd noticed that whenever I stopped for a break on these long and empty desert roads, I did so whilst leaving the engine still running. For some reason, I was concerned that if I turned it off there might be an engine malfunction and I might not be able to restart it. This was complete nonsense of course. It had never failed to start apart from one occasion where it needed to be turned over a second time.

Ever since Peru, I had become slightly paranoid about any mechanical problems occurring that might delay or jeopardise my end goal of reaching Buenos Aires. It was almost as if the closer I got to Argentina, the stronger the pull and the more vitally important it was becoming to get there speedily and in one piece. It seemed totally counterintuitive. I should be more relaxed about the journey, after all, I was nearly there. And yet it felt with every passing mile, the desire to get to Buenos Aires and to get home was increasing. This feeling had grown hugely since my time with Jane in Costa Rica, where it had become crystal clear that this was the woman I wanted to spend the rest of my life with. Her love, support and encouragement throughout the whole venture had been remarkable. All these thoughts were always at the back of my mind on the long, solitary days riding the desert roads of South America.

After several hours of riding across "Mars," the road dropped in elevation and the temperature climbed steadily as I rode into the little town of TalTal where I found a delightfully quaint, and slightly incongruous little hotel. It wouldn`t have been out of place in an English seaside resort, beautifully quiet and peaceful (and of course, expensive.)

I had been aware for the last couple of hundred miles that I was due to do an oil change and air filter change very soon and was waiting for the right conditions to occur i.e. I needed a place with a garage, or safe parking, preferably covered to keep me out of the heat of the baking hot temperatures I was experiencing daily. So far nothing had materialised until my next destination of Copiapo. I rode into town the next day and found a hotel with exactly the right requirements. It even had a motorcycle shop right next door where I could buy the oil. This must have been an omen so I had to get on with it.

I must admit I didn`t really want to do it as it is such a pain in the ass to take everything off the bike to do what is essentially a fairly simple job. Nevertheless, I parked the bike in the shade and set to stripping off the panels and bash plate only to get to the sump plug and discover that I couldn`t budge it. The BMW dealers in Bogota had obviously tightened it far too much. Shit. bloody dealers. The only reason I`d let them do it was because I was feeling far too ill to do it myself when I arrived in Colombia. Luckily, the owner of the bike shop was available (after the mandatory siesta) to take a look, and with the loan of a socket extension and a 2 ft long spanner I managed to get the leverage I needed to get the job done. What a stroke of "luck" to find a hotel right next to a motorcycle shop?

With the last oil change of the journey under my belt, I set off the next day for the town of Vallenar, which would be a stopping off point before I made for the city of La Serena. As I pulled out of the hotel car park and headed down the main street I suddenly became aware of a strange rattling type sound. Stopping immediately, I dismounted and put my ear to the side of the bike and with some growing anxiety listening as carefully as I could. Nothing. I could have sworn I heard something, I thought. Climbing back on I gunned the engine, still nothing untoward. So I slipped it into gear and pulled away. Within a few feet, there it was again. I stopped and tried to logically analyse what it could be, but my anxiety was clouding my thinking. I needed to pull into a safer place and take a proper look so I continued on for a hundred yards and with the noise ever increasing, spotted a garage forecourt and quickly pulled in. Cutting the engine, I took off my helmet and gloves to have a closer examination. I couldn't see anything but as I started the engine and moved the bike forwards, there it was again. Fuck, what now! I decided to head back to the hotel. If there was a real problem I might need to stay another night until I could get it resolved, besides which, the friendly man from the bike shop may be able to help me. Pulling into the hotel car park again, I removed my helmet and gloves and hurried into reception to track down the bike shop owner. He wasn't there. I would have to wait until he turned up and so I returned to the bike and scratched my head some more. Thankfully, he appeared after a short while,

"Tengo un problema," I told him, as I started the engine and pointed to the area with the rattling sound.

He listened, nodded and then took out one of his screwdrivers and removed the front sprocket cover. The rattling magically disappeared. The relief swept over me. My God, was that it? After doing the oil change I hadn't located the sprocket cover correctly and it was making contact with the chain!

"Muchas gracias! Muchas gracias!" I blurted. I was so relieved it had been something so trivial and yet it highlighted again my concern about anything that could delay my quest to reach Buenos Aires. Thanking him again, I climbed back in the saddle and set off for the second time that morning.

La Serena was a big, modern city but with an attractive centre with pleasant boulevards and plenty of cafes and bars. Sadly, my accommodation left a lot to be desired again, all I could find was an overpriced Hospedaje (guest house). Very nice and friendly people but pretty basic facilities to say the least. It didn`t really encourage me to stay longer and I knew I had a big ride the next day to take me to the outskirts of Santiago. My original plan had been to head for Santiago and maybe stay a couple of days if the bike needed anything from the BMW garage, but as I had been discovering, my original plans had been changing on a regular basis. Since, I had already done the oil change and Santiago was further south than my crossing point into Argentina I made for the town of La Calera instead, which would put me within striking distance of the Argentinian border and the realisation of my goal.

I arrived in La Calera around midday and rode around for a while eventually finding a cheap hotel, in fact it looked like the only hotel in town. For 7,000 pesos I got a "cell" with a single bed and my very own padlock to lock the bedroom door. Clearly a really classy place. With no secure parking and the only other option of leaving it on the street being out of the question, they suggested I could park it in an adjacent corridor. I went to have a look and concluded that if I removed all the luggage, panniers and folded in my wing mirrors, it might just squeeze in the tight space. After figuring out how to get it over the high pavement and the equally high step into the narrow corridor and much sweating, cursing and revving, I eventually cut the engine and pulled it onto the centre stand, safe in the knowledge that it would take a mighty effort for anyone to steal it. In fact, I wasn't even sure I could get it out in the morning.

The rest of the day was spent avoiding going into my cell so I was forced to drink beer (they had no bottled water – what can you do) and work on the internet in the hotel bar. There was nothing to do in the small town so I ended up eating dinner there too. I was so excited about the morning and the thought of crossing into Argentina that I went to bed early and tried to get some sleep. It reminded me of Christmas as a little boy! Sure enough, I slept badly, was up before sunrise packing the bike and was on the road before 7.00 am. I worked out it would take me about two hours to reach the border somewhere up in the Andes mountains.

After an hour or so I entered the foothills of the Andes and wondered how high I would have to climb. I had heard that there was a tunnel through part of the route and so I was interested to see how much of the Andes I would climb over and how much I would ride under. Passing through several half tunnels I started to climb steadily and then sharply as I approached what turned out to be thirty one tight, hairpin bends with dozens of trucks crawling around them like giant caterpillars. Still seeing no sign for aduana or migracion, I pushed on until the sharp curves straightened out and the road plateaued eventually leading me to some kind of checkpoint where an official looking woman was manning the road,

"Donde esta la migracion Salida de Chile, por favor?"

"15 kilometres," she said pointing further up the road. It all seemed a bit strange, especially when I saw a sign saying,

"Bienvenidos Argentina". I hadn`t officially left Chile and here I was in Argentina. You`d think after thirteen previous border crossings it would all be easy and straightforward by now, but everyone had been slightly different as this one was proving to be.

The road suddenly ran out and became a dusty, dirt track with visibility limited by a truck in front kicking up the dust and the strong wind blowing it into my face. A quick twist of the throttle took me out of the dust storm and past the truck. Further up ahead I glimpsed a sign indicating the border was near. It appeared I was in Argentina but wasn`t ready to celebrate before it became official.

CHAPTER 42

Malbec and Steak – The Sweet Taste of Success!

Dropping down in altitude I saw up ahead a solitary building, which was obviously the official border crossing. I joined a queue of stationary traffic, turned off my engine and in the heat of the midday sun proceeded to wait, every few minutes pushing the bike ever closer to the checkpoint. Once inside the building I could see the system. It was a joint Chile and Argentina migracion and aduana. You would get your passport stamped at one booth and move a little further and get your temporary import permit for the bike at another one. What a good idea. Central America could really learn a lesson here!

Waiting to cross the border into Argentina!

With minimal fuss I was now officially in Argentina. I had done it! The goal that was a long time in my head, a year in the planning and over seven months in the execution was now achieved! As I rode away from the border a massive feeling of relief swept over me. I expected to be elated and yet that wasn't the over riding emotion. It was relief. Just total relief.

After all the ups and downs, and the physical and mental challenges, I had finally completed what I set out to do, and four months ahead of schedule too. There was of course, the small matter of nearly a thousand miles to get to Buenos Aires, but the actual journey was Alaska to Argentina, and here I was in Argentina. It felt like a massive weight had been lifted off my shoulders. The burden of self imposed expectations to achieve my goal had been removed. If the bike did break down now, I felt like I would get off and push it all the way to Buenos Aires. Nothing was going to stop me now.

The landscape on this side of the mountains was totally different from Chile. I was riding along winding, hilly roads in the foothills of the Andes surrounded by snow capped peaks framed against a bright blue sunny sky. I was heading for the city of Mendoza, the wine capital of Argentina. I had promised myself a decent bottle of wine and a good steak dinner when I got to Argentina. As I rode along the twisty roads and closer to the city, my thoughts turned to home and I wondered what it would be like to return to normality, but I had to remind myself to stay "in the moment". I still had Argentina to cross and I decided to allow myself the indulgence of the necessary assimilation and introspection only when I arrived in Buenos Aires.

My immediate plan was to spend three nights in Mendoza to recover from what had been two long, back to back days on the bike and celebrate reaching Argentina, but first I had to find a place to stay. I made for the centre and stopped at a couple of hostels but they were both full, as were the next two hotels I tried. Peak holiday time again. Nevertheless, I was confident I would find the right place soon because I always did. The very next hotel came up trumps. Secure parking, wifi, air conditioning, cable TV and all for about $40, which was a massive improvement on the overpriced hotels in Chile. I had a feeling I was going to enjoy Argentina. That night I did treat myself to a steak and a half bottle of very nice wine, but Chile had blown a huge hole in what was left of my money so I spent the evening studying the figures and working out how I could eke it out to get home. The next couple of days were taken up with enjoying the sights and sounds of Mendoza, resting, catching up with my blog and pouring over my map of Argentina to plan my cross country route.

I spent the next three days edging ever closer to Buenos Aires. The deserts of Peru and Chile were exchanged for lush, green farmlands, with roads so straight and long (very long) you`d think the Romans had engineered them. For three days I rode across country not too dissimilar to Lincolnshire in England, flat terrain as far as the eye could see. From Mendoza I rode to San Luis, then Rio Cuarto and Venado Tuerto before ending up in the little town of San Antonio de Areco. I hadn`t even planned to stop there, but I decided one hundred and seventy miles was far enough for a day and it would put me within a couple of hours of Buenos Aries. As soon as I entered the town I knew it was a good place to stay. It had a good feel to it.

I was waiting at a traffic light when a car pulled up beside me and the driver wound down his window to ask me about the bike, when the lights changed he wished me good luck and drove off. Two minutes later I pulled over at a corner to get my bearings when another man approached me, also interested in the bike and my trip. This turned out to be Santiago, the son of the car driver Oscar, who had spoken to me earlier! They were both really interested in my journey and since they both spoke good English we had a brief conversation. It turned out that Santiago knew Northampton, home of the Hope Centre, because he had been there to watch rugby games when Frederico Mendez (a great Argentinian player) used to play for the club. I explained I was looking for a hotel,

"No problem. Let me make a call," Santiago said.

"I`ve found a good hotel for you, follow me."

He took me to a place I would never have found on my own and it was better and cheaper than most of the hotels I had used up to now,

"Thanks very much for your help!"

"That`s O.K. Would you like to join us for dinner tonight if you`re not too tired?"

"His wife is a cordon bleu cook," added Oscar.

"I`d love to!" I replied, relishing the prospect of some good, authentic home cooking.

"I`ll pick you up later so you don`t have to ride in the dark."

I spent the rest of the day wandering around the town and relaxing watching some U.S sitcoms. At about 9.20 p.m. (way past my bed time) Santiago picked me up and drove me to his beautiful, big old house in the town.

Santiago`s wife Paula had cooked a beautiful meal and in the company of their friends, Enrique, Florencia, Juan and Ema I enjoyed the best food and wine of the whole trip. Luckily everyone spoke good English so I didn`t have to stretch my limited Spanish. It was such a great night and after many weeks on my own it was a real joy to be in such hospitable, kind and generous company. Santiago dropped me back at my hotel in the early hours of the next morning and promised to return with his daughters before I set off so they could see the bike. Once again I reflected on the synchronicity of the events that had led me to meeting such amazing people. San Antonio de Areco wasn`t even in my plans!

Santiago and friends

A few short hours later, I was up with the bike packed and ready to go when Santiago arrived with two of his daughters to say goodbye. Apparently he had been regaling them with stories of my bear encounters on the roads in Alaska and Canada!

Waving goodbye and with the possibility of meeting up in the city for a drink later, I set off for Buenos Aires and officially the end of my journey. I had arranged to meet up with Sandra and Javier who run Dakar Motos. They are based in one of suburbs of the city and are famous in the biking community. Everyone who passes through Buenos Aires always stays there. They were going to help me with the shipping arrangements to get the bike back to the U.K.

CHAPTER 43

Buenos Aires – The Journey for Hope is over

My next challenge was going to be finding their location in the city without the aid of a GPS or even a proper map of the city. I'd looked on Google maps and had a reasonable idea of the rough location and decided to trust my navigational abilities, after all, I'd come this far and always managed to find my way eventually. Two hours later I'd reached the city and had navigated to an area within a couple of kilometres of their garage when I stopped to ask a local rider if he knew the street, sadly he didn't, nor did the friend he phoned to help out, but we happened to be parked across the road from a taxi driver, so I just paid the taxi to lead me the last few minutes which saved me a lot of time and got me to Dakar Motos more or less on schedule.

Sandra had arranged for me to take my bike to the airport the next Tuesday to deal with the customs and prepare the bike for shipping, so my plan was to stay at Dakar Motos until then where I could keep the bike secure in their garage. They also have four bunk beds where weary overland motorcyclists can stay and if necessary do maintenance on their bikes before moving on. It seems that everyone who rides down through South America usually ends up at Dakar Motos!

I shared the bunk room with two other riders, Ralph and Carol from Canada. They'd just got back from Ushuaia and were waiting to head back home. After a cup of coffee, I met with Sandra who explained the two stage plan to me:

Stage 1.

Tuesday ride to the airport, meet my contact there. Have the necessary paperwork for customs (bike documents plus photocopies, passport plus photocopies, temporary import document plus photocopies). Remove wing mirrors and windshield, let air out of tyres, drain the petrol, disconnect the battery and prepare the bike for being crated.

Stage 2.

Wednesday go back into the city to the shipping company`s headquarters where they would tell me exact cost of shipping (based upon the volume of the crate). Then I had to go to the local bank and pay cash (only!) into their account get a receipt and come back to exchange the receipt for the air way bill.

Simple really!

I spent the next couple of days attempting to get used to sleeping in a bunk bed again, sweating profusely in the intense humidity and being savagely attacked and eaten by the worst mosquitoes I`d encountered on the whole trip. In the meantime, I took a couple of trips into the city to look around and orientate myself. Dakar Motos is about a fifteen minute train ride from the centre. I also wanted to find a centrally located hotel to stay in for the last two nights before flying home and locate the one bank that would give me money on my credit card as the ATMs were refusing to accept it.

On my second trip into the city I had already decided on the area I wanted to stay for my final two nights and now it was just a question of finding a suitably priced hotel. I spent a hour or so walking around and checking out all the possible small hotels, finally settling on one which was the right price in the right location and made a provisional booking for the following day. The plan would be to ride to the airport, drop off the bike and leave as much of my luggage and riding gear as I could with the bike leaving me with just a bag and a small ruck sack to get some transport back to my city centre hotel.

The following morning I was eager to get going and complete

the final few miles of the journey. Although a technicality, I didn`t feel I`d actually finished the trip until I had no more riding to do which meant getting to the airport and strapping the bike on to the pallet. I got some directions from Javier about the route to the airport and was told it would be about eighteen miles. I was carefully monitoring the petrol consumption because I didn`t want to have too much in and have to drain the tank at the airport and at the same time I didn`t want to run out of gas on the way. As it turned out, it was much further than I thought, in fact a lot further, eighteen turned into nearly thirty miles! I ran with the petrol warning light on the whole way and breathed a sigh of relief when the signs for the airport came into view.

The process at the airport was fairly straightforward but time consuming. It took me an hour to get to the airport, three hours sorting the bike and dealing with the customs and another two hours to get back (having mistakenly taken the slow bus) stopping at every bus stop in Buenos Aires and the surrounding area. I was trying to remember the exact area where the hotel I'd booked was located and it seemed the bus wasn't going to stop very near so I asked the driver to drop me as close as he could leaving me with a few hundred yards to lug my heavy bag. As I shouldered my bag and headed down some of the side streets I recognised, it felt distinctly strange to be carrying my luggage instead of having it strapped to the back of the bike. I couldn't quite believe it. The ride was over. I wouldn't have to get up tomorrow and put on my riding suit and boots. It was a very strange feeling.

Everything was now almost complete with only the bank to deal with the following day, so that night I went out to celebrate with a kind donation from Tim and Kris who had suggested when I get to Buenos Aires I should celebrate with a good meal and a nice bottle of wine. It was such a generous offer how could I refuse! I managed to find the perfect restaurant (waiters wearing aprons and table cloths on the table) and had a half bottle of superb cabernet sauvignon and a steak dinner.

The next day would be taken up with sorting out the payment to the shipping company which meant getting a huge wad of cash and taking it to the shipping company to collect my airway bill. In the afternoon I was due to meet up with Santiago who had kindly offered to come to the city and take me out for lunch and show me some of the sights,

"You can't come all this way and not see the best of the city!" he explained. I gave him the address of my hotel and right on time he arrived saying, "my car is just around the corner. Are you hungry?"

We drove to a lovely restaurant in the bohemian part of the city all the time giving me a running commentary on the history and politics of the area. Over lunch he regaled me with the story of his travels.

"When I was very young I spent three years travelling the world," he said.

"What on earth brought you to Northampton?" I asked.

"When I was working in London. We used to come to watch the rugby when Mendez was playing. We had a great time!"

After a leisurely lunch we drove to the river and walked along a short causeway stepping over groups of people fishing right next to signs stating that fishing was prohibited!

"It's the river," Santiago said, "they say it's too polluted."

"It doesn't seem to bother them!" I stated, pointing at the large number of people fishing. Santiago just shrugged,

"This is Argentina. We don't care about rules!" he replied with a laugh.

"Over there you can see Uruguay," he said, pointing across the river.

"This is a huge river!" I exclaimed, taking in the enormity of its width.

"This is the River Plate! The widest river in the world!" he said proudly.

"Really?"

"Well, that's what we say in Argentina!" he said with a big beaming smile. The tour continued for several hours and it was nearly 6.00 pm by the time he dropped me back at my hotel.

"Thanks so much for all your help. It's been a real pleasure meeting you." I said with real sincerity.

"It has been a real pleasure too, meeting a fellow traveller!"

"Take care of yourself and give my love to Paula," I said as I climbed out of the car.

That night I lay in bed with the ceiling fan cranked up to maximum (to keep the mosquitoes a bay) but still found sleep difficult. My head was a maelstrom of thoughts and emotions running through the events of the past eight months, and I wondered how long it would take to assimilate the experiences I had been through. I was very excited about my imminent return and at the same time I was finding it hard to believe it was over. It didn`t seem possible that in a matter of days I would be back in the U.K. The next day, as if to get me in the right frame of mind for my return, the heavens opened and for the first time since I entered Buenos Aires it rained and continued to do so all the way to the airport.

I spent the time at the airport reflecting upon the fact that it was all over. Soon I would be heading for my final destination of Heathrow. It had been eight months since I had left there for Alaska. It was all very hard to take in. The flight was on time, and as I settled into my seat, I was joined by a fellow Englishman who took the seat next to mine. We exchanged the usual pleasantries and as I thumbed through one of the complimentary English newspapers I casually commented,

"The first English paper for eight months!"

"It's been eighteen months for me," he added, "where have you been?"

"I was riding my motorbike from Alaska to Argentina," I said with not a little pride.

"What about you? I asked.

"Oh I've been riding my push bike cycling from Alaska to Argentina."

Of all the people I could have sat next to.......

EPILOGUE

I swapped the humidity and 35 ° temperatures of Buenos Aires for the grey, overcast and wet, 4 ° of England. The flight back was long and uneventful and as we made our final approach I felt the same nervous anticipation I had felt in Costa Rica. I knew Jane would have been there for the past hour waiting for my arrival. After the long flight I was tired but excited as I waited patiently in the queue for immigration and eventually, with passport checked and luggage collected I pushed my trolley through the gates and entered the arrivals hall. I was scanning the sea of faces when I noticed Jane running towards me, I was easy to spot with my bright yellow bag. We hugged each other for what seemed like ages,

"Do you fancy a coffee?" she asked.

"That would be great! A proper cappuccino if they've got one."

We went to Costa Coffee, ordered two cappuccinos and pulled ourselves onto a couple of bar stools,

"So," Jane said, "how was the flight?"

"Great," I replied, "It's so good to be back! And do you know what?"

"What?" she asked.

"I've decided that`s it. There'll be no more challenges. I don't need to prove anything to myself anymore."

Final thoughts....

I had planned to take a couple of weeks to settle in and come down to earth, but as I found on my journey, the best laid plans sometimes go awry. I was brought swiftly down to earth by several events. Clive's death, Claire's brain tumour (thankfully she is making a remarkable recovery) and the Christchurch earthquake had all impacted me profoundly. On a much more mundane level, my car had failed its MOT and would need scrapping, my laptop had crashed and burned before I left and wasn`t repairable, I needed a new phone and I had a big tax bill to settle within a couple of months. And sadly, there was no immediate work on the horizon.

Much later......

My planned period of reflection never really happened. Instead, life`s events took over with a vengeance and I fell into an emotionally demanding maelstrom of trauma, upheaval and change. The business world had changed too. The post recession cuts were starting to bite deep. It was always going to be a risk to leave for a year and try to pick up the pieces on my return, which I would need to in order to repay the significant investment I had borrowed to fund the trip. It was proving even more demanding than I had thought.

My trusty bike had been sold and I confess to a moment of sadness and reflection as it was strapped to the trailer by its new owner. Even though it was bought for a specific purpose, it had served me well and had been my one and only constant companion throughout the whole journey.

In the face of all that has happened and continues to happen, was it all worth it?

I left behind everything and everyone I loved and cared for, stepped well and truly out of my comfort zone, spent a good deal of the time being anxious, worried and sometimes downright scared. I had experienced many "dark nights of the soul," travelled nearly 20,000 miles through fifteen countries, met some amazing people, discovered I have a degenerative spinal condition (which almost brought my journey to a premature end), and in the process raised over £3,000 for The Northampton Hope Centre.

So was it worth it?

Unequivocally yes.

I was privileged to have the opportunity. The journey not only reinforced my faith in human nature, but also took me on a profound inner journey, the findings of which will reveal themselves over time.

> Rest not! Life is sweeping by;
>
> Go and dare before you die.
>
> Something mighty and sublime;
>
> Leave behind to conquer time.
>
> \- Goethe

The Route

Alaska

Canada

U.S.A.

Mexico

Guatemala

Belize

El Salvador

Honduras

Nicaragua

Costa Rica

Panama

Colombia

Ecuador

Peru

Chile

Argentina

15 countries - 20,000 miles - eight months.

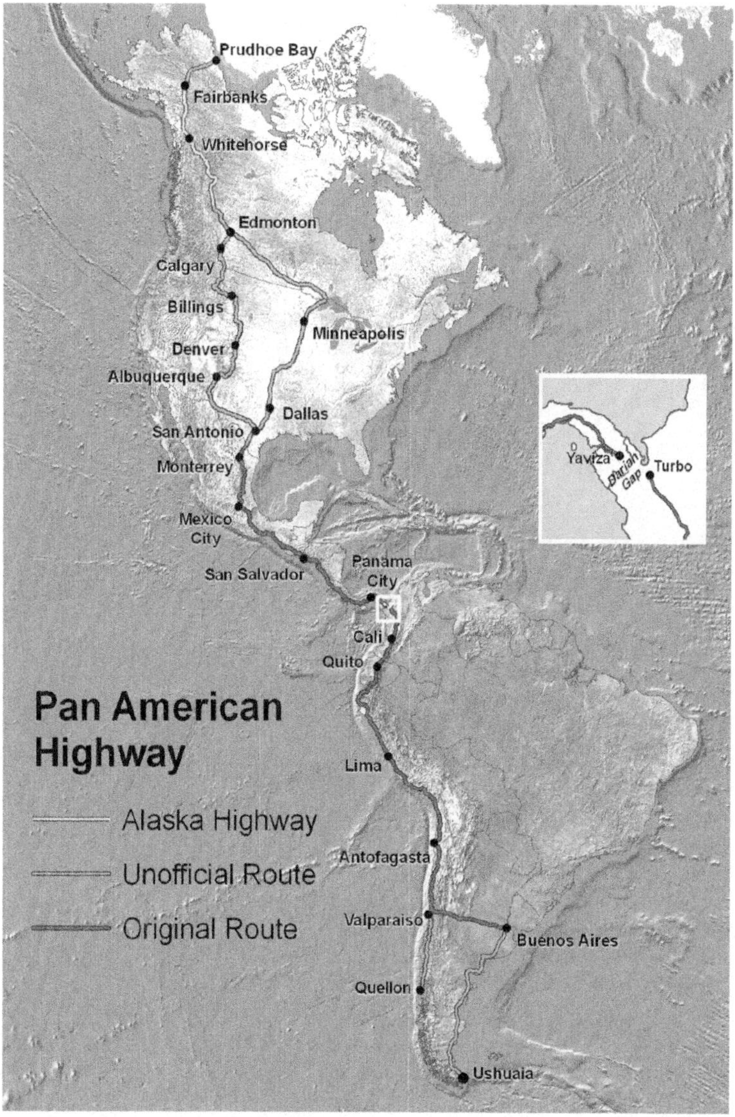
Prudhoe Bay
Fairbanks
Whitehorse
Edmonton
Calgary
Billings
Minneapolis
Denver
Albuquerque
Dallas
San Antonio
Monterrey
Mexico City
San Salvador
Panama City
Yaviza
Darian Gap
Turbo
Cali
Quito
Pan American Highway
Lima
Alaska Highway
Unofficial Route
Original Route
Antofagasta
Valparaiso
Buenos Aires
Quellon
Ushuaia

Printed in Great Britain
by Amazon

83440537R00183